A Mile in Their Shoes

Conversations with veterans of World War II

By Aaron Elson

ISBN 0-9640611-2-0

Aaron Elson

Other books by Aaron Elson

Tanks for the Memories
An oral history of the 712ᵗʰ Tank Battalion in World War II

They were all young kids
*The story of Lt. Jim Flowers and the first platoon,
Company C, 712ᵗʰ Tank Battalion, on Hill 122.*

Visit the World War II Oral History web site

Members of D Company, 712ᵗʰ Tank Battalion, in 1944.

http://www.tankbooks.com

To Dorothy Cooney

Published by
Chi Chi Press
"A good little publishing company"
P.O. Box 914
Maywood, N.J. 07607

Printed at
Ted Weiss Printing
Langhorne, Pa.

Chi Chi

About the author

Aaron Elson has been interviewing veterans since 1987, when he first attended a reunion of the tank battalion his father served with. He studied creative writing with Kurt Vonnegut Jr., and has been a copy editor at the New York Daily News, the New York Post and the Bergen Record.

What people are saying about "Tanks for the Memories"

"A must read for any tanker." – **Armor magazine**

"All the young people really enjoy the book. That doesn't mean the oldsters don't." – **Mary Fetsch**

"It is truly refreshing to read about tankers' war stories. The market is flooded with books on special ops teams, infantry and airmen's experiences in war, but virtually nothing on what tankers saw, felt and did."
– **Capt. Bennie McRae III, 1ˢᵗ Armored Division**

Ask for "Tanks for the Memories" at your favorite bookstore, on the Internet, or call 1(800) 807-TANK

Table of Contents

Preface

On the evening of April 27, 1944 – barely five weeks before the invasion of Normandy – three fully loaded LSTs, or landing ship-tanks, left the port of Brixham, England. They joined five other LSTs off the coast of Devon, and waited to play their part in a major landing exercise.

At 2:03 a.m. on the morning of the 28th, a torpedo struck the auxiliary engine room of LST 507. Within moments, two other landing ships were hit as well.

Angelo Crapanzano was in the main engine room of the 507. He was thrown backward and momentarily stunned. Then, in total darkness, he found one of the two ladders leading to the deck. He escaped from the engine room, but his ordeal was far from over.

After plunging 40 feet into the 43-degree water of the English Channel, Angelo clung to the burned-out shell of a life raft with one arm, while he kept his other arm around an unconscious shipmate. Four and a half hours later, as dawn was breaking, he saw a light in the distance, and experienced a moment of euphoria. Then he passed out.

Pete De Vries doesn't tell war stories. Too many people died, and they're the ones you should tell stories about, he says. Besides, look what happened the one time he did tell a story.

In response to an article about pride in the Marines, Pete wrote a letter to the editor of the Static Line, a veterans' publication. He liked the story by the retired Marine, he wrote, "but I still think the best one was told by an officer in the tank corps. It seems he came upon this lone GI with a bazooka and told him he was being pursued by German tanks and wanted to know the way to the

American lines. After he told the officer the way, he came to attention and said, 'Don't worry about a thing, Sir. I'm in the 82nd Airborne, and this is as far as those bastards go.' I think this shows the pride each trooper had for his unit, and what made him the best soldier in the world."

Pete won't say who that lone GI was. Nor will he divulge the fate of those German tanks. But a couple of years after the letter appears, Pete is attending a dinner, and he hears that someone at another table is claiming to have been the lone GI.

Pete says he didn't confront the pretender, but that if he had wanted to, he might have gone over to the fellow's table and asked him if he could remember the name of the officer from the tank corps.

"How could he be expected to remember that?" I ask.

It was an easy name to remember, Pete says, because he had a famous father and was a congressman himself.

The officer from the tank corps, Pete tells me, was Lieutenant Will Rogers Jr.

A few days before Christmas in 1944, two German Mark IV tanks destroyed every vehicle in the reconnaissance platoon Rogers was leading. A book about Rogers' tank destroyer battalion notes that the survivors reached a checkpoint of the 82nd Airborne Division. Although he's said all he will say on the matter, it is entirely possible that that checkpoint was Pete De Vries.

Have you had breakfast? Perhaps you'll join me at Denny's. I'd offer to pay, but this one's on Cliff Merrill. Cliff is a retired colonel, so who are we to argue?

Cliff's wife, Jan, will join us, along with Ruby and Sue Goldstein. Ruby is fond of reminiscing about the Depression, and is a great fan of the $1.99 Grand Slam breakfast – these are 1994 prices, mind you. Let's take this table in the corner. It's Sunday morning, and the restaurant, in Bradenton, Fla., is crowded. The waitress brings the plates, with their neatly arranged sausage patties, their bacon, their pancakes and eggs. She disappears and returns with a pair of half-empty coffee decanters.

Before long, the conversation shifts from restaurants in the Boston area – a favorite topic of Ruby's – and salmon fishing – which Cliff and Jan do every year – to Normandy in 1944.

Cliff is solidly built even as he pushes 80 with pale, chiseled cheeks and some red beneath his eyes. He looks as if he could still fit into a uniform. Ruby, with the exception of his facial features, bears little resemblance to the rail-thin sergeant in 50-year-old snapshots.

Cliff was a company commander in a tank battalion during World War II, and Ruby was the commander of one of his tanks.

"Do you remember, we had these flare guns in the tank..." Ruby says.

"Smoke," Cliff says.

"Yeah, smoke mortars," Ruby says, although the next time I hear him relate the incident he will still call it a flare gun. Memory is funny that way.

"I had mine wired to the inside of the basket of the turret," he says, "and I took it with me after the tank was hit. There was a machine gun nest in the field. He was waiting for somebody to cross the opening to the field, then he'd let go. So I started to fire it [the smoke mortar] and lobbed it over the hedgerow. It couldn't do any damage, but it must have scared the hell out of them, because I fired quite a few shots. But he caught one paratrooper that was trying to go through the opening, he caught him and killed him."

"It was a captain of the paratroopers," Cliff says. "I tried to stop him."

Cliff pauses amid the clinking of coffee cups and animated conversation at nearby tables. He looks down reflectively.

"Before your tank was hit, you ran over," he says, staring at his plate, his voice barely audible, "there was a wounded German. You ran over him with your tank. Did you know that?"

"No, I just kept going."

Jan Merrill glances at Sue Goldstein. You'd think their husbands wouldn't talk about these things over breakfast, but the two women know it is better to talk about it over breakfast than to not talk about it at all.

"Jesus, you flattened him right out."

"We kept going. Didn't stop for anything."

"He wasn't wounded any longer," Cliff says. "The tracks ran the whole length of him."

For 40 years, Angelo Crapanzano kept his Bronze Star in a drawer, while he drifted in and out of clinical depression. His family knew he lost a ship during the war, but that was about all he would tell them.

On May 3, 1984, Angelo was browsing through the TV listings when the blurb for "20/20" caught his eye. It promised a report about "the mystery surrounding the killing of 750 GIs in a D-Day rehearsal." Could it be, he wondered, that after all these years, there was going to be something about Tiger?

Angelo's brother watched "20/20" as well, and the next morning contacted the show's producer. The producer excitedly asked how she could get in touch with Angelo.

The producer gave Angelo the names of several other survivors, and he began talking for the first time about what had happened.

Today he displays the Bronze Star on the wall of his den, above a small case with a number of books about Exercise Tiger.

For the 50th anniversary of the disaster, the tabloid TV show "Inside Edition" reunited Angelo with John McGarigal, the shipmate whose life he saved, and Joe McCann. When McCann was 11 years old, he witnessed an awesome sight: the battleship Arizona passing through Puget Sound. Two years later, when the Arizona was sunk at Pearl Harbor, McCann couldn't believe it. He was so moved that he lied about his age and enlisted in the Navy. He was still a baby-faced kid of 15 when he skippered the rescue boat whose crew pulled Crapanzano and McGarigal out of the English Channel.

Angelo says the producers of shows such as "Inside Edition" love it when their subjects break into tears. This one was a piece of cake, but still, they weren't taking chances. They brought Angelo by limousine to a ceremony in New Bedford, Mass., and kept the three men separated until the cameras were rolling.

Almost everybody has an Uncle Angelo, or a grandfather like Cliff Merrill, or a father or a husband who gave the best years of his life for his country, or a brother or a cousin who went off to war and didn't come back.

When I began conducting the interviews that appear in this book, I was attempting to reconstruct the stories my father used to tell. As a result, several of the conversations are with veterans of the 712th Tank Battalion, and I have virtually neglected whole branches of the service and theaters of the war. Veterans of these branches have my sincere apology. However, I hope readers will agree that from the discussions in these pages of life in combat – of the meals, the hygiene, the suspension of morality or its sudden appearance where it might least be expected – they will better be able to understand those members of their families who have fought in a war.

Unless you have been in combat, veterans have told me, you can never understand what it is like. I have not been in the military. I have chosen to let the veterans tell their stories in their own words, with an occasional question from me thrown in. I have edited the conversations so as to minimize confusion, and to make myself look a little better. For instance, when Ruby Goldstein was showing me a training manual he had kept, I noticed an inscription on the last page. "Wow," I said. "This was signed by a general?"

I was looking at a handwritten address that began, "General Delivery."

When you're through laughing, I hope you'll sit back, and join me and the veterans in these pages as we walk a mile in their shoes.

"I slipped on vomit. Some guys were throwing up, from nerves, and as we pivoted out my feet went out from under me, and I went out upside down. My hips caught the side door of the plane. The wind was like hell, holding me there, and guys in the meantime as they're going out they're hitting me in the head with their feet. ..."

The last hurrah

Ed Boccafogli
82nd Airborne Division
Clifton, N.J., Feb. 19, 1994

Ed Boccafogli: I was what you'd call a dropout today. It was back in the Thirties, the Depression years. There was no work, so I volunteered for the CCC camps. I don't know if you ever heard of them.

Aaron Elson: Yes, the Civilian Conservation Corps.

Ed Boccafogli: I worked in Pennsylvania for the Dutch Elm division. Then I went out West and spent a year and a half out there. It was rough in those days. I went to California, hopping freights, with a dollar and twenty cents, a bag with peanut butter and a loaf of bread. That's how we lived, two of us. And fighting with hoboes who tried to take our shoes. In those days, they'd kill you for a dollar.

Then the war broke out. I was inducted. In fact, I got called down at the draft board in Passaic, and I'd had an appendix operation. I went to the hospital, and they called up my sister and said, "Your brother is supposed to report today."

She said, "He can't report."

They said, "What do you mean?"

"He's in the hospital."

"Well, have him report Monday." Here I'd just had an operation. So I got a deferment for three weeks. Then I went down to Fort Dix, and from Fort Dix to Fort McClellan. And about a dozen of us were sent to New Orleans as military police.

We were stationed out under the Huey Long Bridge, at Camp Harahan, which was a big port of embarkation. The troops would come in by the truckload to depart on boats for the Pacific.

Also, we had a lot of bad elements there of rapists and murderers and whatnot. The Army was big in those days. We had a prison compound with a lot of men. There must have been three or four hundred at any one time. Most of them were being processed for shipment to Leavenworth. They were bad characters.

Aaron Elson: Had these people been in combat?

Ed Boccafogli: No. The war was just beginning. There were all kinds of elements. Guys who would get in a brawl in a city and end up killing or stabbing somebody. They were military personnel, so they went into the guardhouse and from there to Leavenworth.

I had it made. I could have stayed there the whole war, lived high on the hog. I had a jeep. Go patrolling at night, 11 o'clock, pick up the drunks, bring them back. Then I'd be on the gate many times. And what really discouraged me about that branch of the military, as the people would be coming back from leave, they'd be bringing liquor for the guys inside. As they'd come in the guys were half-bombed. They've got a pint sticking out here, a pint sticking out there. You had to confiscate it. Give them a slip, put it in a box, and after each shift you had to take the box and bring it over to the Officers Club. So the officers were living high on the hog on this liquor from the poor bastards that were gonna go over and die. I didn't take too good to that.

There were a lot of muggings down there, what we call muggings today. What was happening, the guys would go to town, the ones who had money. They'd go out and have a good time, women, whatever. Then they'd get a taxi to come back. They wouldn't come back with the regular trucks. The fellows had to meet at a place where the trucks would be and they'd all get in and come back to camp. But the fellows with money would hire a cab. They'd be bombed, and on the way back they'd pass out, and they'd be rolled. The cabdriver would pull over, go through their pockets, dump them in the ditch and go back.

So my partner and I would lay on the side of the road and wait. Down in the bayous, it's thick, thick cypress trees, and there's just a channel where the light comes through because of the road. And as dark as it was, you could always figure where the road was. So we'd lay on the side and wait. We'd see a taxi coming; it would go by. Okay. Then another one comes. All of a sudden the lights would go out. Oh, man, we'd turn on the ignition and take off. No lights. Follow the road. You could just about make out the road in that dark bayou. We'd go sixty miles an hour, get to where the taxi was stopped, we'd put the lights on and we'd catch the guy rolling the guy that was drunk. We took a club and busted all the windows in the taxicab, beat the hell out of the guy, took the drunk and put him in our jeep and took him back to camp. And nothing was ever said. Because they knew damn well if they complained, they were in trouble.

We did that twice. And then it stopped.

But then I became disillusioned, because the fellows there, they'd turn on you. Everybody was vying for the next position. So I put in for the paratroops.

Then I waited. Three weeks went by, and I knew they needed recruits, so I went in. The man's name was Sergeant Flood. I said, "Nothing came through about my transfer?"

"No, not yet." He said, "Make out the papers again, maybe they went astray."

So I made them out, request for transfer. I waited another week. In the meantime, I'm nervous. A couple of guys were needling me because I wanted to get out. "What's the matter, you don't like this place?"

There was this one big fellow in the mess hall. He kept needling me, "When are you gettin' out? When are you gettin' out?" So that day I went back in, the third time, and the sergeant said, "I don't know."

I said, "Look, I've been waiting four weeks now."

He said, "Make out the papers again."

So the clerk pulled the drawer out, and in all the papers I saw one paper on which I could make out my signature. I reached right down in the drawer and I pulled it out. They'd never processed it.

I was like a wild man. I stormed out of there. It was just lunchtime. I went inside the mess hall, and the guy gave me the needle. It was the worst time he could have done it. I whacked him, right in the mess hall. They had potatoes, cabbage and whatever, all over the floor. And we were wrestling there for fifteen minutes. It was a mess.

The next thing I know, they grab me and bring me in to the provost marshal. A colonel.

He said, "What's your problem, son?"

I said, "Sir, if I don't get out of here within the next week, I'm gonna be behind that compound."

Then I explained what happened.

He said, "Is that true? Sergeant Flood, come in here."

Sergeant Flood told him, "Well, we. ..." He gave him some excuse.

The colonel said, "I want those papers processed immediately." Then he said, "Why do you want to get out of here?"

I said, "It's a nice place here, but I just can't get along with most of the fellows. I'd rather be in a fighting unit. If we're gonna be in a war let's get over there and get it over with."

He said, "I commend you."

Papers come in, boom-boom-boom. Two days later, three of the guys that were giving me problems, they were noplace in sight. I was gonna bomb each one of them. I was really hot. In fact, I had one fight in the barracks, knocked a guy right through the window.

So I get my transfer and go up to Fort Benning. The next day I'm doing fifty pushups. I said, "What the hell am I doing here? I must be nuts." Running. Everything running. You couldn't even stop to take a leak; you had to turn and take a leak running. You had to doubletime wherever you were. You couldn't get caught walking. You went to the latrine, you had to doubletime, even when you were ready to let loose. It was rough. The training was unbelievable. I passed out twice. A lot of guys passed out. You see, they'd get you with the Indian war clubs in front of the big hangars. This was in July. Hot as anything down in Georgia. They've got the war clubs and you're doing circles. Then you're doing deep knee bends at the same time. And then in the front. And then overhead, you've got these ... they're like bowling pins. And the pain in your arms is unbelievable. Next thing I know, from the heat and everything, I'm on the ground and they're slapping me. "That's all right, you're okay." They pulled me on the side, gave me a glass of water with some salt in it. "You'll be okay." Another guy passed out; they go over there. They give you a kick in the rump. If they see you blink, they grab you and pull you on the side. "What's your name? Report to the orderly room." Boom. Out. They don't want anybody that's faking. If you pass out, that means you went over your limit. But if you fake it, they don't want you there. We had some fakers. I had one guy that I sent back with seven prisoners and those seven prisoners would have been dead except that I sent him back. He had tried to goof out on me during the Bulge. Monahan that guy's name was. I had to chase him all the way back to a regimental aid station. There was nothing wrong with him. He was looking to get evacuated. I beat the hell out of him. I hit him fifty times on the head, knocked his helmet loose. I got him up to the front line, we went into the attack, lost quite a few men, took seven prisoners. I had one guy, I think his name was Wood. One of his sergeants, Sergeant Savage, shrapnel took his head right off. He was laying there and there were brains all over. Wood came over, he wanted to take the prisoners back. He's got a Thompson [submachine gun], and he's shaking like a leaf. I wrote a story for a book but they didn't put it in, because it's showing that the American, too, was a killer, not only the Germans. The Americans, some of them are vicious. Not in this case. It was a matter of he lost his brother, the equivalent.

So I grabbed Monahan. I said, "Monahan, take the prisoners back."

Meantime, the Germans are over there, and they're shaking like a leaf because they could understand English and they could understand what it was all about. Go back 200 yards, he would have killed every one of them. So there's seven Germans that are still living. They owe me their life.

But anyway, going back, now where the hell was I? Oh, so I got into Benning. In the training, we'd run around Lawson Field, which was quite a distance. It's six or eight miles around. In the morning you got out and you had to doubletime all around the field before breakfast, then fall out. The first two weeks you'd think you were gonna die. You were walking dead. After two weeks you were an angel. You were floating through the air, because the body now started to acclimate to the rigors.

Then we'd go on forced marches, and there's always some guys that are gonna drop out. But you evaluate, did he go his limit? And you'd get a big gorilla. You'd think he was like [Mike] Tyson, strong; or what's his name, the actor, Rambo, would turn to a big bowl of jelly. But you'd get a little bit of a guy, he'd go to the end. Another big guy would collapse very easy. But is it his limit? You can run them until they collapse. So you evaluate the man according to what his limits are. That's the reason for that punishment. The same thing in the Marines, to find out how much you've got in you.

Aaron Elson: At this point were you still a private or were you a sergeant?

Ed Boccafogli: I was a private. Right after I got wounded I became a corporal. Then when we jumped into Holland I became a sergeant. A squad sergeant. And then a platoon sergeant, but I never got my bottom rocker, because of one boy. I forget his name. I don't remember names now. You get 75 and all of a sudden everything starts to…Kleinfeld! Kleinfeld, my platoon sergeant. As we moved up into the Bulge, the truck overturned. Quite a few guys got hurt; he was one of them. He was evacuated to the States, and he came back after the war. So they kept his rank open. In the meantime, I was the acting platoon sergeant through the worst part of the whole damn Bulge. From Christmas right straight through to the end.

Aaron Elson: What was it that drew you to the paratroops? What did you think about jumping out of a plane?

Ed Boccafogli: Oh, that was nothing. Once you got up there, the first time, you look out, you say, "Boy, I must be nuts."
They tell you, "Don't look down." I looked down but then I looked up again.

Aaron Elson: Did they have a simulated tower?

Ed Boccafogli: We had training towers like they have out in Coney Island. You're standing there, and it's worse than actually in an airplane because you're looking at the ground. You're looking at all the guys sitting; they look like ants. And you've got the cable up there, you hook on, and now you've got to jump. So as you jump you fall down, "Zzzzooop," the slack is taken up. You go flying down into the sand pit, and it's beautiful. Once you do it, you climb back up there and you jump again. Now you're getting a thrill out of it.
Then you had mock doors. You had to jump out and go into a roll, all the different things. And then you had to hang on harnesses and pull, to adjust the height. It would control your parachute. Not like today. They can stop in midair. They have equipment today, if we had that, we'd have won the war in half the time.

Aaron Elson: Really?

Ed Boccafogli: No, but see, parachuting is only a method of getting there. Once you're on the ground, you're an infantry soldier. You're high class, well-trained, but you're an infantry soldier. And the idea is to use what they call vertical envelopment. Send your troops in behind the Germans. If you've got to outflank them and try to get around, it's hard. By throwing them in behind, you attack from the rear. The thing is, if you don't succeed then you're stuck. So that was the idea in Normandy. The 101st jumped at Carentin, and they dropped us at Ste. Mere Eglise, Chef du Pont and Beaulieu. The Merderet and

Douve Rivers, the two principal rivers, were not big, but the area is something like the Meadowlands was fifty years ago. Imagine trying to get armor from here into New York if you don't have the causeways. You can't get across those swamps. So that was the idea of the Merderet and the Douve rivers, to get the bridges and the causeways, and the road net at Ste. Mere Eglise. Those were the critical points. Because once the Germans could get through to the coast, they could drive them back into the ocean. We had to prevent the Germans from getting to the coast. Then we had to hold so that our troops, when they reached us, would have the bridges and the causeway to get through the marsh area and then continue on, circle around and go up to the Brittany and the Cherbourg peninsulas.

Nobody ever realized how important that operation was. They say Eisenhower waited all that morning before the invasion to find out how the paratroops made out. He said if they failed it would have been another Dieppe. And when he heard that everything was going, he proceeded with the invasion. There was mass confusion, but the confusion also caused mass confusion for the Germans, because they couldn't understand what the hell we were after.

I was lucky. I landed within, I'd say, maybe hundreds of yards of where I was supposed to. Others landed five miles away. Many of them were killed, because by the time they tried to work their way back they ran into German units. A group of four or five guys against let's say a company, it's only a matter of time. They're taken prisoner or killed. And as we moved south later on, in this village we found rifles in the cemeteries with a helmet on top, meaning there was an American soldier there. Out in the fields, too, we'd find them.

Aaron Elson: Who buried them?

Ed Boccafogli: The French people. In that case. In the other cases, we had to bury them there. We ourselves didn't have to do it, but the graves registration, if they couldn't evacuate the bodies they covered them, and put the rifle and the helmet on. Later on other units would come and take the body out.

They had a lot of bodies. One guy was telling me, he was in a graves registration unit, he said it was the most horrible thing. They'd just take the bodies like pieces of, you know, down at the butcher shop. They've got the lambs and the cattle, they'd just throw them up on top of the thing, human beings, throw them up there, one on top of the other; any kind of soldier. Then at the collecting point they'd find the tag. It was very horrible.

Aaron Elson: Tell me about that first jump.

Ed Boccafogli: You mean the first jump in practice?

Aaron Elson: No, the jump into Normandy.

Ed Boccafogli: We prepared for the jump – I'd gone through demolition school, so when I jumped I had TNT and a C-3 pack of explosive. I had fulminate of mercury blasting caps strapped to my boot, and a land mine. Everybody had to carry a land mine. I had the front parachute, the back parachute. Musette bag. Rifle.

Aaron Elson: Why a front and a back parachute?

Ed Boccafogli: The front one is reserve, in case of malfunction. In combat, you very seldom pull it because if the back one doesn't function you're already on the ground. You're only jumping at four or five hundred feet. But in a higher jump the reserve is helpful.

Another thing – we left on June 4th, because the invasion was supposed to be June 5th. Many people don't know that. We left on the night of the 4th. We circled around for about a half-hour. We were the lead unit. Circled around, picked up other units from various aerodromes. And then the crew chief said it's being canceled because of the storm. Christ. It's like a man going into a ring. He's gonna fight now for his life or death. You could hardly breathe. It was a complete letdown, because you're keyed up. Your mind was thinking of every little thing, the sand tables [models], where the church was, where this is, where we're supposed to assemble, where the river is, where the La Fiere Bridge is. All these are in your mind, and you're trying to orient yourself to when you hit the ground. You want to know exactly where you're gonna go, where your buddies are, and hope to hell you don't all get killed.

And you're green troops. By green I mean we hadn't had combat before. Some of the 504 of the 82nd were in Sicily, so they'd had experience, especially the noncoms. But we were green.

Then we landed, and we went back to the tents. Some guys were inside the hangars and some guys in the tents.

That night there was a storm. I mean a storm, lightning and everything. They had the regular squad tents, with a pole – square ones. And the tent next to mine got hit by lightning and collapsed. Nobody was hurt, but everybody had to start moving canvas to get them out.

The next morning we had breakfast, and I'll never forget – I was standing in the tent and there was this kid John Daum. We called him Johnny. Skinny kid, didn't look any more than 16 years old, tow-headed. And he's standing there like a statue, looking into space.

I went over. I said, "Hey, Johnny!" Being I was older and was more rugged, I used to take him under my wing. I said, "What's the matter, Johnny? 'Ey?"

And he's there like in a stupor.

"Hey," I said, "what the hell's the matter with you?"

He says, "I'm gonna die tomorrow." Just like that.

"Ahh, come on," I said. "Chrissake. Some of us will, some of us won't, but you ain't gonna be one."

He was one of the first guys killed. I didn't see him get killed, but one of the fellows said he ran up the incline, and he saw him drop. He got hit with a bullet.

These things are with you the rest of your life.

Anyway, then we had to strip all our bundles; the parachutes, the bundles with extra parts, machine gun, mortars, ammunition, rifle ammunition, plus bundles with medical supplies. Strip 'em. Repack 'em. This is all just to keep you going.

While they're stripping them – these things are never written into the history – they have bundles with land mines. You need them. You get over there, you've got to block a certain area of road for protection.

Somehow, one of the land mines must have been activated. They figure the pin must have fallen out of one of them or somebody had activated it stupidly. It fell, and as it hit the ground, "Boom!" A whole damn bundle of land mines exploded. Six or seven people were killed and seven planes were damaged.

That was a disaster right off the bat, like a bad omen. The jump was canceled. Then this had to happen.

That night, we got back in the planes. Now your tension was twice as much, being you went through it the night before. Especially the first group, which was ours.

We took off at 9:30 or 10 o'clock on the night of the 5th, and we circled until 1 in the morning of the 6th. We had to pick up, I don't know, a couple of thousand planes between the 101st and the 82nd. The 101st had a different route. They went north to south, and we went between the Jersey and Guernsey Islands and we came in from the west. Then we reached the Merderet and Douve rivers.

There were cloud banks and then the ack-ack coming up, shrapnel hitting the planes. You'd see these balls of fire. You can hardly sit in there because you had so much equipment. You're looking out the little window, and you could see those damn balls of fire all around, like in Desert Storm. All that stuff going up, we were going through it.

My plane was hit after I got out. That I know because the guys were missing.

I fell out. I slipped on vomit. Some guys were throwing up, from nerves, and as we pivoted out my feet went out from under me, and I went out upside down. My hips caught the side door of the plane. The wind was like hell, holding me there, and guys in the meantime as they're going out they're hitting me in the head with their feet.

Finally I twisted and broke loose, thank God. Then as I'm coming down I hear crackling through the air. And what was it? Bullets were going through the parachute. I could hear crack-crack-crack-crack. And Jesus Christ, as I came down, I climbed up the risers [to collapse the parachute] and I came flying backwards, and went into a hedgerow. I was hung up on a tree about a foot off the ground.

I took my knife out, and I'm slashing all the rods, because now I figure the bullets are gonna be coming through the brush. I hit the ground behind the dirt bank, and I threw everything off. I threw the land mine away. The hell with this, I figured it wasn't worth dying for. Plus we had a Mae West [life jacket] and a gas mask. The Mae West was in case we were shot down in the water. We had all this unnecessary equipment. I'd rather drown than carry that damn thing.

All this extra equipment, you'd get killed if you had to keep it. You couldn't crawl through the brush. I threw this, I threw that, cut everything loose. I even cut myself [in the leg] getting out of the parachute.

I took off like a rabbit. I go and I'm getting to a hedgerow. I get over to a little gate, one field to another, and I hear somebody coming. So I lay down on the ground. I lay flat. They're coming. I hear click-click [paratroopers had clickers to identify themselves].

I'm looking for my clicker, and I couldn't find it. So I lay flat on the ground, and I'm looking up, and I could see this silhouette go by. It was one of our men. "Yo!" I said. Oh, man! I was glad to see one of my own men.

Then we grouped together. There were four of us. We got over to a road, went down the road, and then we ran into the Germans. The Germans were coming up the road. We shot like a sonofagun, fired all the bullets we could, and took off backwards, because our objective was to get to Hill 30. That was the main objective. And to try to group into bigger forces.

Then we heard some fighting off to the side, and you could tell the difference between the German and American weapons. The German machine gun is like a rip, like the Uzis today. Our light machine guns went donk-donk-donk-donk.

We finally hooked up with another small group. Then another one. By daylight we had quite a group.

At one point we got into a big firefight, and I jumped into a ditch. The

Germans were on the higher ground, and they were firing down. There was a dirt road with ditches on either side. Bullets were hitting all around. I got into the ditch, and I'm laying flat on my back. The road bed is here, and the bullets are striking the bank. The bank on that side was a little higher. If it was lower, the bullets would have come right down.

Then they let up. In the meantime, the other guys were firing, but I was in a spot where I couldn't even get up. If I would have got up, I'd have got hit.

Also you're frightened. And you talk about frightened, you stop breathing actually. In Holland, too, in the town of Weiler, we got in one hell of a fight with the Germans, and there I actually stopped breathing. Stopped breathing. I ran I'd say 200 yards without taking a breath of air. My heart even stopped. This is what it's like when you get into a fight. You see these pictures on television, it's such a joke. There's no such thing as these so-called hero-baloney. Everybody I knew of, they were frightened stiff when they were really into a fight.

But anyway, we finally got to Hill 30. Just before that we got very heavily shelled. They were using aerial shells that burst above the ground. I don't know that much about artillery because I was never in the artillery. But that shrapnel's coming down, and one guy got a big sliver like this [about four inches] into his rump, and I hit the ground. I lift my head after they stop shelling, and there's smoke in front of me. I look, and there's a hole. A piece of shrapnel had just come down into the ground. And the hot shrapnel, with the moisture, was making smoke come up. It missed me just by inches. The other guy got hit in the rump.

We finally got to Hill 30. We had a lot of casualties. Some minor. We left a few dead here and there. We got to Hill 30, and we set up.

Aaron Elson: About how many men were in your group?

Ed Boccafogli: On the hill, there were 180 to 200 men. Across the river, in Chef du Pont, Colonel Lindquist had assembled another 200. So between the two sides we had control of the causeway.

Now we had to hold it until the 4th [Infantry Division] finally reached us four days later, and then they could get across and continue their drive.

Then we went south, to Beuzeville. We took the bridges there.

Aaron Elson: In that three-day fight, what kind of equipment did you have?

Ed Boccafogli: We had mortars. And one light artillery piece. That was it. I went on three different patrols to try to get ammunition, because we ran out. When we jumped we all had four bandoliers of ammunition across our belt. And by the second day we ran out. That's how much we used. I was down to one clip and six or seven rounds. Then finally we got some ammunition.

Aaron Elson: What was it like going on the patrols?

Ed Boccafogli: We went down through the swamp. We went all the way down to where the water was there [in an aerial photograph]. There were some farms in there. It looks very small but that's a big area. We only took a section because we wanted to get the causeway.

There were ten or twelve of us. Warnecke, he was my platoon sergeant. Eventually he was made a battlefield commission, stayed in the military, and retired a full colonel. He sent a tape, too, to the Eisenhower Center, [in which] he says, "And can you imagine me, with the name Adolph Warnecke, and with a slight German accent. ..." They couldn't find better soldiers, though. Knapp, another one, Jannigan, all from B Company, became battlefield commissions. I had been put in in the Bulge, but the war ended, and then the whole thing stopped.

Getting back, so they attacked us, and during the early morning we tried to go down and get some ammo from the parachute bundles in the swamp. Some of the parachutes had different colors, and the colors represented what would be in that bundle. But half the parachutes were already sunk. We'd see part of it standing up. Mixed in, we'd see a red, white and blue one, or a white and red one. A lot of them landed in the swamp. Some of them had a body on them, too. The white ones.

We spread out along the edge and waded into the swamp. I got out maybe from here to across the road over there, grabbed a parachute, and the water was about [up to my chest]. I'm trying to keep my head low, and me and this other kid are pulling the parachute. And as we're pulling, bullets start ricocheting off the water from the other side. The Germans spotted us. I go under water, the helmet and everything. I come up, get some air, pull.

We get to the bank, and as we're pulling the parachute up, this kid Maloney standing right beside me, "Poom!" Right dead in the chest. We had to leave the body there.

We brought the bundle up, and what we were looking for was mortar rounds and rifle ammunition. I forget what was in there, but there was very little of what we needed. Then we had to go down and get another one. And then they sent other patrols. Finally, little by little, we retrieved about ten bundles.

Aaron Elson: Were these patrols at night or during the day?

Ed Boccafogli: Daytime. Then I went out on the second day. We had a patrol, and there were six of us, to see if we could round up some fellows. We were walking along a hedgerow, when all of a sudden a guy screamed.

And he's down in the ditch, all covered with hay. It was a young lieutenant. He had been shot through the legs. He crawled into the ditch, and pulled all the weeds and stuff over him, and he lay there. He said all day the first day and part of the second day he watched Germans go by. He saw the silhouette of the helmets. Night patrols, day patrols.

All of a sudden he saw us and let out a scream. He was so happy.

Another time we went out, and we got into a hell of a firefight. There's a lot of ditches there, a lot of sunken roads. We got into a firefight and one of our men was killed, one guy wounded, two or three Germans. They finally broke off, and we captured a flak gun, which they had been dragging.

We got it back [to the hill]. We had no ammunition for it, but at least we had a gun. They had one less to shoot at us.

To give you an idea of how many casualties we had, out of 2,010 in the regiment, on the 14th of July I think there were 900 left. Three hundred and some killed. I think six hundred or so wounded. And four or five hundred missing.

When we went to the reunion in 1976, there were only about 24 of us, but from my company there were only four of us. Everybody was crying. It's unbelievable. Because when I got discharged from the Army, I had 90 days to reenlist. They picked out about 20 of us noncoms and brought us up to headquarters, gave us a big spiel that they were gonna form a new training unit, and that we would be raised in rank and we would be the cadre to introduce the new unit, which was the Green Berets at the time.

So we had ninety days. When I got back I met my wife, and then I said I had enough. I didn't want no more war. But a couple of them stayed in. In fact, one guy, his name is De Vries, from Wallington, he stayed in. He went through Normandy, he went through everything; he went all the way through to Korea, to Vietnam. He was a command sergeant major; got every god darn decoration. I wrote to him, and he wasn't home, because then he was still in the military, and never got an answer.

You know who was in my company? Bill Windham, the actor. He was one of my riflemen. He came to a couple of reunions. He plays the doctor in "Murder She Wrote."

Ed Boccafogli: I always say the fortunate part of the Depression was that it toughened that era of kids. They were brought up in adversity. They'd go to school with holes in their shoes, patched up clothes. They didn't have the food like they have today. They eat too god darn much pizza. People lived on corn meal and potatoes during the Depression.

These are the kids that ended up being the tough soldiers that we had.

It's very sad, now that I look back, at all the guys that died. Go back to Holland, I lost one kid there. I put him in for a decoration. If it wasn't for him quite a few of us would have been killed. He set the barn on fire. The Germans had gotten into it, and we had nothing but a quarter of a mile of slightly inclined [land] going back with nothing but haystacks. There was no way of getting out of there, and he broke it up.

My wife and I were over in Europe, and we went to the cemetery to find his grave. We had to leave him there, in Weiler, when we pulled out. We felt him for a pulse, and he was dead.

We went to the graveyard, and I asked at the office, "A fellow named Ellerbush is supposed to be in the cemetery, a kid from Kansas." So he looks in the book. He says, "No name here. If he was killed, he isn't here."

Then when we were ready to leave he came out and said, "Pardon me, sir, there are some late entries." So he went to another office and got the book. He said, "There he is." They had built a wall, and had the names of all those that were found. Some of them were found buried, and they didn't know who they belonged to, because some of them were buried with the Germans and later on they found out it was an American, and there [his name] was on the wall. It made me feel better.

Aaron Elson: Let me go back to this [reading from the transcript of Boccafogli's taping session for the Eisenhower Center]. "We had quite a confused mess. We had men from the 505 PIR and we had men from the 101st Airborne Division mixed in with us. So we dug in the positions there and tried to hold Hill 30. We had several attacks later in the day and there was quite a bit of shelling coming in on us. That night, they attacked us from two sides. The next day they attacked from three sides. Each time we'd throw them back. The artillery was bad, because it was coming in and we were getting casualties more from the artillery."

Ed Boccafogli: Our own artillery, coming in from the coast. They were shooting big stuff in, and the stuff would come overhead. A lot of it would land on top of us, and then go down into the valley there. That helped break up the attacks, but it also gave us quite a bit of agita. It's terrible when that big stuff comes in from the coast.

Aaron Elson: I've been told they sounded like freight trains.

Ed Boccafogli: Oh yeah. Christ, in Holland, I'll never forget. They must have had the Big Berthas because when they would come in, you'd hear 'brrrrrrrrrrrrrrrr' way high up in the stratosphere. And you're in a hole, half sitting in water. And then all of a sudden "BOOOM!!" Then it settled down. It seemed like we were floating on the water. Damn hole. You'd be in there and you'd hear plop-plop-plop-plop-plop, big blobs of crap and mud, trees coming down. This stuff would blow in the air and come down at you like cow flops. And then the hole would partially cave in. There were dozens of holes like that, all through the area. And then at night, if you had to take a poop you had to crawl over into the edge of those holes. You couldn't go down too far because they'd fill up with water. They were as big as this room, as this house.

Aaron Elson: [reading]. "It seemed that most of the heavy fighting was to the north of us at La Fiere Bridge. There was another unit there, and they were in some battle, because day and night you could see the flashes in the sky. It was like the Fourth of July.

"Eventually our troopers did take the bridge. Later on, I think it was the fourth day, one of the regiments of the 9th Division finally reached us, and that took a lot of pressure off us. We were organized to start to push south, and we headed down to another bridge crossing."

Ed Boccafogli: I can still see the town on the other side. And there, too, we got shelled from the coast. And a lot of them landed on us. I mean big stuff. You could hear them screeching through the atmosphere. They come in, and we're over here waiting to cross, and they're hitting the village on the other side. They blew that village to pieces.

We were more afraid of that than we were of the Germans. That's why in Desert Storm when those poor Arabs got bombed over there, I wouldn't have wanted to be in their shoes for nothing. They were ready to surrender. There's nothing like a devastating bombardment. Your nerves get shattered. You can't stop shaking. People don't understand that. You see the movies and they get bombed. A guy says, "Yeah, all right, well, let's see, we'll open a can of Spam." Like it's almost a joke.

Aaron Elson: What is it like when you hear the shells?

Ed Boccafogli: You're shaking. In Holland we got hit so bad when we crossed the Nedercanal, the Neder Rhine. See, you've got two parts of the Rhine there. You've got the one up at Eindhoven and the one at Arnheim. Arnheim was where the British went and were wiped out.

We finally crossed over and we were going up to relieve them, and that's it.

We stopped at Lint – Lint or Alst. And then the Germans started shelling us. They even hit the bridge. And this stuff would come in, big, heavy stuff, and all Holland would just pick up and come down. And you're shaking. You can't stop shaking. You're safe in that foxhole. That shell's got to come in to kill you. Or come close enough to bury you alive. But your nerves get shattered, and you're squatted down in there like this [bringing his knees up to his chest]. Because you're in the water, if you go down further you drown. And the ground is above you. Usually you'd dig buddy holes, in other words two guys in a hole. And there was Moline, a big Swede who was with me. And he's in there shaking; you can't stop. Your knees hurt, and the tension is so high you want to stand up to relieve that tension, but you can't because your head would be above, and the shrapnel would cut you right in half.

I said to Moline, "I can't take much more." And he said, "Me neither." He says, "I'm gonna crack up."

I said, "I'm gonna crack up before you."

You go hours with shelling like that. We were in an orchard, a beautiful orchard, whatever they were, apple, pear trees. And then when it finally lets up, you look out, and you could swear a giant lawnmower came over there and just cut it clean. There wasn't one tree that wasn't just cut to pieces. And all that time I don't think we lost two or three men, because it had to get in the hole to actually kill you. The holes would cave in on you, and they'd just throw the dirt out. But even when it got bad, you'd dig down there and poop right in the hole, throw some mud on it. Miserable. Then your legs itch, because you're in there for weeks, and you didn't take a bath or nothing. There's mud and everything and your skin starts to itch. Especially where your clothes are tight.

It's hard to describe. I'll tell you, boy, the mind just cracks.

Aaron Elson: Did you see anybody get combat fatigue?

Ed Boccafogli: Oh yeah. In Weiler we had one. I was on a patrol. I was always the lead scout. They used me and this Mexican kid as the lead scout, all the time.

We went down off the high ground, Bergendahl, which is high ground, a hundred feet higher than anything around. That's a mountain in Holland. We went down through the gullies, and into Weiler.

We didn't know at the time that that was German territory. So they decided to occupy Weiler, a small village on the Donhoevel Road, which comes from Bergendahl and goes all the way down to Groesbeck, which the 504th had taken. And then beyond Weiler was a big forest. And they were afraid that there was armor in there.

So me and Lieutenant Glein and the Mexican kid, we go down through the gullies, get into the town, walk around the town. There wasn't a thing. When you don't hear a cat, a dog, or see a civilian, you know that's occupied. Because people, the first thing they do is take their pets and disappear. They go in the cellar, they go anyplace, hide, or leave the village.

We went in the village and said Jesus, nothing in there. Went all around. At the edge of the town it dropped off another 30 or 40 feet down into a swamp. From there you could see all the way to the bridge at Arnheim, about eight miles away.

We came all the way around the edge, and went in a couple of buildings, looked inside. In one building there was some German gear. And it's strange, because they don't leave and leave their gear. And then I'm thinking, back in Normandy, I was in a similar situation. I started getting butterflies. We figured there's something wrong in this town.

Still, we went around, went all the way down, came all the way back. Then we headed back up to the hill, and reported the town was not occupied.

They radioed back, and I guess headquarters says, "Okay, move Company B down there and occupy it." So just before dark, we moved down to the first part of the town. It was a whole town, but there was a double apron barbed wire fence, and a trolley line and a road. So we figured that's Weiler, and this must be another town.

Then we dug in and set up a roadblock, because the road coming from the one end was where the Germans were. I dug a hole. We set up weapons. And there was a pile of railroad ties. So we just pushed them up nice, and dug a hole, figured what a beautiful parapet. The bullets come and it'd stop them. I dig down. The ground was real soft, and all of a sudden I hit a glass jar. I said, "Sonofabitch, I've got to get cut," and I'm taking and throwing the jar out the side. I look, and I see money. So I clean around nice, and I pull this big jar out. It's full of money. I took all the money, gelders, kroners, what the hell. I figured this money is worthless now, the country's invaded. That's how stupid I was. I took all that money, rolled it up in a big roll, stuck it in my pocket, and took all the coins and filled them in my steel helmet. Then I said, "What the hell am I gonna do with this?" So I called the guys over and gave them some money. I got rid of it. I had these two big wads of paper money.

Then orders come to pull out and move to the other end of the town. So I left the foxhole there.

When I went back [a few years ago] I wanted to go and see that farmhouse, but I figured the people would take me and throw me in jail for stealing that money.

We move to the other end of the town, and we set up where it dropped off. I'd taken a grenade – there was a sunken road going down to the lower part of the town, there was a big field over here and there was a road coming out of the forest. I had a 57 Bofur lined up with the road.

Aaron Elson: A 57 what?

Ed Boccafogli: Bofur. That's like a 57-millimeter antitank gun, with machine gun ammo. Beyond that, I don't know. All I know is you fire them, they do damage.

So I get out on this open spot to see the flank, because we couldn't see down below. I told this one kid to dig in over there where he could see. I took a grenade, and I took some string out of one of the buildings, and I put the grenade with the pin anchored to the string. I figured anything coming up in the dark is gonna trip it, the grenade would go off, and it's a warning. Also, nail the guy who's coming up.

It got dark. Everything's quiet. I figure, well, I'm on a corner and I had a grenade launcher. So I put my grenade launcher on, with the grenade on top. And I sat there nice and comfortable, looking at the road.

Comes dawn, it's all like a mist, a heavy mist, just starting to clear to where you could see. All of a sudden, "whirrrrrr," there's a motor coming. A truck comes out of the mist, coming right straight toward us. A German truck with troops.

Evidently they didn't know we were there, and they thought it was still their troops occupying the town. There were Germans in there. They had gone into the church and hid when we moved in. This we figured out later.

In the meantime, everybody's asleep. It's a nice morning, the fog, everything quiet. I hear this motor coming. So I anchor my rifle, and fire the grenade. "Poom!" It falls short, by about 20 feet.

He put the brakes on, and he stopped. The guys woke up when they heard the explosion and opened up. They hit the cab of the truck. Germans were spilling out. Everybody opened up, machine guns, everything. We must have got at least half a dozen, a couple of them escaped. Blew the truck apart.

Then we start getting fire. They must have realized what happened when they heard all the shooting, and they started shelling us. And they were hitting everything in the town.

Then they started coming across the open ground, but there are a lot of culverts. You could see them come through the ditches and then they'd jump the culverts where the little farm roads were. We were picking them off left and right. And me, I've got the M-1, and I couldn't fire. It jammed on me. When I fired that rifle grenade, the thing ruptured inside. I couldn't open it up. I had cut my hand all open trying to get it unjammed.

I'm running around the town trying to get this damn thing open. In the meantime everybody's opening up, and the Germans pull a full-scale attack. They come from all over.

I run over towards the church. I get over by the church, and there's Evans – the kid Evans, he was a sergeant – and a lieutenant.

By then orders had come to pull back onto the other side of the road because we were outnumbered. I don't think we had a hundred men there, and they pulled a full-scale attack.

I got over by the church, and as I'm by the church, two Germans came around a corner and were looking straight at me. Now they could have killed me. I'm up against the parapets on the side of the church. I'm jammed up against there and I'm shaking. I couldn't breathe, that's how scared I was. And I'm looking at them. And one of them's looking at me, he could see part of me. And he's saying something – now, whether he saw me or saw the other kid, Evans, I don't know. Evans was behind a tree and the lieutenant was a little further over. I don't think they could see them. And he's saying something I couldn't understand. He's not saying "Hande-ho," but what he was saying I didn't know. I was so scared. I put my gun down on the ground, my hand was bleeding all over from trying to pull that damn lever. And I stood up on top of the lever – this is all in a second I did this – Rrrrrrr, I jammed, and "Poom!" It ejected the shell. And I took the rifle up, I emptied the whole clip, and I nailed one of them. The other one, as he went around the corner, I saw him fall. There were three of them altogether. Two of them came out, but one went back.

Then I started running. Evans and the lieutenant started running. We were the last ones out of that part of the village. We go across an open field. There's a fence, and the fence comes to the Donhoevel Road. At the Donhoevel Road there's a trolley line, and a double apron barbed wire fence. That's why we thought the barbed wire fence was a border. But it wasn't. And the fence goes right up to a barn. We ran across, bullets flying in all directions. It's a miracle we didn't get hit. All three of us go in through the goddarn barn, and then we went over a stone wall on the other side of the road.

I went over the wall. Believe me, I didn't breathe once, from after I shot until I got to there. And I think my heart even stopped. That's how fast I was running, how scared I was. I got over that wall and "Aaaaahhhh, Aaaahhhh" [heaving sounds], finally I started breathing.

I stood there a minute, and there was Mackey. Mackey, my friend, he was over on the side. He came over to see how I was. Man, my heart was stopped.

And then I had this kid Ellerbush; that's who I mentioned. The Germans got into the barn, and all along the line there, everything opened up. All our guns were opened up. It was one of the most brutal battles we had. And Ellerbush crawled out in the open. He had the bazooka, and he fired into the barn. The first one didn't do anything.

He loaded up again, and fired. In the meantime he crawled way out in the open, and he got hit through the side.

The barn caught fire. And at the same time, the British reached us. They're up on the high ground. These are British tanks. And they're firing down into the town on us. They're hitting the buildings, they're hitting the stone walls. The walls are made out of stone and mortar. God darn bricks, stones and everything are coming down on top of us. So the Germans are shooting at us, the barn is on fire. The flames must have gone two hundred feet in the air. The Germans spilled out. As they're spilling out the guys are shooting and knocking them down, and I'm yelling, "Don't kill 'em! Don't kill 'em! We want to get prisoners." Then we motioned them to come in, and so we took quite a few prisoners.

Aaron Elson: And the British were shooting at you?

Ed Boccafogli: The British are on the hill shooting at us. Our radio operator went crazy. We're on different frequencies. He was at the other end, where the captain was. They say he tried to get them. He couldn't get them, and he felt a responsibility. He started going across the open ground, to go up on the hill to try to tell them. "Boom!" They nailed him out in the field, killed him. Finally, after about an hour or so the British must have realized somehow that we were in the town and they were shooting at us. Then the tank firing let up. But the Germans and us were still firing back and forth.

This was late in the afternoon. Now we had to get out of that town. There was no way we could hold it. We were outnumbered like 20 to 1. There was only one solution. Get the hell up to the high ground.

So orders came to activate all the mortar ammunition, pull the pins and leave it all there. And I went over. Ellerbush got hit. He was stone cold, and we had to leave his body there. But if he didn't hit that barn, the Germans would have crossed that road and got behind us.

As it started to get dark, we got the German prisoners to carry the wounded. The walking wounded walked, and other guys we'd put on doors, ladders, anything we could get. Oh, cowardice, that's what I wanted to bring out. This one kid, Sergeant Vento, a good sergeant up until that point, left his whole squad. And they found him underneath the crawl space, because there are no cellars over there. He was down there shaking like a dog with the tail between his legs. He was broken down, and we transferred him out to supplies later on.

At the time I had nothing but contempt for him. But then later on I thought, how many men used every method not to be there. At least this guy went his full measure. He went through Normandy, all the way to there, and then all of a sudden something just went "Poom!" That's it. Battle fatigue, whatever you call it. Later on I had compassion for him. But he left his squad, and most of them were either killed or taken prisoner.

Aaron Elson: Is this many years later?

Ed Boccafogli: No, it was while we were still in England. You start to think. And then we had the young punks come in. We're in Germany as occupation troops, and the young punks had never even seen an enemy. "Hey, ya goddamn Kraut." An old man. This old man could be his grandfather. "Get out of here ya goddamn Kraut." They act nasty to people. We'd go to the mess hall. We had the three garbage cans where we'd put the edible, non-edible. You'd see an old lady there with gray hair, a little kid over there with a bucket waiting to get something. You're not supposed to fraternize or give them nothing. What, are you kidding? All of us would say, "Hey, Hans. Come over here, Fritz." We'd call the woman over, give her whatever we saved – a potato or something. Then you think, it could be my mother. The suffering these people went through.

But anyway, that guy left his squad, and as dark got in, with phosphorous shells we started setting all the haystacks on fire. We went back with these ladders, and the Germans carried them, too. The prisoners carried the ladders with our wounded. We went in a long file, up the hill, till we finally got to the high ground.

Then for two days they attacked us with everything. They never dislodged us from the high ground. That was it, we stopped them dead. There were a lot of German casualties; they just couldn't take the hill. Then we pulled out after the British finally reached us and stabilized everything. But of those tanks that were shooting at us, every one of them was knocked out by German 88s. As they came up on the knoll, they'd nail them like clay pigeons.

Aaron Elson: Which tanks were these?

Ed Boccafogli: The British tanks. I think they lost seven of them, they all got knocked out. Those 88s were accurate, like rifle fire.

Then we moved across the river there, the same thing. The British, they got so far, and then they refused to go any further. Poor bastards up there. The British bastards up in Arnheim. That's it, they were lost. The ones that finally got back looked like they had gone through hell. Their eyes were coming out of their head. Out of 10,000 men that were dropped into Arnheim, they lost 8,200 men.

Aaron Elson: Tell me about when you were wounded.

Ed Boccafogli: After Baupte finally fell. Baupte was bad. They were shooting antitank shells. They were coming right through the trees. There's nothing like an antitank shell, which is armor piercing. When it hits a tree it ricochets. That's worse than shrapnel. That thing is slapping trees and ricocheting and it doesn't explode unless it hits point blank. Boy, that was the weirdest sound.

Then we pulled out, and I was put ahead, Hernandez and myself, as head scouts. We were moving along this dirt road, and they said they spotted a large body of Germans from the air. Another company, a quarter of a mile away, was moving forward, trying to see if we could contact and flank them.

I'm going along this dirt road. All of a sudden the road drops off on the side of the hill and goes down, then levels off, and there's farmhouses. And they opened fire on us. Well, my job was done. I drew fire. I hit the ground. And the next squad deploys immediately and opens fire. I can't fire back. If I stand there, the second shot's gonna get me for sure. So I hit the ground and let the squad take care of it.

Now two Polish soldiers come out with their hands up. "Me Polski! Me Polski!" That was bad, because up ahead was the main body of Germans, or enemy. The enemy had everything there. They had Poles, they even had Russians that were taken prisoner and were put up in the front as soldiers. Now they heard the shooting, so they knew that there's a movement coming towards them.

We took the two prisoners. The old man, Millsaps, says, "Okay, move ahead." So I go ahead. We're two hundred yards ahead of the main body, one on each side of the road. We're going along, and we come to thicker brush, and then thicker woods. On the side it was low ground and fields up above. So as we're coming in I hear a high-pitched screech. I stop, put my hand up, and move over to a wall. I look and see a farmhouse inside the walls, like a chalet, and another building. So I stop. The old man comes running up and says, "What's up?"

I told him what I heard. I said, "It sounds either like a woman screaming or a high-pitched voice yelling."

He said, "You and Hernandez take off on the right flank." He called up Thomas and another kid and said, "Skirt those buildings and keep going." That scream was the angel on my shoulder. The old man must have thought I was starting to get jittery. So we go off about a hundred yards to the right flank of the column, as side riders. We're going along, going along, maybe another six hundred yards. The two scouts ran right smack into the German positions, and instead of waiting, to let the main body come forward, one of the Germans opened up and killed both of them.

Then the company deployed, and the firing started.

We had some battles that were brutal, but this one was unbelievable. There must have been thirty or forty machine guns going at any one time. Bullets were cutting everything apart. Mortars were coming in.

We're out on a flank, and I'm trying to work my way back in. I work over to a hedgerow. I get to this dirt bank, and I climb up, trying to see ahead, and I look out and I see something shine, and I open up. Next thing I know, "Poom!" The dirt flies up against me. I get down. Crawl away from there. Climb up on the bank again, and look, look, look. I'm next to a tree. I'm looking, looking, and see something out there like brush moving. I open up. Then, "Pow!" The bark and everything flies off the tree. I figure this guy can see me. I didn't know where it was coming from. I go down the third time. I get up again. I get down in the brush. I fire two or three rounds. The next thing I know, "Pwwaaangg!" That was it. I got nailed beautiful. The bullet came from the right. The bullet went through the stock [of my gun], through my first aid packet, and tore my arm.

I'm laying on my back with my arm under me. I'd rolled off the bank and passed out. Then I start to come to, and I figure I'm dead. All I see is clouds, like a mist, and I figure I'm going to heaven. Then I started to feel pain, and in the tree above me I could see the leaves start to form. I said, "Holy Christ, I'm still here." Then I hear machine guns going. Everything comes back, and I think I must have been hit in the face. I'm numb from [the top of my head] down. I had one pain all through my body. I didn't know where I was hit.

Finally I look and I see the blood squirting out. My arm is under me. And I thought, "Jesus, they blew my arm off." I rolled over, finally got my arm out, stuck my hand in and squeezed the blood into the hole.

Hernandez came over. In the meantime, I'm going into shock because of all this blood I'm losing. "Ahh," he says, "You're okay." He takes my canteen and he gives me a drink, and I'd milked a cow just before, and I got some milk. The milk was sour. I spit it out. Just like Jesus Christ on the cross, they give him vinegar. So he gives me some of his water. Then he takes off and he gets hit in the shoulder.

Then I got a handkerchief and put a tourniquet as tight as I could get it around there. I worked my way over to where the kid from Peoria ... what the hell is his name? I used to call it the whiskey capital of the world, Peoria, Illinois. I get over to him. He had the machine gun. The machine gun was firing so much that it was squealing. The bullets were squealing trying to get out. That's how hot the barrel was.

And then I went crazy. I had a luger, and I started firing, going from hedgerow to hedgerow. The old man's yelling at me to get the hell out of there, and I refuse. I went berserk. I started going after the Germans through the hedgerows. Finally they got me and they calmed me down and made me go back.

I got the Bronze Star, because when I went back I told Captain Taylor, he was back where the mortars were, I said, "You've got to come in closer. You're firing way the hell beyond." So they brought the mortars in and started pounding them. And then eventually, after about twenty more minutes, the fighting broke off. The Germans pulled out and we pulled out. It was too big. We hit a tremendous force there. We lost a lot of men. I think that day alone, I was one of them, but we must have lost fifteen to twenty men right there.

Aaron Elson: Where did you get the luger that you were firing?

Ed Boccafogli: Someplace between there and Baupte. We'd gotten in a fight and there was a dead German officer. I took the luger off of him. The luger had blood on it, and I cleaned it off. I always thought that was a curse. I should have never taken that gun. I took it off a dead body. These things hit you later on, when you look back. When I got wounded and was being evacuated, I gave that luger to somebody. Then I found out he was killed.

Don't touch the dead. We had one fellow, he had every kind of trinket you could imagine off dead bodies. He was a ghoul. He'd cut the finger off a dead body to get the ring off. He didn't give a damn.

Aaron Elson: He survived?

Ed Boccafogli: Yeah. He came to a reunion. We used to call him the Ghoul. A dead German ... he'd take the arm and cut off a watch.

Aaron Elson: I guess that happened a lot.

Ed Boccafogli: The Russians did that to the Germans, because the Russians were a lot of peasant people, and the Germans were more advanced. They all had watches. And the first thing they do is go for the watch, take it off the dead German. Rings and watches.

Aaron Elson: Towards the end of the war, were you with them when they entered any concentration camps?

Ed Boccafogli: No. We were stationed at Frankfurt, Germany, as honor guard, the 508th. I pulled sergeant of the guard at SHAEF [Supreme Headquarters of the Allied Expeditionary Force]. Two times. You had all the dignitaries there, and you were shaking in your boots because you had to march around and come in front, with the parade and everything, and salute. It was quite a show. I was even in Eisenhower's office, and I was in the war room with the officer of the day. All plush rugs. Maps all over the wall, the Pacific and everything. I got in there because I was sergeant of the guard with the officer of the day. Otherwise I'd have never gotten in there.

My wife and I are going back in June [1994] to Normandy. That'll be the last hurrah. I'm going to pay tribute, visit all the graves, the cemeteries, in Belgium. There are a few of us. I don't know how many men from my company are going. Some of them can't afford it, and some of them are too old now. A lot of them have died. We've lost 11 men since the last newsletter. They're dying left and right now.

"This friend of mine, Dan Donovan – he was in Guadalcanal during the war – he says, 'Hey Lou, you know where that guy's going?'

"I said, 'No.'

"He says, 'He went there last year, and he's going again this year. He's taking his vacation and he's going to England. Then he's going to take the ferry over to France, and he's gonna start going from hospital to hospital, and different churches. He's going to go look for his son.'"

Man Overboard

Lou Putnoky
USS Bayfield
Edison, N.J., April 16, 1994

Lou Putnoky: In 1939 I lied about my age and got into the Civilian Military Training Corps. I spent two summers at Fort Dix. If you went four years, you became an officer in the Reserves, in the infantry. After two years, however, I said, "I'm not going to any infantry," and I immediately switched. When I enlisted in the Coast Guard, I never even told them about this training so that they wouldn't get any ideas.

Aaron Elson: You must have been about 15 when you went to the CMTC.

Lou Putnoky: That's right. I had my mother sign for me. As long as she signed, and I lied about my age, it was okay to go. When you're young, you're enthusiastic about things like that.

Aaron Elson: What soured you on the infantry?

Lou Putnoky: We went on a 15-mile hike this one summer, down in Fort Dix. It was over a hundred degrees, and we had one canteen of water. That was the thirstiest I have ever been in my life, until this day. They say that if you haven't been thirsty, really thirsty, you don't know what it is to really have a drink of water. If you haven't really been hungry, you don't know what it is to sit down and enjoy a meal.

Until this day, when I'm real thirsty, my mind goes back to that day in Fort Dix. We trained with the 16th Infantry. We had to go 15 miles with full packs, and then they brought us our meal by Army truck, and they brought us water. They gave us a pretty good meal, considering it was field training. They had butter in ice water so that it wouldn't melt. It was a 2,000-man training group. You drank out of these rubber lister bags, and I couldn't quench my thirst until 11 or 12 o'clock at night.

We drank the water that the butter was being cooled in. You just couldn't get enough. That's how wrung out we were. This was my second year. The third year is when the war broke out and they eliminated this whole program. Then they went right into full training.

I graduated from high school in June of 1941. Pearl Harbor was on December 7th, and like all young people at the time I figured I'm going to have to go into the service eventually, so I was looking at the services. There were three and a half million people in the Navy, and another three and a half million or so in the Army.

Good Lord, little old me. I thought I'd get lost in either of those. Then the Marines had so many. So I started looking, and I always admired the Coast Guard. I knew that the Navy took them over during the war, and it was harder to get into the Coast Guard than it was to the Navy. I'll bet you have no idea what the total amount of people in the Coast Guard was in World War II. It was in the neighborhood of 125,000. So I thought I'd give the Coast Guard a shot.

When we got over to England, our ship got the attention of Admiral Moon, who was looking for a flagship. He picked the Bayfield. When he came aboard, he had additional staff, so we fell under the admiral's staff. But we had a Coast Guard captain, Captain Spencer, who after Normandy and Southern France ended up being made an admiral and going to Washington.

After the Normandy and Southern French invasions, we were coming back for repairs to Norfolk, and he addressed us.

He said, "I'm being transferred, and there's only a handful of people being transferred off your ship, because you are so well-trained and you are so badly needed."

He said, "We're going to be in port for 30 days for repairs. Half the crew will go home the first 15 days. When they come back, the second half will go home."

Then he said, "I shouldn't tell you this, but I know you can handle it. Go home, get everything in order, and when you come back your ship is going to the Pacific," and he told us with a lump in his throat, "You will not come back until the war is over."

Then we went out, we made Iwo Jima and Okinawa, as flagship once again. And when I say flagship, that means carrying an admiral attached to your ship, and that flagship is in charge of that whole task force until those men get ashore. Once they get ashore, they come under their own commanders, but it was that admiral's job to get those men on that beach in the safest way he possibly can.

It proved to be a real job, and a beautiful job they did. I'm more amazed today as to what happened during World War II than I was at the time. And they accomplished all this without computers. Today we can't move without computers. That was all done by hand, calculations and everything else and your personnel records following here and there. It was so ancient, and they did such a magnificent job when you stop and think about how complex it was – what they accomplished in both theaters of war. I think they could never do it today.

The way the American public backed the servicemen during World War II was phenomenal. If you got off the ship and you were in the States and you went out to the highway and you were thumbing a ride, every car would stop. Everybody had their heart behind the war program. It was something to behold, and to feel. I know when I tell my son the story, once in a while, because once in a while he gets me talking, he's still amazed by it.

I can never forget that feeling of coming home and visiting the plant and seeing the women that took the place of the men, and seeing women crane operators in the plant. It had 2,000 employees. Of course this is all gone now [showing an enlarged photograph], this is all bulldozed, this is all warehouses now. And this was there for 100 years.

Aaron Elson: Which plant was this?

Lou Putnoky: This was the U.S. Metals refinery here in Cartaret. We produced one-eighth of the world's copper. We always had between $30 million and $40 million in precious metals. That was a byproduct that we had gotten from the smelting operation.

Lou Putnoky: I washed socks with Caesar Romero. He was on our sister ship, the Calloway, and we were on Ellis Island, and I went in there to wash socks and who's there but Caesar Romero. I said, "Caesar, you've got dirty socks, too?"

He said, "I sure do." So we washed socks together. Victor Mature was in the Coast Guard, too.

Here's a photo of Danny Delanowitz, a very good friend of mine from Brooklyn. We had a German helmet, and every once in a while when things would get dull, we'd get Danny and we'd put a big raincoat on him. We'd put the helmet on his head, he'd get a comb and put it under his nose, and then in German he would imitate Hitler. He had him down to a science, and he was always good for a laugh. God bless him, he had such a good way about him.

These are the first six Japanese prisoners taken on Iwo Jima. They had their heads shaved, and they were aboard our ship. There were a few others. But Iwo Jima, you figure between American and Japanese casualties, 26,000 men died. Twenty six thousand men. I mean, it's mind boggling.

Aaron Elson: This is the flag at Mount Suribachi?

Lou Putnoky: This isn't the actual one, although maybe it is. I saw that the following morning. When we saw that flag up there it sure made us feel good, because that was their observation point. They had the island all zeroed in. Actually, being perfectly honest, that whole operation was a bit of a fiasco because they never guessed that there were that many Japanese dug in there. That operation was supposed to last at the most two weeks, and it was supposed to be maybe one-tenth of what it was.

One out of three Americans that hit the beach was either wounded or killed. The beach was black gravel. And you just got so high, and you couldn't get any further in the beginning. They would just lob mortar shells in there, and they'd bounce off the beach, about a foot high. You had to get inland and get the hell off of there. There was just no protection. The Japanese were fierce fighters, and they were dug in so deep, and they expected this invasion so they were prepared for it, and they were taking their toll, unbelievably so. We just had to get Mount Suribachi because that's where all their observers were. After that they were just shooting blind, and they were still hitting Americans. In fact, I remember one of my details there. I was on the bow lookout, it was towards dusk, and I hear bup-bup-bup. I didn't think anything and I look behind us and

I see a couple of flashes in the water. And I thought, that's strange. Then I hear another bup-bup-bup. And I got on the bridge. I said, "You'd better move," of course we never dropped anchor, we just drifted and floated. I said, "They're trying to get our range." Slowly we just pulled out of the area.

Lou Putnoky: In Normandy you had a 20-foot drop in tide, from high to low tide. I saw ships on the sand, with smoke coming out of their stacks. In the meantime, the whole harbor was mined by electronic mines. The Germans set up these magnetic mines. For instance, when the minesweeper came in and swept it, let's say he swept it 15 times, that mine could have been set up for 18 sweeps. So the minesweeper would say okay, I'm not getting anything, so you go in there and all of a sudden a ship would blow up here, a ship would blow up there. It was horrible. And you're out there in this area, you never know when you're going to trip one of these mines.

Here's an interesting picture. This is a ship that was sunk right alongside of us. See the silhouette? These are bombs dropped by enemy planes, and this is all antiaircraft fire. The whole sky was lit up. This appeared in Liberty magazine, but they could never mention the name Bayfield. They didn't want to give it away, so that was eliminated off the caption. Of course we knew it was our ship. The photographer gave me a copy of this. This is a fantastic picture, that whole sky, now all the shrapnel came raining down like hail. These 20 and 40-millimeter explosives would explode up there and then come raining down, that's the main reason for the helmet, to protect you from those shrapnel pieces.

Aaron Elson: Did it really look like that?

Lou Putnoky: It looked worse. It lit up the whole sky. These are tracer bullets, and you could smell the cordite, because your ship was also contributing. You could smell it and the explosions. I don't even know what you'd compare it to. Have you ever seen the finale of a fireworks display? That's the closest to the sound, especially when these 90-millimeter guns and five-inch cannon would be going off. You could feel the heat in the back of your neck.

Aaron Elson: How long would the firing last?

Lou Putnoky: Until the enemy plane was gone from the area. If they were a wave, it would be a burst of maybe half a minute. Then it would ease up. Then another plane would come, then you'd get another ten, fifteen seconds. It would be in spurts. But you never knew what's happening, and that's the part that's so trying on a serviceman. Of course, in a case like this, all your troops have to be below decks, and this kills them. I've seen Marines at Iwo Jima who were screaming because they heard the gunshots coming and everything else. They'd say, "We're trapped like rats!" We had to lock the hatches to keep them down there because they wanted to see when they got hit. They'd say, "I want to get off this fucking ship. I want to dig a hole, because at least on land I know what I'm doing." So they don't want to have any part of our life and we don't want to have any part of their life. Of course we saw, and we felt better, but they didn't see and they only heard. This drives a man nuts. It makes old men out of young ones, believe me.

Aaron Elson: I didn't know that the Germans got that many planes over the Channel. I was under the impression that the Allies had complete control of the skies.

Lou Putnoky: So much so that we shot down our own planes also. In fact, one of the pilots that was picked up by one of our landing crafts was brought aboard our ship, and he was cursing a blue streak. He was a young pilot. I wasn't actually there but some of the radio men told me. They went up to Admiral Moon, and Admiral Moon says, "Take it easy, son. You weren't supposed to be here." See, he came out of an overcast sky. "We feel bad about you being shot down. Calm down." And he settled down. He was lost up there, so he broke out of the clouds, and when he broke out of the clouds, we were told anything up there is going to be enemy at this particular point.

There was another incident that happened during Normandy. It happened to me personally.

On D-plus two or three we got a radio message for help from a PT boat. First of all, I'll tell you how the PT boats came over. This was Commander Buckley's squadron from Corregidor. He's the one that got MacArthur off Corregidor. So because of this gigantic invasion, they brought that whole squadron over to Normandy. And one of the boats called our ship for assistance. He said they're broached on a reef. So real fast we hustled up a crew, and two landing barges. The plan is to pull alongside, and we're going to try and broach on each side and tie the PT boat up, and bring it onto a safe shore, because it was laying off an enemy shore.

So we're heading over, and it's laying two or three hundred yards off an enemy shore, and just the skipper is with it because he told everybody else to get off.

The skipper is sitting in the bow, and he's got a Navy machine gun in his lap.

I can understand why he stayed with his boat. He knew if he lost his boat – he was a lieutenant junior grade – he would end up being a subordinate somewhere else, and god knows how long it would be before he got another boat, so he was staying with his boat. I admired him for that.

We pulled up on each side, real fast, and tied up, and from a distance the battleship Nevada was lobbing shells in to cover this rescue. We pulled out with full power on both landing crafts and we were able to back him off the reef. We brought him over maybe a mile and a half, onto a secure beach.

Everything is going pretty good. We're coming over to our beach, and it just so happens one of our planes had been shot down. This plane is going down, I see the pilot parachuting, he's heading right for the beach that we're heading for. This is all adding to this picture of the strangest day I ever had.

We broached this PT boat, we backed off, in the distance this pilot landed, and then we headed back. On our way back, an LST loaded with wounded hits a mine and blows up in the distance. We picked up six survivors, and other landing barges picked up some of the others.

Now we have to get back, because it's getting late. As we're heading back to our ship we get hailed by the battleship Nevada. We went over, and they said, "We had a man overboard," and asked us to look for him.

We made two passes around the Nevada, and we motioned to them that we couldn't find anything. Then we said we have to leave.

We went back to our ship, and they said, "Where were you guys? We thought maybe something happened to you."

Then, it was a strange thing. I don't know what made me even ask. I said to the radio operator, "There was a man overboard. The next time you're talking to the Nevada, ask them where the guy's from," because in the service you always asked that sort of thing.

That night I'm having a sandwich in the mess hall, and the radio operator said, "Hey Lou, that guy off the Nevada, he's from Jersey, from Carteret. His name is Duffy."

I said, "Oh, God." Just like that, it hit me. I knew the kid because I had gone to grade school with him. He didn't go to high school. But I knew the kid. He said John Duffy. I felt weird.

What happened is they lowered a gangway, and whenever any small boats came alongside the Nevada, it was his job to guide that boat in. The seas got rough, slammed him up against the ship, and he slid under. He must have had on his life jacket, but the seas were too rough. We never found him.

After the invasion of Normandy we had Southern France, Iwo Jima,

Okinawa, and I got discharged and went back to my job as timekeeper down at U.S. Metals, so this is two or three years after the war. We're doing payroll, and this man comes into the office, Scotty – I knew this boy's family. They lived on Chrome Avenue; there was a row of company homes. But you never spoke about any of this, especially when someone was killed in the service or missing. And I knew that this was his father. He was a little man, a very good-natured individual. He had two sons and his wife was an invalid; she had a back problem.

One day a friend of mine, who happened to be on that payroll, asked him, "Where are you going Scotty?"

He said, "I'm going on vacation. Two weeks."

So okay, he gave him the slip to get his money. As he left the office, this friend of mine, Dan Donovan – he was in Guadalcanal during the war – he says, "Hey Lou, you know where that guy's going?"

I said, "No."

He says, "He went there last year, and he's going again this year. He's taking his vacation and he's going to England. Then he's going to take the ferry over to France, and he's gonna start going from hospital to hospital, and different churches. He's going to go look for his son."

I said, "You mean he doesn't know what happened?"

"No. All he got was a missing in action telegram from the Navy."

So I stopped everything. All of a sudden I got this picture in my mind. I ran out, and I caught him at the railroad tracks as he was crossing over. I said, "Scotty!" I don't even … I hate to talk about it because it upsets me sometimes. I said "Scotty, you're going on vacation?"

He said, "Yeah."

I said, "You lost a son in Normandy?"

He said, "Yeah."

I said, "Your son was on the Nevada?"

He looked at me real strange, and said, "How do you know?"

I said, "Scotty, they never said anything?"

"No, I just got missing in action." It was hard for him to talk.

I said, "Scotty, I don't know how to tell you this. I was there." And I told him the story. And I felt every single emotion that this man felt, and it upset me terribly. He was elated, relieved, just knowing. See, a person doesn't know when you get a missing in action what that does. It would take a serviceman that's had some experience about something like this. And this little man with his little bandy legs, he turned and he jogged all the way home, across the field from the plant. And he never took his vacation.

Lou Putnoky: Just before the Southern French invasion, Admiral Moon committed suicide aboard our ship. He was the highest-ranking serviceman to commit suicide during World War II. But it was kept very quiet, because they didn't want the enemy to know. He shot himself with a .45. In fact that's documented in a book. There's an incident that happened in April of 1944, just before the Normandy invasion. It was the final training exercise. The name of it was Exercise Tiger, and a book was written about it by a British author. His name is Nigel Lewis. It's very enlightening. And it was kept quiet for many, many years.

Aaron Elson: Were you participating in it?

Lou Putnoky: Yes. Our admiral, and our task force was involved. The reason why this was hushed up was because the British fouled up. See, the British, it's a hard thing to say – they're good sailors, but the one thing that trips up the British is tradition. They get involved in these little traditional things that are extremely dangerous to warfare.

There were about five LSTs coming over, and one of their escorts had gotten into a little bit of an accident and had a little hole in the bow, and they radioed back to their base. You see, the British answered to the British admirals. It was a strange coalition that took place. Because of pride and tradition, it got to be very touchy, so you had to use kid gloves. They called their admiral, and their admiral told them to come on back, and nobody told Admiral Moon. So they go back to port, and it left this whole group of five LSTs exposed.

Now these LSTs were only a short distance, maybe 80 miles from the French coast. And there were these E-boats – an E-boat is over 100 feet long, they're narrow boats equipped with two torpedoes and 40-millimeter and other machine guns and cannons, and they could do about 25 knots. So they went out on the prowl, and they were devastating some of our shipping lanes, because they would sneak in, torpedo a couple of ships and then leave. They were black; you couldn't see them, and in the confusion of darkness …believe me, the confusion during war is the thing that kills you.

So they picked off and sunk three of our LSTs that were loaded with troops. Altogether we lost in the neighborhood of 750 men.

And they kept this so quiet. We knew aboard our flagship that something was going on in the distance, but we were getting it in dribs and drabs. I didn't find out until I read the book. I knew that there were a couple of LSTs, only because of what the radio operators had picked up. And the radio silence is very, very strict during a condition like this, and everything is in code. You can't get this kind of information until after, and this was kept quiet for in the neighborhood of 40 years. It's one of the biggest disasters of World War II.

Lou Putnoky: If you saw the picture "The Longest Day," we had aboard our ship General Roosevelt, "Lightning Joe" Lawton Collins, and another two-star general. We were going to Normandy on June 5th, and that night there was a cloudy sky but you had the moon breaking out every so often. We were standing on the fantail of the ship. We weren't at general quarters yet but close to it, so we were just talking, and we knew that it was some Army personnel that were with us. We knew that it happened to be an officer because we could see from the shadows, and all of a sudden the moon broke out and it lit up the fantail of our ship. That's when we looked and we saw the star, it was General Roosevelt. So we immediately apologized. We said, "General, we didn't realize you were a general," because he was talking so nice.

"Oh, son," he says, "don't let that bother you."

Olga Putnoky: [While Lou is talking on the phone with a former shipmate about an upcoming reunion] This has been so funny, because Lou has been getting calls from all over the United States. The best part of it is, in 48 years I've never been able to get him to go to Las Vegas. I've been dying to go. He's been getting calls from all over the United States, and the conversation will start out, "Are you that tall, skinny, curly headed kid?" And Lou will say "Are you the redhead that I pitched the football to and fell off the dock," and so forth. It's the nicest thing, it's wonderful.

Aaron Elson: How did you and Lou meet?

Olga Putnoky: Lou and I lived in Carteret, and we belonged to the same church. I was five years old and he was six. I was in the church play, and he and his mother were sitting in the first row. He said, "See that dark-haired girl? When she grows up I'm going to marry her." And we went to different schools. I went to Woodbridge and he went to Carteret. We started to date; nothing serious until after he got home from the service.

Aaron Elson: And you have how many children?

Olga Putnoky: We have two. We have Bruce, he's 44, and Diane, who's 40. We'll be married 48 years in May. We just had four 50th anniversaries of close friends. And our children were invited to all of them. They just could not get over it. Lou's parents were married over 70 years. His dad was 102 when he died. We had him for six years, taking care of him. Most of our friends have been married since around the time we got married. Lou's closest friend, his shipmate, called this morning from Long Island. We're godparents to his children.

We don't live for just today. I think that's the thing of it. Today's youngsters live for today. I was at a checkout line of a supermarket a couple of years ago. There were two very pretty young girls, and one said to the checkout girl, "I hear you're getting married. What made you decide?"

She said, "If it doesn't work out, I'll get rid of him." I was just shocked. I didn't say a word, I just listened, but what fools. Don't get married if you have that kind of an attitude. But we've just been very lucky in our relationship.

Aaron Elson: Did you work in a defense plant?

Olga Putnoky: I worked in U.S. Metals. I was the first girl hired in personnel. They hired me in 1941, and I stayed on until '49.

Aaron Elson: Did they make ammunition?

Olga Putnoky: Oh, yes. Our bosses used to go to New York, or North Carolina, South Carolina, Florida, to recruit labor. All the boys and the men from around here were in the service, and they [U.S. Metals] were a very big copper industry. We had the war bond rallies. It was really nice. I have some pictures of the women who worked there. They had such an attitude, these nice, quiet old ladies. Even the elderly women came to work, and they put their noses to the grindstone and worked. We had a lot of women during the war. And then slowly as the men came back, they were replaced.

Lou Putnoky: Admiral Moon flew back to Washington after the Normandy invasion. When he came back aboard, the guys noticed that he was a little bit nervous, high strung. But other than that they didn't pay much attention. I think it was two days before the Southern French invasion. He [pointing into his mouth] mmph, he shot himself. And the rumors aboard ship were, well, battle fatigue. They said he got into an argument in Washington in regards to the Southern French invasion, and they didn't want to follow his plan. He wanted to go up and hit the tougher beach at St. Rafel, and their plan was to hit around Marseilles. Marseilles was like a horseshoe, a natural harbor, and he said, "If we hit in here, they've been there so long, they're just gonna cut us to ribbons.

We're better off hitting a tougher beach. We're experienced enough, we can go in there," and sure enough, we hit the St. Rafel area, which was a tougher beach. But it was easier as far as casualties were concerned.

Aaron Elson: So they did hit the beach that Moon had wanted.

Lou Putnoky: Yes. But I definitely feel, now that I've read about this Exercise Tiger, that this played on his mind. In fact, there was one incident that happened during Exercise Tiger. Admiral Moon was up on the bridge, it was still dark, and there was either a DE [destroyer escort] or destroyer. It's hard for me to give you the picture. During a time like this it looks like one big mass of confusion, because ships are big and long, and they're drifting. As we're drifting in a little bit of moonlight, with all these other crafts there, this DE or destroyer cut across our bow, and you've got radio silence, and they were communicating mainly by lights. But this ship got real close, and the admiral went out and he had the megaphone, and he hailed this ship. He could make out the number, and he shouted, "Ahoy 624. You are out of position. Return to your position."

And they came back with their megaphone, "Who are you?"

And he answered, "This is Admiral Moon. I'm in charge of this whole fucking task force."

Lou Putnoky: One day we're standing on the fantail, and this redheaded kid from Brooklyn says, "I've got this awful urge. When I was a kid, I used to make kites." And we had some orange crating, some wood. He says, "I'm gonna make a kite." So he gets a couple strips of wood, and we got string, and a couple of socks to weigh the tail. Somebody's playing chicky [lookout]. We let this kite go off the fantail, which is the perfect place to fly a kite. We're letting it up, and we tie it to the rail.

Now we notice all the other boats. We see this activity happening all around us, and we see a big grin like on the faces of their crews. Here's a flagship and they've got a kite flying with a couple of socks for a tail.

Everybody knew what was going on except the staff and the officer of the day of our ship. All of a sudden here comes the o.d. on the run. "What the hell's going on?" He got a knife and he cut the kite loose, and you could see it going down. You could almost see the hysteria, everybody is laughing. But he didn't want it to happen on his watch. The admiral would call and say, "What the hell is going on? I'm a goddamn flagship, you're making a fool out of me." It was like the movie "Mister Roberts." When I saw that kite, it was something that you should put into a movie. And everybody enjoyed that moment.

There was another little incident. When we were at Saipan, every so often to ease the tension we'd have a beach party. You'd load the landing craft full of men and you'd go on the beach. They'd give you two cans of 3.3 warm beer, just to get off the ship, because after a while that steel got to you.

It was a rough day, and there was this one lieutenant. He wasn't too well liked, and he was in charge of the boat crew. And they had this real cocky little Southerner, who was the coxswain of the boat. As he's going to shore, the spray would come up, and because the barge was flat, you'd hit it and the spray would come and everybody would get sprayed. The coxswain was here, and you'd turn your head and the spray would hit you in the face, and the lieutenant was right alongside him. So the lieutenant says to him, "Watch what you're doing." He's reprimanding him. These two didn't get along.

The coxswain saw another wave coming, and just before that he caught some water in his mouth. As the next wave hit, this lieutenant turned his head, and the coxswain would turn so that literally he was only a few inches from the lieutenant. Then, of course, everybody closes their eyes except the coxswain. And when the officer closed his eyes he'd go "Pffft!" He sprayed his face with a mouthful of spit. We were dying laughing. Everybody knew what was going on except the officer. Every spray, "Pffft!" To this day the lieutenant doesn't know that this guy, his nickname was Spooky, that Spooky was spitting the spray right in his face.

Aaron Elson: What can you recall about Yogi Berra?

Lou Putnoky: He was a coxswain on one of the rocket boats. He was attached to the admiral's staff. Let's figure they brought maybe a hundred men to supplement our crew of 500, and Yogi Berra was attached to Admiral Moon's staff. He latched onto our particular group because that's where the action was, and he said to us that the admiral was such a nice man. He said that when he was in England, with thousands of sailors, he was able to recognize men and he would stop his jeep with the two stars and he would pick up seamen that were part of his ship. He didn't know them by name but he knew them by looks, and he would pick them up in the staff car, which was very, very unusual. But this was the kind of man he was, very well-liked.

Yogi was very personable. Of course it always would come up in conversation when you had new people, "What are you gonna do after the war? What did you do before the war?"

And he said, "Oh, I played ball, at Norfolk, in the minors."

And we looked at him, with his bandy legs. What the hell kind of ballplayer is this; are you pulling our leg? Were you a batboy or something? And we never paid much attention. He didn't elaborate on it too much. It would come up every now and then, and we would kid him about it.

Then after the war I'm looking through Life magazine and I recognize his picture. I knew him as Larry Berra, not as Yogi. And I said, "Larry, good God, he did play ball!" And he was a fantastic, phenomenal ballplayer. He could hit any kind of wild, crazy pitch. You never knew what the hell he was gonna hit.

Other than that, during Normandy I remember him pulling alongside our ship with his rocket boat. And I know, like everyone else, he was deathly scared.

Aaron Elson: When you say like everybody, what was it like being so scared?

Lou Putnoky: It's a crazy thing that happens. Today you could be a hero, tomorrow you could be a bum. You don't know how the hell the damn thing hits you, or when it hits you. We had a very, very close hit by a bomb in Normandy. We had these open toilets. I could never get used to that. We've got four toilet seats in a row, with running water, in a trough. No partitions. And there were two sections, half a toilet seat made up one, half another.

This 500-pound bomb came, and it just missed us at general quarters. It sprayed us. We got shrapnel aboard, and it knocked all these toilet seats off the toilet. This is the vibration, the shock. Those four pieces literally fell off. I was at my general quarters station, and I would have sworn that we got hit. I'm on the radio and I look down, and literally, my knees were like rubber. I couldn't control them, actually couldn't control them. They were just shaking. That was my own personal reaction. Because I visualized my crew members being mutilated. I would have sworn that we took a hit.

One time I felt something similar. I had a fender bender in an automobile, and I stopped and I had a dent. And it's very strange; I couldn't control my legs at all.

Aaron Elson: In the invasion of Iwo Jima, did the Bayfield come under any kamikaze attacks?

Lou Putnoky: Yes, but kamikazes hit us more in Okinawa. In Okinawa, we came in in three columns. Because we were the flagship we were in the middle. The ship directly to our left was hit and sunk by a kamikaze. It came in about six feet off the ocean, hit it right in midship and it slowly sunk. Other escort vessels came in and picked up the survivors. We couldn't get involved because we had to continue with the operation.

Aaron Elson: What goes through your mind at a time like that?

Lou Putnoky: You're so young at the time; you could never do it at our age.

Once you have a family, you're not worth a darn anymore. But because you're young, you get so caught up in it. But I did notice one thing. You get very, very superstitious. When I went to Europe I had $5,000 [life] insurance. The limit was $10,000. After the Normandy invasion I went down and made out the necessary papers to change it to $10,000. It was just a formality.

Now we went to the Southern French invasion, and the chief yeoman says, "Hey Lou, I notice here that you're one of the few guys that still has $5,000. What the hell are you doing, with what we're going through?" Today, it would be the equivalent to a hundred thousand dollars at least.

I said, "I put my papers through."

He said, "They're not changed."

So after the Southern French invasion, I went down and changed it again.

We get out to the Pacific. Once again I'm reminded that it wasn't changed. Do you know, I couldn't bring myself to change it, and I'm not a superstitious person. I was afraid that if I put it through a third time, now something will happen.

And you end up, you wear your lucky belt – you don't say this to anybody but yourself – now we're gonna go into the invasion. We went through four, which was very unusual. I don't know anyone else except this particular crew aboard this ship that ended up in two theaters as a flagship, going through four of the biggest invasions.

I had my lucky belt, my lucky shoes, I had my lucky shirt. I kept all this to myself. I can't speak for other people, but I know we got superstitious about little things. And I can remember one of the last times, at Okinawa, we picked up sixty bogeys, they called them, enemy planes. Radar picked them up at forty or fifty miles. My buddy was in the sack opposite me, and they sounded a general alarm, and I looked at him and he looked at me, and we would chuckle, but only out of fear. It wasn't a happy chuckle. It was more like, "Here we go again." And the damn thing was closing. I don't know why that particular one scared us more. I know it scared me more, because we knew that if these sixty kamikazes picked us up, with the firepower that we had at the time, they would rip us to hell. So the orders were, "Don't open fire. Don't give away your position." Maybe they might miss us in the clouds. And we kept getting the radio report. I'm on the phones. It's thirty miles. It's twenty miles. "Jesus Christ," you're saying, and nothing's happening. And then they went. They missed us and they caught Task Force 58, which was covering us further out, and they had a donnybrook.

Aaron Elson: I saw that photo there of you with the jacket on, hunched over those wounded men. What was that like, bringing back the wounded from the beach [in Normandy]?

Lou Putnoky: It's heartwrenching. An awful feeling. These are all seriously injured men from all parts of the service. One of them I remember vividly. He was shot just forward of the temple, right across both eyes, the bridge of the nose. Both eyes were blown out. And he was just bandaged up. That one I remember more than any of the others. I don't know what ever happened to him, because after a couple of weeks a hospital ship took over. When it got safer, a hospital ship came in and we transferred all our seriously wounded.

We had a special staff. We had a specialist in most fields of the medical profession because of us being the flagship.

Aaron Elson: Did you have any further contact with the guy who was wounded in the eyes?

Lou Putnoky: No. It upset us so much. There was nothing any of us could do for him. It was one of those things. You saw it and you ran away from it, because you didn't even want to remember. You're almost sorry that you knew the situation. You're a little ashamed to even say this, but you didn't want anything to make you feel worse than what you felt, because it would hurt the overall picture as far as your performance. And you never knew what would affect your performance, as things went on. That's something, you had to take it one day at a time, otherwise you couldn't handle it.

Aaron Elson: Do things like that ever give you nightmares?

Lou Putnoky: Oh, you have maybe restlessness. It comes and goes. Now, if I actually saw the bullet, that would be different, but the rest was imagination. Different people it would affect different ways. All I know is we wanted to get the hell out of there afterwards. We knew he was in good hands. But because we knew we couldn't do any more for him, we were almost sorry that we got this involved. And we saw guys torn up with holes. We were putting the sulfa drug in by the spoonfuls, small teaspoons. They were putting it in the open wounds, and closing them up, for the initial dressing. Because it just ripped big gouges.

Aaron Elson: Where was the Bayfield when Hiroshima was bombed?

Lou Putnoky: We were in San Francisco getting repaired, getting ready to go back and invade Japan. Truman saved our lives. Where the hell are the people like Truman, a simple man but an honest man that had the gall to drop that bomb? That to me took more than a man. That took something that's beyond comprehension, and yet the bomb had to be dropped, in my view. It's easy to say, "Well, we could have shown them what it does." We didn't have time to show them. You had to act. You had to do it fast. And thank God that Truman did it.

"I wore the same damn clothes for 31 days"

Mixed Nuts

Bill Druback, John Miller, Frank Miller, Len Goodgal and Mickey Cohen
101st Airborne Division
West Point, N.Y., Dec. 3, 1994

Frank Miller: Some of the stuff that I've seen happen to us, and tell me if I'm wrong, most people wouldn't believe.

Bill Druback: They don't understand.

Frank Miller: They don't understand how this could ever happen, especially if they've never been in the military or in any kind of a situation where it's life-threatening. So if I ever told them some of the things that actually happened to us, even by accident, they wouldn't believe it.

Bill Druback: It's like I was telling somebody the other day, with all this new technology that they have in the service like these high-tech night glasses. Back then there was nothing like it. But we were in a position there one time where we had a company firefight, and it got dark, and I was with this Oscar Dolens. He and I were on a machine gun team. The firefight stopped, there were some guys hurt and killed, and things got quiet. All of a sudden, right across the road, we could hear this German saying, "Kommen Sie hier. I'm hurt."

So Oscar, out of the clear blue sky, says, "Don't you move, you sonofabitch! I've got night glasses."

I looked at Oscar, and I gave him a smirk, and he says, "Keep quiet."

Sure enough, the morning came, we went across the road and there was this German. He was still living, and he had a couple of grenades by him and ammunition. The reason I'm bringing up this story is, here in true life now they have these things where they can see at night. Maybe Oscar was thinking ahead of himself, or maybe he knew something that we all didn't know.

John Miller: And you know, too, back then they used to teach marksmanship, right? With the M-1 you had an eight-shot clip, and you put one here, one here, one here, each round. Now with the M-15, it's just like having a machine gun. They don't have to aim; they just point it and spray. There's a big difference in the way they teach them.

Frank Miller: I think that happens, but they do teach them how to shoot, and they still shoot marks. We had the Director of Civilian Marksmanship courses. When I was a kid I used to go to those. I belonged to the NRA and the Boy Scouts and I learned to shoot in high school. It helped. You may never need it, but if you ever need it it's good to know instead of taking a guy raw, and he's afraid of guns because his mother told him he's not allowed to have them.

John Miller: Now they're taking toy guns out of the toy stores, because, oh, Jesus, there'll never be another war anyway the way we had it.

Frank Miller: It's just not the circumstances. Bosnia is the closest thing to World War II in a sense, because they're fighting with conventional weapons. And they have, well, they call them firefights, we used to call them skirmishes. That's a hangover from the Civil War, skirmishes.

Bill Druback: I still say that one of the toughest winters I ever spent was in Bastogne, throughout my 72 years.

John Miller: That was the worst winter they had in Europe in 100 years.

Frank Miller: I remember times where they said it was 13 above during the day and at night it went below zero, and we had on all kinds of clothes. I had a regular tank-type undershirt and a flannel undershirt, and the wool o.d. [olive drab] shirt, and the Army khaki, you know the knitted sweaters that we had? Then I had the field jacket, and on top of that I had that green combat jacket.

Then finally I had an overcoat that was much too big for me which was what I needed to go over all the other stuff. When some guy, unfortunately, got killed I got his overcoat and I cut it down to three-quarter length because when you ran in the snow, it used to melt, the snow against the heat of your body, and then it freezes, and it would slap you in the legs when you ran. So we cut it down to three-quarter length, just took a knife and sawed it off. And you're just trying to keep warm. But at night you'd take a canteen if you had one, if you kept it inside your coat, the next morning you'd shake it, there was ice in it. So you'd heat snow for water most of the time.

You know, if you tell people this, they don't believe it. So you don't talk to, I guess in fifty years I never really talked to what we called civilians in those days. Because they didn't believe it. Even my own family. Sometimes your kid will say, "How come you never told me things like that?" when they see these documentaries. TV has been the biggest informative method for the younger people. Like they saw the Battle of the Bulge, not the movie but the documentaries that A&E puts out. Some of those have done more to educate individuals than almost anything because they show the actual conditions.

They've got captured films and everything we never had access to. We had some pictures, a few snapshots here and there, but we didn't run around with a camera in those days like we do today.

Bill Druback: You carried your ammo, what you had.

Aaron Elson: How about the extremities, your hands and your feet? How did you keep them warm?

Frank Miller: A lot of guys didn't. They lost fingers and toes.

John Miller: They issued wool gloves, right? And some gloves had leather palms and some didn't, some were just plain wool. And then they issued us a pair of yellow leather driver's gloves. They were light, with no lining. And we put both of them on. If you could get part of a parachute or anything that was silk, you could put that on, because silk is a very good insulator, and you put silk on first. Then your gloves. The same thing with your feet. It would help if you could put anything with silk on your feet, under the socks.

Frank Miller: I was a Boy Scout. I was almost an Eagle Scout, and I had done a lot of camping. I used to always get extra socks. I usually had eight, ten pairs of socks. Other guys would put cigarettes [in their musette bag]. I didn't smoke so I put socks in it, and I changed them whenever I could, but I wore the same damn clothes for 31 days, literally. The underwear and everything. And I changed my socks a couple of times. One time I changed them in a barn in the middle of the night in the dark because you couldn't light lights, but that was the only way you saved your toes.

I used to wear the gloves and I never put my fingers into the tips. I had my fingers curled up inside the gloves, and you'd be like that trying to keep them warm. And whenever you could, you'd stand. You never put your gun down as a rule because if you let it lay in the snow it would get frozen, so you'd hold it in your arm and you'd stick one hand underneath just trying to keep warm.

If a building got blown up, you would run over to it and get warm, and stand there about ten minutes, then you'd move, because the Germans would shell it again. They all figured the same way because they were doing the same things we were.

Bill Druback: I had a pair of socks that I always kept in my helmet liner. It sort of kept them dry from the heat of my head. I guess that was taught somewhere along the line and I retained it.

The morning when they woke us up to get going, half the guys were on leave. They came and woke us up. They just told us to take whatever equipment you could get your hands on, and you grabbed what was available. That's the way we went on these big semis. Biggest truck I'd seen.

John Miller: The first couple of days it was warm. A lot of guys left their overcoats behind.

Aaron Elson: What it was like going into Bastogne, with everybody going the other way? Did you have any idea what you were getting into?

Frank Miller: No, not actually. Nobody knew what they were getting into.

John Miller: Because we started out going one place, and then on the way up there they changed it, and sent us into Bastogne.

Frank Miller: They told us to take our patches off, and we get there and the Germans' radio was saying, "Welcome to the 101st." They knew more than we knew, as members of it.

John Miller: They were going to annihilate us. They knew who we were, but we weren't supposed to have any patches or anything, no identification, right?

Frank Miller: So I put them back on.

Bill Druback: Don't forget, when we first got there, we got off the trucks and went into a field. They told us to dig in and you couldn't dig into the hard ground. You just dug whatever trench you could make. In the morning we got up and we headed into Bastogne.

Frank Miller: Even before we got to Bastogne, there were troops going the other way.

Bill Druback: Just the opposite of the way we were going.

Frank Miller: Some of them looked pretty harried. They'd say, "Where are you guys going? The Germans are that way." We got weapons even from some of them, because we didn't have enough equipment. We said, "If you're not gonna use them, we'll take them." I saw guys actually jump off a truck and get a gun from somebody else, because they weren't gonna use them, not if they're running the wrong way. But a lot of them were service and supply companies that were back and got caught. I mean that they weren't combat troops, per se.

Bill Druback: The 28th Division is the one where they broke through.

Frank Miller: How many guys are actually combat, in a division? They claim out of 10,000, maybe 4,000 are actual fighters, the rest are backup.

John Miller: But when they put the 28th in there, that was a quiet sector.

Frank Miller: It was supposed to be a rest area.

John Miller: And this was their first combat experience. They put the division up there to bring them into a quiet sector. And then they got overrun. I don't know if they didn't or they couldn't put up a fight; they were just overrun and they took off.

Frank Miller: I think some of them lost their officers and they just weren't taught to be independent. We were no good bastards, we were always independent.

Bill Druback: We'd just got back from Holland (where the division had fought in Operation Market Garden). It was a little after Thanksgiving. I think half of the outfit got diarrhea from the turkey.

John Miller: At the end of November we got back out of Holland, and then we were supposed to be on R & R, for recreation and retraining and regrouping and everything, right?

Frank Miller: I had just gotten out of the hospital from Holland. I got shot up in Holland. It was just the arm, but I got back a day or two before, imagine, just in time. But we had hardly anything set up. You didn't know which way to go, but you were ready to go, that was it.

Aaron Elson: How were you wounded in Holland?

Frank Miller: I got hit by shrapnel from an 88. I was behind a tank when this guy O'Brien got killed in our outfit. He was up on a British tank. It was buttoned up and they wouldn't move and there was an 88 down the road firing point blank. So O'Brien jumped up on the tank and he pulled the hatch open and said, "You open up on [that 88], or I'm gonna drop a grenade in on you."

And they finally started moving forward, and when they did he got machine-gunned. We took him to the aid station the same time I went back. I got blown out of the middle of the road, and nothing happened but a little shrapnel.

Aaron Elson: What happened to the tank?

Frank Miller: The tank blew the 88 away, with him directing [fire], and when the 88 went out, there was always support infantry. One of the infantry guys who was moving away from the 88 machine-gunned the tank and that caught O'Brien. He had about five bullets in him.

I was behind the tank with two or three other guys running behind me. We usually followed behind the tanks, the same as the Germans did. The shell was timed probably, and it exploded behind me to my right. It blew me a good 20 feet into a ditch. I remember getting up out of the ditch. You're sort of groggy for a second, but I was fine, I thought. And when I went to pick up my rifle, I couldn't bend my arm. That's when I knew I got hit. I had no feeling in the ulnar nerve. I didn't even think I was hit. I thought I broke my arm from the fall. I didn't see any blood. And when I finally got back to the aid station, about a mile away – I walked back because they needed the ambulance for the guys like O'Brien – the doctor asked me if I could bend the arm.

I said, "No, it just doesn't move." So he cut the coat off, and it was all matted with blood, and he said, "You've been hit." And it affected the ulnar nerve, which paralyzed three fingers on my left hand for a couple of months. They cut about eight pieces of steel out of me. I still have about three pieces in me.

But I was lucky, because guys maybe ten feet away from me, one of them was killed and another one was really wounded bad. I never saw him again. I don't even remember who he was.

Mickey Cohen: What are you having, a private meeting?

Aaron Elson: Sit down.

Mickey Cohen: I am sitting. When I get a little taller....

Frank Miller: He said, "Do you know any battered bastards?" I said, "I know a few battered people but the only bastard I know has just walked up."

John Miller: Here's two more guys you can interview. He wants to know about Bastogne.

Len Goodgal: I'm talking, I've been talking about it.

Mickey Cohen: They had no pro station.

Aaron Elson: No what?

Mickey Cohen: He doesn't know what a pro station was.

John Miller: They don't have them now.

Len Goodgal: All I know is, in Bastogne I never saw any men. I saw women and children. I didn't see any men. They just disappeared.

Frank Miller: But do you know why? The Germans had taken most of the Belgian men away as prisoners two or three years before. All the guys who fought against the Germans when they invaded Belgium; there was a small Belgian army. Remember the little guy I told you I met in Bastogne in the mayor's office? He was ten years older than me, and he's up to here. He was the only guy I ever met shorter than Mickey. He was in the Belgian army. I've got a picture of him and me; we exchanged hats. And this little old guy, he couldn't speak English, but one of the fellows we met there was translating for us. He said he was captured four years before, when the Germans invaded Belgium. He said he was transferred to Germany, him and a lot of his friends. A lot of them died, but they were like forced labor.

Mickey Cohen: They were worse than prisons, the forced labor camps. They worked until they died.

Frank Miller: Yeah, that's what he said. He said very few of them came back.

Mickey Cohen: Fed them poorly, chained them to machines.

Len Goodgal: I noticed that there were no men around, just women and children.

John Miller: That's why.

Len Goodgal: I remember being in a cellar in Bastogne, in a house. We had two women that were making crepes for us. We had champagne and cognac up to here in that place. I don't know where the booze came from. She used to pop the cork and the ceiling was low, it would hit the ceiling and make a dust mark, and we thought that was fantastic. We'd take a couple swigs of champagne, get another bottle. And they were cooking crepes suzettes for us, put jam inside the crepes and we would eat it. That was really fantastic.

Mickey Cohen: There were liberated countries, and they organized — you've seen this, right? They organized the European prisoners of the Germans. The insignia was a little piece of barbed wire you'd see on the lapels, remember, Frank?

Frank Miller: Yeah. And this is all people, it wasn't just Jewish people.

Mickey Cohen: And kids.

Frank Miller: Kids over 14. If they were big kids, they took them, a conscription of a form.

Len Goodgal: The Jews they were gonna eliminate. They didn't want to mix them with the population, they wanted to eliminate them. Actually Dachau was a camp for anybody. Originally they had anybody thrown in there.

John Miller: Well, all of them were originally.

Len Goodgal: Actually, the extermination camps sprang up later.

John Miller: In the beginning they were forced labor camps. Then, when they came out with their final solution, that's when they started all kinds of … they didn't originally go to exterminate everybody. They wanted to make forced labor out of them, and then they started exterminating everybody. It was Jews, it was Poles, it was adults, it was Belgians.

Len Goodgal: They murdered 12 million in those camps and 6 million were Christians. They were the people that resisted. And they murdered a lot of priests in there.

Frank Miller: In little towns, the priests – rabbis of course would be in hiding – but priests and ministers, in little towns, they're a big figure. They have a lot of clout with the population. If a guy says do this, they do it; if he says resist, they resist.

Len Goodgal: If you split Germany in half, the northern half is mostly Lutheran. The southern half is very much Catholic. And as we went through the middle and then down to the south we saw a lot of the Catholic part of Germany. If you go to the north, you're seeing the Saxons, who are Lutheran basically. So it's an interesting relationship.

Aaron Elson: What were the civilians like in Bastogne?

Frank Miller: The civilians were very cooperative. There weren't too many.

Mickey Cohen: And if they were there, they made themselves scarce. There was heavy bombardment all the time.

Aaron Elson: What was the city itself like?

John Miller: They had a convent, and they made it into a hospital. The nurses and the nuns took care of a lot of the people.

Mickey Cohen: Do you know what a corps of artillery is? That's what surrounded the town. A corps of artillery.

Bill Druback: It's like five battleships.

Len Goodgal: Mickey, he was interested in knowing were there black soldiers in Bastogne.

John Miller: There was a colored artillery battalion up there that had 155 Long Toms, and they had all white officers. When the Germans broke through, all these white officers told the battalion to blow up their guns and get out of here. And the white officers left. The colored guys in the battalion said no, they weren't gonna leave. They stayed there all the time with us. I forget, 330 something, 337? I forget what the number was.

John Miller: That colored battalion, they stayed there all the time.

Frank Miller: In those days you stood and fought. You didn't run.

Len Goodgal: You know, when I first went into Bastogne I went up the railroad tracks, and I saw these guys coming down the track, and I said, "What the hell's going on here?"
[One of them] said, "The Germans are up there."
I said, "I don't see any Germans." I didn't see anything, just these guys coming down. There's one guy from one outfit, a tank outfit, artillery outfit, all kinds of outfits, and all of a sudden it started popping. We're getting artillery fire. We're getting tank fire. They're shooting at us. That's where we set up our lines. This was just laid out there. It was along a railroad track that I first saw these guys. I saw guys from all different outfits streaming back in towards Bastogne. Evidently they broke up these outfits, and whoever could walk came back. So they were just stragglers. They organized these guys. And first, as I can

recall, they organized them, and put them to work back in Bastogne, in the kitchens, or whatever they were doing. And then they put some outfits together, because I saw 75s, antitank guns, up on the line outside of Foy, on top of the hill. We had some 75s out there and we didn't have any ourselves that I knew about.

Frank Miller: Which [regiment] were you in?

Len Goodgal: The 506th.

John Miller: I was in division artillery.

Frank Miller: I was the 502. We were up near Champs. We were in a different area, and I never got near anything that was artillery. I never saw any of that. I did see a couple of tank destroyers, those fellows that were trapped in there with us. You know, a lot of stuff got caught in the thing when the Germans went around and made a pincer to go around Bastogne. Whoever was in the area, automatically these officers like [General Anthony] McAuliffe gave orders, "Okay, now you're attached to the 101st." And that's how they had so many heavy guns. Otherwise we'd have had nothing. Because we came in on trucks with what we could carry.

John Miller: The only artillery that we had was 75 pack howitzers. Then they had part of the 10th Armored, two groups of them. Then they had the 705 antitank outfit. Those guys, after the end of it, they all tried to put in a petition, they wanted to be attached to the 101st permanently. At that time no airborne outfit had an antitank outfit because they're big guns, it wasn't feasible. Now they drop tanks and antitank guns together. But at that time it wasn't feasible. They asked to be attached to us permanently. Anyplace you guys go we want to go with you, but they wouldn't allow it.

Frank Miller: You know, Bastogne, people don't realize how big a perimeter that area is.

Len Goodgal: There was a lot of area.

John Miller: Bastogne, here's one city. Then you have several little towns around it, and that whole area was surrounded.

Frank Miller: It's like New York and the suburbs, and they were surrounding outside the suburbs.

Len Goodgal: An interesting thing is we took all the high ground. We were always on high ground. Our regiment was all around the town. There was flat land in the center.

One time I think they said the Germans had 32 tanks behind the lines, and when the fog lifted, our planes came in. Between us and the planes they knocked them out. But when the fog was there you couldn't move. You couldn't knock the damn things out unless you got close.

Aaron Elson: There were 32 tanks inside the perimeter?

Len Goodgal: At one time, I recall them saying they had about 32 German tanks behind our lines. That's a big area, but it was hard for them to get anyplace except by going down the road because there were wooded areas, and they couldn't go through the forest.

Frank Miller: The woods were thick.

Len Goodgal: It was very heavily farmed in the area, and there were wooded areas that separated the fields. So if they didn't take those tanks down the road, they weren't going to get through. Our town, Foy, outside there, the first day I remember there were halftracks and tanks burning along the highway. It was our stuff that was burning. The Germans pushed that off with their tanks, but they still couldn't get up the hill, and we just went and knocked out a couple of tanks and they couldn't move them at all. As long as there was anything in that highway, they couldn't come up the sides.

Aaron Elson: The sides of the road were too steep?

Len Goodgal: Not only that, it was wooded. It was so heavily wooded at the top, they had to come through the road. That was a main road. And on other roads I assume they had the same kind of problem. It was very cleverly defended. Whoever set up the defense set it up so cleverly that they had to come through us.

Frank Miller: Wasn't that Kinard? I remember they were amazed when they realized how young he was.

Aaron Elson: What about, Frank, what you were talking about before, when you were shooting at the lights.

Frank Miller: That was Christmas morning. We had a lot of shelling after the 22nd for a couple of days there. Then when we were coming down a road, single file on each side, it was 6 o'clock in the morning, just getting light. It really didn't get too light until about 8 o'clock or so, till the fog cleared. And we were going along this road when somebody started shooting. And all these tanks were coming in through the fog. There were five or six tanks, maybe seven. But Captain Cody said we were like sitting ducks on the road. He ordered us up the side of this little hill, and at the end was a forest. He said to line up along the perimeter of the forest. The idea is so you're not silhouetted against the snow completely.

We were in a long line, more or less, and all we had were the weapons we were carrying. We didn't have anything heavy. But these tanks came up and started firing. And they apparently had a bunch of infantry guys riding on the tanks. So when the Germans started firing, we said, "Fire at the flashes," because with the ground fog that was all we could see. Then they were firing and we were firing. We just kept shooting back and forth. It seemed like everybody was firing at once, and there were lots of flashes. You'd fire at the flashes.

Around 8 o'clock it was over. The ground fog rose up a little bit and you could see everything. There were a good hundred Germans, and at least 60 of them were dead. These must have been the guys riding the tanks. And two of the tanks had gotten knocked out. Somebody knocked them out with a bazooka. The rest turned away and went down the road, and that's when we found out the tank destroyers were in the woods. There were two of them that hadn't done anything previously because they couldn't get a shot at the German tanks. Once the German tanks turned abreast, these guys opened up and knocked out a couple more.

Aaron Elson: This was Christmas morning?

Frank Miller: Yeah. Christmas day.

Len Goodgal: There was snow on the ground.

John Miller: There was a lot of snow. It snowed all the time.

Len Goodgal: I recall going over a field down that hill into a wooded area in the evening, and observing the German tanks and artillery that was lined up in back of Foy on the other side. We were sent on patrol with an officer that hadn't been in combat before and two other guys that hadn't been. Nobody would volunteer. Somebody go out? Why me? This officer had to take three other guys. Finally I said, "Okay, I'll go with you." I figured the guy, he didn't know where he was. He'd just got into combat. These other two guys volunteered, too.

We crawled through the snow till we got to the woods. And they were firing shells at us on top of the hill while we were out. We waited till evening to come back up that ridge. And I remember when you say the fog, the fog lifted about 10:30, 11 o'clock. It was foggy and we took that much time to go up the side.

Frank Miller: It depended on the area. In the lower areas, the fog would rise and hang on the mountains or on the hillsides.

Len Goodgal: Do you recall the planes coming in and strafing us?

Frank Miller: I didn't say it lifted entirely. At one point walking down the road we were strafed.

Len Goodgal: By our own...

Frank Miller: Yeah. We didn't know that at the time. I thought they were German planes.

Len Goodgal: I remember we called for aircraft support, and the planes would strafe the woods in front of us.

Frank Miller: They didn't know the difference between the Americans and the Germans. And we had no identifying thing, like in Holland we had those yellow panels.

Len Goodgal: That's true. A number of guys were being strafed, but when they would come out, they knocked the hell out of German tanks. When that fog lifted, the Germans were in trouble. When it settled, we were in trouble.

Frank Miller: See, the fog was intermittent. It would rise, and then it would dissipate, but it would be up a little higher.

Len Goodgal: There were times when the sun came out.

Frank Miller: That was after December 26. That was after the first resupply. Then it started, after the weather got a little better. But then the fighting got worse, if you remember.

Len Goodgal: I wasn't there then. I came back.

Frank Miller: When did you come back?

Len Goodgal: I got wounded and I was sent back. But the guys went from there to Hagenau.

Frank Miller: He had socks in his helmet so his head didn't get trenchfoot.

John Miller: Oh, that's what it was.

Frank Miller: But your feet got hit by a trench.

Len Goodgal: Oh, it isn't funny either, they nearly cut my toes off.

Len Goodgal: Christmas Eve, they bombed us. They were throwing anti-personnel bombs back in the town. We'd hear the planes. We used to call them Bedcheck Charlie. They came over and they would drop anti-personnel bombs. You could always tell the German planes. Their engines were not synchronized and I didn't ever understand that, because ours roared like all one engine. Theirs go "rrg-ghh-rggh." You knew it was their plane when you'd hear them cranking over. They'd drop anti-personnel bombs.

Aaron Elson: What was an anti-personnel bomb?

Len Goodgal: When they landed, they gave off fragments.

Frank Miller: Some bombs are made to blow up buildings, and other bombs are made just to wound people. They had a lot of crap in them, I guess, that would do damage.

John Miller: Same as artillery shells. Some were meant to blow things up, then they had anti-personnel shells that were fragmentation, the same as grenades. When they exploded, there were all these little sections.

Aaron Elson: Which was the concussion grenade, the potato masher?

Len Goodgal: There was a potato masher that didn't have a fragmentation thing on it. It had metal ribs on the outside that would explode. Those things, the concussion was just, it was powder put together to blow up. But the other ones were heavier.

John Miller: And they didn't throw them like we did. They took them and whipped. We could get ahold of them.

Len Goodgal: GIs could somehow throw those things with a whack! You'd get them going and they'd go up in the air and just really go. Some guys have been known to grab them and throw them back, but you didn't know whether you're gonna get it or not. If you saw it and threw it back quick, a grenade had around five or six seconds.

John Miller: Five seconds.

Len Goodgal: You pull it and say one ... two ... three and throw it. What the hell, when we were in training I'd pull the thing and throw it.

Frank Miller: And then count.

John Miller: You'd throw it. One. Two. Three.

Frank Miller: It's like when we jumped. We used to go out the door, hit the ground, then the chute would open.

Len Goodgal: Did you ever see a box mine? It was an Italian mine. They would plant it in the ground, and if a tank or something ran over it it would blow it up. And I didn't know what they were. It looked like a flower pot to me.

Frank Miller: They had all kinds of things.

Aaron Elson: Len, you were wounded at Bastogne?

Len Goodgal: Yes.

Aaron Elson: What was the medical treatment like?

Len Goodgal: They were back in the monastery.

John Miller: It was a convent, actually.

Len Goodgal: I was in that convent. I was laying next to a guy that had a shell in his head. His brains were hanging out and he was still breathing. They were just waiting for him to die. I mean, what could they do for him?

Doc Feiler was there, and another doctor was there. Two doctors. They jumped some medical guys in a few days later. The Germans had captured our medical company, and that was a big problem.

John Miller: The first couple of days, the whole medical company was captured. So the only medics that we had were...

Len Goodgal: Feiler and another doctor. Feiler was a dentist, but he was doing all the surgery with some other physician.

Aaron Elson: Did they have morphine?

Len Goodgal: Everybody had morphine. We had morphine kits.

Frank Miller: No, we didn't have those kits then.

Len Goodgal: Sure you did, in the jump kits. Your first aid kit had a morphine shot in it.

Frank Miller: We had that little packet with the [sulfa] powder in it. That's all I had. In Holland we had the thing we jumped with on our helmet. That little pouch that had morphine in it.

Len Goodgal: That little pouch that they gave you, when we jumped in Normandy we had it, and we had it in Holland. And we had it in Bastogne. It had a morphine syrette. They told you to put it above the wound.

John Miller: Jam it in and squeeze it out.

Len Goodgal: And we had a sulfa packet in there, too.

John Miller: That was the powder he was talking about. Put it on the wound.

Frank Miller: Later on, when Boone got shot, Cokenauer was cutting his pants off and Boone was yelling, "You're cutting my balls off! They shot my balls!" We said, "Lay still." I guess Cokenauer was so nervous, he's got his trench knife and you could shave with those damn things we sharpened them so much. And he's cutting his pants, and he's cutting his leg. Finally, one of the squad sergeants took the knife and he cut the pants off and he said, "Ahh, it's only a flesh wound." It went through the fat part of the leg. The pain probably went up that way when he initially got hit. That's when we used that pack and I never used it for anything else. But I had opened it up, and I remember scraping all the sulfa powder on him and then giving him the thing, but I never saw any syringe.

Len Goodgal: We had a little syrette.

John Miller: It had a little needle on it.

Len Goodgal: I don't know if they had more than a quarter or half a gram maybe. It wasn't too much, but if you shot a quarter gram of morphine it could addict you.

I was going to tell you about Zeole. He was in Holland and he was cleaning his .45 and it was loaded and he shot the head of his pecker off. Cleaning his .45.

Aaron Elson: Who was this?

Len Goodgal: Zeole was a cook in my company.

Frank Miller: How was he cleaning it if it was loaded?

Len Goodgal: He was cleaning a .45. I don't know what the hell he was doing.

Frank Miller: Oh, you mean he was wiping it clean.

Len Goodgal: Whatever, and he had a shell in the chamber.

Frank Miller: That's why he was a cook.

Len Goodgal: Charlie Shettel said he saw it happen.

Aaron Elson: When did General McAuliffe get the ultimatum to surrender [to which his reply was the famous "Nuts"]?

Frank Miller: The 22nd. I looked it up because this guy had asked me about it for Newsday. He caught me unaware, so I said, "It was just before Christmas, but I don't remember the date." So I checked it out in one of the books, and, you know, he had given out that letter that day.

Len Goodgal: Yeah, "It's Christmastime, and we've got to be thankful for…"

Frank Miller: The 22nd was the day they gave it to him, and the Germans said, "Vas ist das?" What does it mean?

Aaron Elson: After he made that response, what were those next two days like?

John Miller: A lot of shelling. A lot of bombs.

Frank Miller: Constant firing, and noise.

John Miller: Constantly. Constantly.

Frank Miller: I mean, you couldn't listen to a radio if you wanted to, if you had one. But it was constant shooting. It was like they were trying to do what they said they were going to do. Obliterate everybody.

John Miller: They were gonna destroy the whole thing.

Frank Miller: And they had an awful lot of equipment around us.

Aaron Elson: What goes through your mind at a time like that?

Frank Miller: What the hell am I doing here?

John Miller: That's for certain.

Aaron Elson: Did you see anybody crack under the strain?

Len Goodgal: I never saw a guy crack at any time. At any time. Although I heard stories. Good ones. I heard a story of a guy freezing in a foxhole during the damn siege. But I never saw a guy freeze. I never saw a guy chicken. I never saw a guy do anything dishonorable all the time I was in this outfit. We were talking about guys doing things. But they're always secondhand stories of guys doing something dishonorable. Did you see anybody do anything dishonorable? No. He didn't either.

Aaron Elson: How about the food? Maurice said that, by the way, did Maurice have a nickname? You wouldn't call somebody Maurice in combat. My father's name was Maurice.

John Miller: We called him Tydor. Everybody called him by his last name. People very seldom called anybody by their first name. You called everybody by their last name.

Len Goodgal: Unless you had a nickname.

John Miller: Because if you answered a roll call, they wouldn't say, "John Miller." They would say, "Miller, John."

Frank Miller: We had so many Millers in my company, there were about five of us named Miller, so they used to call me F.J. Then Freddie Haddock, Fritz Haddock was killed in Bastogne, this is a guy that was really something, he was a machine gunner, and he used to call me Kid, all the time. They wrote something about him in "Rendezvous With Destiny," they said he did this, he did that, like clips from different people, a lot of names. And there's one listing, that's the only place I was mentioned in the book, they said he used to say to me, "Stick with me, Kid, and I'll get you home." We were in the same platoon. Fritzie was one heck of a guy. And when he got killed, one guy went crazy, oh, what's his name, Ball? One of his closest buddies. Freddie got hit in the back of the neck, a downward shot, it was from a sniper, and it was at a quiet point, we were on a hill, and when he got hit, Yurecic, he was a medic, tried to patch him up. And when they carried him down the hill, Captain Cody wouldn't leave him up there because he was that kind of a guy that he wouldn't leave anybody out in the field, they brought Fritzie down to the C.P., and they claim he died on the way down the hill and Yurecic used to think that it was his fault because he didn't bandage him right. But you know, it was nobody's fault, in those days, it's just like Frank Wasenda, when we left him somewhere after January, we were in a rough area and Frank got shot in the shoulder. We thought he got a million-dollar wound, he'll go home. The medics didn't pick him up for a few days. When I saw him in 1967 in Chicago, the first time I saw him since the war, since we left him, he was without an arm. He got gangrene. But he was one that went into a shell after, for the longest time, didn't go anywhere, or tell anybody about anything, you talk about people who wouldn't talk. Frank was like that. He felt not complete I guess, [because] he lost an arm. Who knows why. But there's so many guys that have had this happen, and we can't even talk for them because we never had that much of a, you know, we've all been shot up but are fortunate enough to have all our extremities and still capable. But some guys really had it bad. I never saw anybody crack up, though, to answer your question. Not per se. When we were getting shelled, I remember guys in the hole, you know, two guys would get together, you'd try to keep warm at the same time because it was still freezing, and we were out in the open because if you were in a building they dropped it on your head. If you were under trees you could get killed by the branches. So the safest place was sort of if you found a ditch or a low spot because you couldn't dig a hole it was so frozen, so it was a combination of just surviving. And where were you gonna go, there isn't a bus on the corner to take, what are you gonna panic and run for?

Aaron Elson: When you were wounded in Bastogne, how were you wounded?

Len Goodgal: I lifted my head up. We were making an attack on Foy. We were gonna take the town back. And I lifted my head up, a kid named Cross was next to me and Raymond Crouch was right in front of me, and there was machine gun fire across the field. I wanted to see where it came from. I just lifted my head up a couple of inches and it went right across my face and it hit the kid next to me, Cross, up the side. I saw him wince, that's all, he was laying there.

Frank Miller: Did it kill him?

Len Goodgal: I pulled his shirt up, and he had holes right up the side. Oh, Christ. And that's when I saw the medic. We had just broke through to the second battalion which was surrounded, that's what we were attacking for, to break through to them. The jeep came down the road, a medical jeep had four stretchers on it, two on each side, and I saw one was empty, and I stopped that jeep. I ran across the road and I got Cross, and we dragged him and put him on the jeep. A guy looked at me and he says, "Christ, you're bleeding like hell." I didn't realize it. It didn't hurt. It hurt, you know, like just, you figured you scraped yourself, you don't care. Then I wiped my finger over it, and there was blood all over me.

I caught up to the rest of the guys. It was all over at that point. The sergeant says, "What happened to you? Where the hell have you been?"

I said, "I don't know, I got hit in the face."
So he forgot about it. He thought I took off or something, which I didn't do.
I was with Crouch. We took this guy, dragged him up there. But he died in the convent.

Aaron Elson: What was his name?

Len Goodgal: His name was Cross, he was from Iowa. Idaho or Iowa. The reason I can remember him so well is that incident, but he got off a truck with Joe Chivas, all the C's got off in Holland when they came to my outfit, and Chivas said to me when I was out in Colorado Springs, "You know, I wonder whatever happened to that guy Cross." I guess he knew him from getting off the truck in Holland when they came up as replacements.

I said, "He got killed right next to me." He practically died in my arms. I felt bad. I was a kid myself. The guys looked out for me, and I was looking out for him. To me, he was just a kid because he just came to the outfit. He couldn't have been more than 18, 19 years old.

John Miller: We were all the same age.

Frank Miller: Except the old guys like ... I was 19 the day we jumped in Holland. That was my birthday, the 17th of September.

Len Goodgal: The 17th of September. It was a beautiful day.

Frank Miller: Remember, they were singing Happy Birthday to me on the tour bus? You know, that's an important date in Holland, so when they found out it was my birthday they're all singing Happy Birthday in Dutch and English.

Len Goodgal: The sun was shining. You could see the fields, we just jumped in the field, there was no artillery at us, no fire or anything.

John Miller: That was a beautiful day that Sunday we jumped in Holland.

Frank Miller: I had a leg pack with a bazooka, and my rifle was in three pieces in a case.

Len Goodgal: I hated that leg pack. Man, you'd break your leg with those things.

Frank Miller: You were supposed to pull the wire and let it drop below.

Len Goodgal: I can only say that we went over the bridge at night.

John Miller: I went over the next day.

Len Goodgal: So the bridge was blown, we went over on boats. Slept in the fields alongside that road, part of my company was on the right and part was on the left. We went down the road. Captain Kylie, who was Lieutenant Kylie, he became a company commander after Normandy, he got killed. A sniper got him out of the church steeple, and that's when they decided to blow every church steeple that they saw. Whenever they came to a town if we were having any kind of fighting at all, "Whoom!" The church steeple.

John Miller: That's something that amazed me, this last trip to Holland, all of these church steeples, fifty years ago every one had a hole right square in the middle. Now they've patched them all up. No more holes in church steeples.

Frank Miller: Yeah, it was different. Did you notice all the steeples that look new on top, like an ice cream cone?

Len Goodgal: You know, in Holland, I remember the brick factory out in the flats that we were in.

Aaron Elson: Now Johnny, were you with Tydor when he was wounded in Holland?

John Miller: Not in Holland. Me and Maurice were in a room in Bastogne of a building, and a shell came through the wall, and he maintains that we went out that hole at the same time. I don't know if the shell came in first or made the hole as we were going out, but we wound up in a hole outside, so Mickey calls me and Maurice foxhole buddies. I still don't know who landed on top.

Frank Miller: That's a fact, sometimes, when something happens. We were on the Moder River, it was a static front, and I had a .30-caliber machine gun that I inherited for the period. There was a point across the river and you could see the Germans in the trees moving back and forth, it was quiet, and they were doing things, and this one guy, I don't know what he was doing but it looked like he was doing laundry, hanging stuff. So I take the machine gun, and I put the sight on, I'm figuring how far that is and everything, this thing is on the other side, so I set the sight on the machine gun. It was a light caliber .30 gun, it was like a pistol grip, the one with the serrated barrel. So I figure I'm gonna try one shot and see what happens. So I pull the trigger and fire one shot. And there were five of us there, we had a dugout that belonged to the Germans when they pulled out, it was like a mound with a doorway that was maybe 22 inches wide, and just about three feet high. And it was myself, Wylie J. Myers, Krupp, Connors, there were five of us. And these guys, we couldn't even light a fire in those days, you couldn't do anything, the Germans would drop a mortar on you. They were good, they were so damn good. So I take one shot, "Ding!" I see the branch shudder, a couple of leaves come down. And this is maybe 150 yards across the river. And the minute that happened, say 30 seconds went by and you hear, "pop." I knew what the pop was, the mortar going into the tube.

Well, I'm not exaggerating, five of us went through at the same time into that dugout. I wish we had a picture, it must have been just stacked. And Wylie's on the bottom. "Get off me! Get off me!" We're all on top of one another. We come out and the damn thing didn't wreck the gun but it knocked it over. It landed in between that dugout and where the gun was in like a little enclosure of logs. And Wylie says, "Don't you do that anymore."

Len Goodgal: The thing about a mortar is this, when they go off, you could hear them go off, you hear a pop. When you hear that pop, you'd better move, because it's got a high angle trajectory.

Frank Miller: It doesn't shoot at you. It goes up in an arc.

Len Goodgal: And when you hear it coming in, it's all over. Forget it. So when you hear it go off, you've got to take action right away.

Frank Miller: When we heard that pop, we knew that was for us. I mean, the funny parts, you laugh afterwards but at the time...

"I always wanted to shoot a clock out of a bell tower."

Interview with a tank driver

George Bussell
712th Tank Battalion
Indianapolis, Ind., Oct. 25, 1993

Aaron Elson: Were you drafted or did you enlist?

George Bussell: Well, my father never knew it but I volunteered. My mom knew it. In front of my name there was what looked like a check but it was a V. Dad went to his grave never knowing I volunteered. Because he told me, "Don't you volunteer. They'll get you soon enough."

Well, my buddy and I, we got three sheets to the wind, and I said to him, "Hell, let's volunteer." So we went downtown.

They took me first. Then he got ready to sign up, and they said, "Are you married?"

And he said, "Yeah."

They said, "Then you can't sign." But he ended up in the Navy. He got the hell blown out of him. He's all right. But he really got shook up bad. We were figuring on going into the same outfit together. Instead he waved goodbye to me.

Aaron Elson: How did you become a driver?

George Bussell: I was up at Pine Camp, New York, and they had these old tanks with double turrets. They called them Mae Wests. They had them dug in, where the bottom sat on the ground, and they had the tracks dug out where they could go around. And they took you over on the field and said, "We're gonna teach you how to drive tanks."

I said, "That's all right."

And this sergeant got up in there and he said, "Now this is the way you double-clutch." He said, "You think you can do that?"

I said, "Hell, yes." Oh, and I loved it. Man, I loved it. I drove the hell out of it, too, boy. That's how I got to learn to drive tanks.

Aaron Elson: Ruby Goldstein told me about a barroom brawl that you and he got into in Phenix City, Alabama.

George Bussell: Oh, hell, we got into a fight in Phenix City, right across the river from Columbus, Georgia. Shoot, I ended up with a busted nose and a black eye. I had six stitches in the top of my head. That guy really whupped me over with a walking cane. I was in this place, and in the back you could dance. So I was back there playing the jukebox for this girl, and I put a nickel in. Before the fight started there were beer bottles and everything else laying around on the tables. Whiskey bottles. I asked her if she wanted to dance. And this guy was standing there. He said, "What did you say to her?"

I said, "Hell, I asked her to dance. You don't mind, do you?"

That's all it took. He peeled off. There was nothing in there for me to get ahold of and there were three or four of them coming at me. And when I backed up I fell over a chair and fell right down on a table. And this one guy jumped up there with a walking cane and hit me about four times across the head, busted my head open and broke my nose.

Of course, with all that rumpus back there, a bunch of other GIs came in and stopped it.

There were two paratroopers in there, and one of them got stabbed behind the ear and the other got stabbed in the back.

And the only thing they asked me, when they were taking me out the door, they said, "What happened? What happened?"

And the other guy said, "Don't worry about what happened. It don't concern you."

And hell, all three of them beat me to the hospital. Because I had to go to jail. I walked in that jail, I just stood up in front of the judge and he looked at me and said, "Take him right out that door." Right on to the hospital.

Shoot, my whole outfit would've went to Phenix City if I'd have said, "Let's go." The whole outfit wanted to go over there and wipe the place out. Because there were a lot of boys getting the shit beat out of them. See, they did that down in Fort Jackson. They had a bunch of young policemen down there, and boy, those young policemen were beating the hell out of the soldiers with their nightsticks. So this general, he went to the round table discussion right downtown and said, "I'm gonna tell you right now, the next time that I go to the hospital and I see the way these boys have been beaten, the whole Army's coming in your town." Boy, they put a stop to that. Oh, some of us guys really took a beating down there.

Aaron Elson: Forrest Dixon says you were going to drive the tank in the front and out the back of the place where you were beat up.

George Bussell: Sonofagun I wanted to do that! I was afraid of a basement. I said to Dixon, "Let's take it through the house." Boy, I'd have loved that.

Aaron Elson: How many tanks did you have hit?

George Bussell: I lost three.

Aaron Elson: Can you tell me about them?

George Bussell: We were at the Falaise Gap, and it was all camouflaged, we had a big tree sticking out there, and [Eugene] Crawford was my tank commander. We used to call him Mother Macree.

Aaron Elson: Why was that?

George Bussell: He couldn't hear himself fart. He had perforated eardrums. We'd be going down a road and hollering to get his attention so he'd turn around, and when he'd turn around we'd act like we were gonna hit the ground, and he'd fall. We'd just do that to see him fall.

Aaron Elson: His eardrums were perforated from concussion?

George Bussell: I don't know. He had bad eardrums when he went in the service. But they took him in anyway. I said, "Why don't you get out?"
He said, "Hell fire, they won't let me out. I had bad eardrums when I went in."

Aaron Elson: At the Falaise Gap, did the Germans go through your platoon?

George Bussell: No, that's where we stopped them. But boy, I mean to tell you it was a mess. After we got through, I don't remember whether it was Dixon or not, he said, "Come on, boys, down here to the road and see what you've done." So we walked through the hedgerows and fields and got down to the road, and no matter which way you looked, [there were] German vehicles just bumper to bumper, burning and, oh, hell, we wiped out the whole Seventh Army. And two of the guys in my outfit got the damn Seventh payroll and I didn't know what it was. One guy says, "Here, you want some money?"

I said, "I don't want none of that damn paper."

Sheeeee! Finally Patton called it all back in. But boy, some of them got away with it. There was one guy, I think this fellow sent enough money home that his old lady bought a big fur coat.

Aaron Elson: Tell me about the first time you got scared.

George Bussell: [Bob] Hagerty was the tank commander and I was his driver. We were coming down the road. We stopped at this crossroad, and boy, one came in close. I mean it was close. Because they had everything zeroed in out there. And I said to Bob, "We'd better move." So we moved on up into a hedgerow, and backed around so we could get a shot at something coming. I got out of the tank, and went in back of it and was eating a sandwich. I leaned over on the tank with my hand, and in that shroud that comes up just below the end of the tank there was a big hole. That 88 went clear through it. I said to Bob, "That's pretty damn close, ain't it?" And we were carrying Bangalore torpedoes on the back of the tank.

Ahh, we sure had a lot of fun, though. God damn. That ol' Mother Macree there said we were gonna get some eggs.

I said, "How the hell are we gonna get eggs? We don't speak French."

He said, "I know how to ask for eggs. You go up and knock on the door. When they come to the door you say, 'Avez vous des erf.'

I said, "Is that right?"

He said, "Sure."

That's all he knew how to say. So he knocks on the door, this woman comes out, and he says, "Avez vous des erf." And she shook her head no and he says, "Well where in the hell can I get some?" That sonofagun.

One time, on the breakout from St. Lo, there was a small cliff, not too high, and there were trees on top. And we're going along there driving the tanks and looking around. And way up in this one tree, I mean way up there, there's a cow. And he was hanging by his neck right in the fork. It was like somebody'd put him there. He got blown up there, and when he came down his head landed in the fork of the tree, and that's what was holding him. I said, "Man oh man, look at that!"

I always wanted to shoot a clock out of a bell tower. I never did. Old Hagerty did, though. I believe it was Hagerty. It was either him or [Morse] Johnson.

Aaron Elson: Tell me the story Dixon tells about you, when you went out a little ahead of where you should have been.

George Bussell: Oh, hell, yes. We went about three miles past the German lines. We went up there and turned around and came back, and on the way back they started firing at us. We turned broadside, and came back down a hill. Coming back down there were two German soldiers. That's when my tank got hit, but the only thing they hit was my suspension. Tore it all to hell. It's a wonder we made it in.

Aaron Elson: Dixon says you turned a corner and you saw three German motorcycles.

George Bussell: Yeah, they were parked. I ran over them with the tank. Shoot, you can run over anything in those tanks. Just like a Caterpillar.

Aaron Elson: You got out three miles behind German lines, and on the way back they started shooting at you?

George Bussell: Yeah. That's when one just missed my gas tank. They were shooting at me, but they weren't getting enough lead, that's what the trouble was. I was coming to hell. See, I'd spread the governor on my tank. I could outrun a jeep. That sonofagun, that medium tank I had, they couldn't catch me in a jeep. They'd say, "What in the hell did you do to that?" They opened it up and the seal wasn't busted. They couldn't accuse me of busting the seals on the governor. I put that sonofagun up against a tree, came down on the accelerator, and spread the governor. It scared me. I thought the tank was gonna turn over.

Aaron Elson: That's how you broke the governor?

George Bussell: That's how I spread it. Might as well. See, when I spread it, hell, it wasn't any good then. Then you could really throw the coal to it. We had one lieutenant who said, "What in the hell did you do to that motor?"

"Didn't do anything."

"What kind of motor is it?"

"Wright-Whirlwind." That's what I had in there. Boy, would that sucker run. The only thing, every time you fired it up, they knew right where you were, from the smoke. But outside of that, that sucker would run.

Aaron Elson: When was the first time your tank was hit? Before the Falaise

-74-

Gap?

George Bussell: To tell you the truth, I don't remember. Oh, I got hit in the Battle of the Bulge. That's when it got hit. Hell, I'd have jumped out of the tank if it hadn't been for Mother Macree. He told me to sit still, don't get out. Because they hit the tank with white phosphorous, and phosphorous was coming through the tank, through the cracks. It wasn't a whole lot, but it was enough to make me think the tank was on fire. I was getting ready to jump out of that bastard. And old Crawford said, "No, sit still. Sit still. They don't even know we're here." And they didn't. This German tank came over. Hell, he was as close as I am to that chair in there where you've got your sack. And we're sitting there with this big tree in front of us. That tree was right up against our gun. And that tank sat there for a few minutes and backed off and went someplace else. Then when the fight got going, old Crawford said, "Traverse." We traversed, hit that tree, knocked the whole damn thing down, and boy, we were sticking out there like a wet hand. Out there in a wide open space. Then we got a lot of small fire, didn't get anything big. That's when we closed the Falaise Gap.

Aaron Elson: That was the Falaise Gap or the Bulge?

George Bussell: The Falaise Gap.

Aaron Elson: But you said it was in the Bulge that you were hit with white phosphorous.

George Bussell: Yeah, shoot, I was setting there one day, and we were all outside of our tanks. The lieutenant said, "Pull into this field and leave yourselves about 50 yards apart, and get out and stretch, and if you want to eat something, eat, because I don't think there's anything around."

So we're in back of the tank, I've got a combat suit on, sitting and drinking coffee and batting the breeze, when "Psheeew! Psheeew!" Mortar shells. You can't hear 'em coming. But you hear 'em when they hit. A couple of 'em came in, and of course when they came in we flinched. But then they were getting pretty close. One of the guys went underneath the back of the tank, and two of them went up over the turret. The only thing I could think of was to go underneath the front. And we'd just pulled in over a bunch of cow shit. Boy, when I came out of there I had that cow shit all over me. I mean all over me. The guys laughed. I said, "Laugh, hell, I'd have ate it if I had to." Man, I had that cow shit all over my combat suit.

Aaron Elson: Did you have a change of uniform in the tank? How did you get it off?

George Bussell: Scrape it off, and if you get a chance wash it, and if you don't, smear it with mud, dirt, anything to get rid of the odor.

Shoot, that steel helmet did everything. Fried eggs. Boiled eggs. Made coffee. One day you shit in it, and the next day you ate out of it. That's the truth.

One of the guys – there were always five in a tank – would keep his helmet back, and keep it clean. Because that helmet would catch hell. You'd eat out of it, do everything out of it.

Aaron Elson: Do you remember the crossing of …

George Bussell: The Moselle? Yeah, I remember crossing it. I think we waited about three days to get across it. Then we went across it on pontoons, and they had the pontoons sunk in the water about a foot deep to keep the shells from busting them up. After we crossed it, Patton's on the other side waiting. Sure as hell was. I was as close to Patton as I am to you. That sucker was there. "Give 'em hell, boys. Give 'em hell." Yessir. I'd have followed him to Japan if I'd had to. I don't care what they said. To me, he was a general. The one and only.

Aaron Elson: Did you ever hear him speak?

George Bussell: I heard him over in England. And I mean, have you seen that show "Patton"? That's just like it was. He walked up to that crowd, only it was a lot rougher than what he says on TV. He says, "The sons of bitches…."

Aaron Elson: Did you ever get into any tank to tank duels?

George Bussell: No. Hell, we wouldn't have had a chance. The only way you could get 'em was to get 'em on a tree. I saw a light tank knock one out.

Aaron Elson: You saw that?

George Bussell: Yes, a light tank. He went up to it, he maneuvered that big tank around, that German tank, and when he went to move, his gun hit the tree. Because it was so long, a German 88, it hit the tree and when it hit that tree that little tank went up, and "Tooong!" He knocked the doors open on that tank. He hit her with a 37-millimeter and he busted that German tank all to hell. He maneuvered him around. Boy, those little tanks were fast.

Aaron Elson: Did you ever get wounded?

George Bussell: No, I made it through without. I got limited assignment on account of, well, they said I had a heart attack. I don't think it was. Because I've never had any trouble since. They classified it as a heart attack. I ended up in a general hospital, driving a jeep. That was a good job. Shoot, you'd just go out on Sunday and get booze.

Aaron Elson: Tell me about going up into the Bulge.

George Bussell: I remember going north to the Bulge. For a long while we drove with the lights on, the blackout lights.

Aaron Elson: And the roads were slippery?

George Bussell: Hell, yes. God damn, we went down that mountain, and the only way we could get down it was to drop one track down in this here ditch and go down that way, because if we didn't, if you slid over, by God, you didn't know where you'd go after you hit the bottom. I was going down that hill, and after you get down the hill, of course you let off of it, and there was a tree down there at the bottom of the hill. That sonofabitch must have been as big as this dinette. Boy, and if I didn't smack that sonofagun head-on. And my gunner was looking through the sight; it cut his head. Knocked all the rest of them out of their seats. Shit, I couldn't help it. And then Dixon had to go back and rob a turret lock off of a tank that was knocked out and bring it up and put it in my tank. Because I broke the turret lock. Cracked the turret ring.

Damn it was slick over there. And cold. I had an assistant driver, Johnny, from Tennessee, I forget his last name. He told me, "George, if I get home and it's in the middle of July, and I think how cold I was, I'm gonna build a fire." You could take your finger and scrape the frost off the inside of the tanks. Because they didn't have heat. Air-cooled. And once you crank one of 'em up, there was a Homelite heater in there, but that Homelite heater didn't amount to nothing. It was to keep your oil thin on the motor so you could get a fast start.

Aaron Elson: How would you do guard duty when it was cold like that?

George Bussell: We'd pull it in the tank. Set in the tank. Once, at Niederwampach, we had our tanks down at a corner. There was a house there, and we'd stand in that doorway, two of us. Damn, it was cold. I don't believe I ever was so cold in my life.

Aaron Elson: How would you sleep?

George Bussell: With your clothes on, and anything else you could find. We had five blankets, and we had them all in a roll. We had the roll in the tank. And each one of us would take a blanket and stay right in the tank. You'd sleep right in your seat.

Aaron Elson: Sitting up?

George Bussell: Yeah. The guys in the turret, some of them would lay down on the floor. Lay over the gun shells and everything else. A tank's got a ready rack in it. You put your foot on it, so we'd get ready to stow a tank with shells. I forget how many 75s it held. I know it held 18,500 rounds of .45 automatic. And I think it held 70 or 79 75s. And I forget how many thousand rounds of .30 caliber. But you could reach around and get a box of .30 calibers anyplace. Then we'd take our 75, there was a ready rack on the floor – well, that top of the ready rack, we took it off and threw it away, because it wasn't nothing but in the way, and we'd stack the shells. We'd stack maybe 20, 25 inside. And what we couldn't stack inside, we put them on the back, near the motor. Shit, you didn't know whether you were going to go to a cookout or hunting. I've seen them tanks come by and one of them will have a little stove on it. Went in this one house, a guy had this little stove, put the chimney on it, put a pipe on it and everything. He couldn't figure out where to get rid of the smoke, so he just went upstairs and knocked a hole in the upstairs floor, let the smoke go up there and out the windows.

Aaron Elson: What was it like inside the tank? Was there smoke from the shells when it fired?

George Bussell: There wasn't too much smoke. And your recoil wasn't bad. I think it was a 21-inch recoil on a 75, and 27 on a 76. So the recoil wasn't bad, and the smoke wasn't bad.

Aaron Elson: Your rank was corporal?

George Bussell: I was a T-4. Well, I'd been a sergeant and got busted. So they made me a T-4 and made me a lead tank driver. I said, "I'll drive the lead tank, but I want my stripes back." So instead of a sergeant, they made me a T-4. I made the same kind of money. I don't know how I could have got out of driving. They could have court-martialed me for refusing to drive. Anyway, I got my T-4 back. Oh, I wouldn't take a million dollars for what I went through. But I wouldn't want to go through it again for a million. You know what I mean? It's really something.

Aaron Elson: What about after the war? Big Andy [Bob Anderson] said he would go out in the field at night and he'd see Germans behind the barn. Did you have any after-effects like that?

George Bussell: When I first came home, my dad and mom were both still alive, and we lived over on Pleasant Street. And I had the back bedroom, it had French windows, and I went up there one night and I was laying there. Of course I was asleep, and my mom came in and caught me. If she hadn't, I'd have probably jumped out the window, because it was thunder and lightning and I kept saying, "Here they come! Here they come! Here they come!" And I'd sat up on the edge of the bed and I was heading for the window. I had the window open. But she grabbed hold of me. After she grabbed hold of me I was all right. That's the only time. But I probably would have jumped.

Aaron Elson: What do you think when you see films about the war?

George Bussell: I love that Patton show. And you know, there's a lot of that true, too. If he'd have went to Japan, it'd be altogether different today. He wouldn't tell his men to do anything he wouldn't do. I liked it there in the movie where that guy says, "Where are you going?" He said, "I'm going to get that Hitler sonofabitch."

Aaron Elson: Did you ever see any of the Hitler youth?

George Bussell: No. I saw one little kid. Oh hell, he was talking Hitler and Hitler and Hitler. I stood there for a while and listened to him. And when I got ready to go I just stepped on his toes. "You cute little bastard you." I did, I stepped on his toes.

Aaron Elson: Did you receive any citations?

George Bussell: Only thing I got was a Bronze Star.

Aaron Elson: Only thing!

George Bussell: Heroic achievement in battle.

Aaron Elson: What were the circumstances?

George Bussell: I pulled up to knock out a German tank. I forget where we were. And there was a light tank and a medium tank, German tank. I hit the big tank, but shoot, our 75 was no good against a German tank. But anyway, the second round, I hit his turret ring. He couldn't traverse. Then I knocked the little one out.

Aaron Elson: Were you at the gun or were you driving?

George Bussell: I was driving. That's the only two tanks that I ever really came in contact with.

Aaron Elson: Did the big one fire back?

George Bussell: No, it couldn't, because I'd jammed his turret. He couldn't turn his gun. I'm tickled to death I didn't run into any of them big ones, boy. The big ones would cut you wide open.

Aaron Elson: Hagerty said that he felt that there was a sort of special feeling between tank drivers. People like Big Andy and you, because you had to have so many extra skills.

George Bussell: I don't think so, outside of seeing which one could bullshit the most.

Aaron Elson: The third time you were hit, the last time, did you tell me about that?

George Bussell: I got hit at, I forget the name of the town. They had me zeroed in. We pulled in. There was a railroad station, and I backed up right beside the station, because I was supposed to watch the road ahead of us. So I heard a couple rounds come in. The corner of the building was blown off. We had tank destroyers there, and they caught this German, and they tried to give him to me, and I said, "I don't want him. What am I gonna do with him?"
They said, "We don't know."
I said, "Do what you want to do with him. I don't want him."
You know what they did? They walked him across the street, stood him up against the building, and put a .50-caliber slug right in his head. One shot. Because they carried a .50-caliber. And then, we're sitting there. I could sit here in my tank and see that building where the whole corner got blown off. They zeroed in on it, and they hit the railroad station. When they hit the railroad station, that's when I moved. We were going down the road, and the lieutenant was with me. So we picked up this doughboy and he dropped his helmet. So the doughboy said, "Stop!" So I pulled up to a stop and I stopped at a crossroad. The kid had to jump down and get his helmet, and come back up. And as soon as he picked up his helmet, "Psshhoooom!" Here comes a round in. And then another one. I said, "Jesus Christ!" The tank shook. I said, "That was close." Then we took off. Went down the road, and we got into the hedgerows. I pulled around a hedgerow and I pulled up there and stopped. Hagerty was with us. Hagerty was back there eating a sandwich. I got out of the tank and I said, "God damn." I went around the tank and there was that hole, where that 88 went through it. That's when I got rid of the Bangalore torpedoes.

Aaron Elson: But that was the first time you got hit. You started telling me about the third time. When they had you zeroed in.

George Bussell: Oh yeah. They had me zeroed in, but I moved out. Because if you set there, three brackets, they got you. They're smart.

Aaron Elson: So once you got hit with the white phosphorous. There was the time they put the hole in the shroud. You said there were three times your tank was hit?

George Bussell: And I got hit ... no ... I didn't get hit in the Battle of the Bulge.

Aaron Elson: Did you ever drive for Lieutenant Bell?

George Bussell: I drove for one lieutenant in B Company.

Aaron Elson: How did you get switched?

George Bussell: They were short of drivers, and they wanted me. I told him, "I'll give you a ride like you never had." Oh, I'd love to get in one of them and drive today. Just to see how it feels.

Aaron Elson: What would you say was the most amusing thing that happened over there?

George Bussell: The most amusing thing was when we went to Paris. Hell, we went to Paris on a three-day pass. I went to Paris with $500 and came back with 75 cents. Man oh man, what a time I had. I told them guys, "Look at me, I'm gonna piss right on the main drag of Paris." Eight o'clock at night I was right out there, directing traffic, pissing right on the main drag. Hell, yes. I went to England, I went to Piccadilly, and France was Pigalle. I was in both of them. Oh, what a time. You could be in Pigalle, and I don't give a damn who she was or who she was with, you could walk right up there and ask her, and if she said no, she wouldn't get mad. She'd say no, but she'd show you a girl that's just as good looking as her and built just as nice. Yessir. Boy oh boy, I had a good time. But like I said, I wouldn't want to go back.

Aaron Elson: What was the most scared you were?

George Bussell: I don't know what you'd call the scaredest. Anytime they said "Move," you were scared. We were down on the Moselle River and had a bunch of these Germans in this pillbox, and the GIs were shooting at them. Every time they'd open that door on the pillbox, "Ping!" they'd get a bullet in it. Because they were machine gunning the engineers putting a bridge across the Moselle. They called us up there, and we were gonna shoot the pillboxes with our 75, knock 'em the hell off. But they said they didn't need us, and finally they opened them up and the Germans came out. They were all young kids, just young kids.

I left my outfit just before they hit Czechoslovakia. Man, I had a German dress sword. It was a beautiful thing. Somebody stole it. Boy, it was pretty. The blade was all engraved.

Aaron Elson: How would you place the war in the context of the rest of your life?

George Bussell: I don't think it made any difference to me, because a lot of guys can't even talk about it. But it doesn't bother me. Just like I told you, I wouldn't take a million dollars for what I went through, but I wouldn't go through it again for a million. I can talk about it to anybody. It doesn't make any difference because it doesn't bother me. A lot of guys go crazy, start biting their fingernails and everything else.

Aaron Elson: Then you went to work for the railroad?

George Bussell: I worked for the railroad before I left. Then I went back.

Aaron Elson: What did you do for them?

George Bussell: I was a machinist on the steam engines. And I worked 52 years for the railroad. No, 32 years. My dad had 52.

Aaron Elson: Which line?

George Bussell: New York Central. Yep.

"Don't worry about a thing, Sir. I'm in the 82ⁿᵈ Airborne, and…"

This is as far as those bastards go

Pete De Vries
82ⁿᵈ Airborne Division, 2ⁿᵈ Ranger Battalion, 10ᵗʰ Special Forces
Wallington, N.J., May 10, 1997

Aaron Elson: How did you come to get into the Special Forces?

Pete De Vries: I started in 1952. I had met Colonel Aaron Banks, and I met Bull Simon when we were in the Rangers. And when they started the Special Forces he got in touch with me. He told me they're starting a new outfit, and they were taking all former Rangers and paratroopers. Also, they were taking a lot of the ex-German soldiers, because they started them in Europe. They weren't even intending to go to Vietnam or the Pacific. They were strictly trained at that time. They had the trouble with the Russians on the German border, so the Tenth Special Forces were going over to help train these different countries around there to fight the Russians. That's how it originally started.

Aaron Elson: What was it like training with the Germans whom you'd been fighting against a few years before?

Pete De Vries: Well, a lot of them were just like we were. They didn't want to fight, but unless you got with the real Nazis, you know.

Now, these are some of the things over here...

Aaron Elson: This is the citation...[reading] "Private Peter De Vries distinguished himself on 19 December, 1944, while assigned to the 508th Parachute Infantry Regiment at Werbemont, Belgium. Though wounded and with disregard for his own life he attacked two enemy tanks that were advancing on his company's position, destroying one and disabling the other. This action prevented the enemy from breaking through these positions and saved the lives of many soldiers and civilians. His bravery against such odds was in keeping with the highest tradition of the United States Army and the 82nd Airborne Division."

Is this the citation for the medal that was just upgraded?

Pete De Vries: No. See this?[pointing to a citation on the wall] This was from Canada. See, in World War II I jumped with the Canadians and the British, in England. I trained with them. So it tells you right on the bottom if you can see it.

Aaron Elson: [reading] "...Has successfully completed 16 parachute descents with the British and Canadian airborne forces while training in England with the United States Army Rangers." Now wait a second. If you trained with the Rangers, how is it you went into Normandy with the 82nd Airborne?

Pete De Vries: I got out of the Rangers because I got hurt, and when I was in the hospital they moved out.

Aaron Elson: Otherwise you would have been at Pointe du Hoc?

Pete De Vries: I would have been at Pointe du Hoc.

Aaron Elson: [reading a letter to Don Lassen, editor of the Static Line, an airborne veterans' publication]. "I just read the story by John E. Fitzgerald, but I still think the best one was told by an officer in the tank corps. It seems he came upon this lone GI with a bazooka and told him he was being pursued by German tanks and wanted to know the way to the American lines. After he told the officer the way, he came to attention and said, 'Don't worry about a thing, Sir. I'm in the 82nd Airborne and this is as far as those bastards go.' I think this shows the pride each trooper had for his unit, and what made him the best soldier in the world. Take care, Don. Peter De Vries, 508.' "

Now, you wrote that letter in response to an article?

Pete De Vries: Yeah, there was an article that some guy from the Marines put in. He was talking about the pride the different units had. So when I read it in one of the Static Lines, I figured I'll write this. I didn't use any names. I don't believe in that.

Aaron Elson: And then what happened?

Pete De Vries: When I wrote that in, nobody said anything for a couple of years. Then all of a sudden we went to a dinner in this place called the Drop Zone. There was this big poster, and it had this guy standing up there with all the equipment, and the caption of, "I'm the 82nd Airborne. This is as far as those bastards go." Then they had a couple of guys [who claimed to have said it] after that. One guy said it happened in Bastogne.

Aaron Elson: And you were by yourself at this outpost?

Pete De Vries: Well, I'm not saying too much about it. But you've seen this whole thing (DeVries' "Airborne Room"), right?

Aaron Elson: No.

Pete De Vries: I thought you did.

Aaron Elson: I saw it briefly.

Pete De Vries: This here, we took this, I think it was last year. This is Colonel Jones. He was a very outstanding Special Forces, 101st Airborne – one of the heroes of World War II. And this is Roy Benevides and myself. This is on the Real People show.

Aaron Elson: Roy Benevides was a Medal of Honor winner?

Pete De Vries: Yeah, he was the last one in Vietnam to win the Medal of Honor. So while we were on the show here with him, they didn't want to give him any Social Security money, I guess because he was getting money service-connected. They were giving him a hard time as far as Social Security goes. So he went and a lot of people got behind him, and he got the Social Security.

Aaron Elson: Who's this here?

Pete De Vries: He was Chaplain Watters. He was killed in Vietnam. He was going to save these guys at Dak To, and he got killed there. He was one of the few chaplains there that got the Congressional Medal of Honor.

Aaron Elson: Who was Frank Funk?

Pete De Vries: You mean Lenny Funk. He was from the 508. He won the Congressional Medal of Honor in Belgium. What happened on that one is he had turned these prisoners over to his men and then he went out scouting again. While he was out scouting, they pulled some shenanigans and the German prisoners took the Americans prisoner. So when he came back, the Germans were all holding the Americans. He had a sub Thompson slung over his shoulder, and when they told him and a couple of guys that he was with to surrender and turn over their weapons, he said okay. While he was unslinging it, he hollered to the other guys to get out of the way and he swung the machine gun and let 'em have it. And by him recapturing the guys he saved a lot of lives, because they were right behind the American lines. These Germans could have really done a lot of damage. He passed away. As a matter of fact, this is his citation right here.

Aaron Elson: Can I just quickly read that? "Sergeant Leonard Funk distinguished himself by gallant intrepid actions against the enemy at Holzheim, Belgium on 29 January, 1945. After advancing 15 miles in a driving snowstorm, the American force prepared to attack through waist-deep drifts. The company executive officer became a casualty, and Sergeant Funk immediately assumed his duties, forming headquarters soldiers into a combat unit for an assault in the face of direct artillery shelling and harassing fire from the right flank. Under his skillful and courageous leadership this miscellaneous group and the third platoon attacked 15 houses, cleared them and took 30 prisoners without suffering a casualty. The fierce drive of Company C quickly overran Holzheim, netting some 80 prisoners who were placed under a four-man guard, all that could be spared while the rest of the understrength unit went about mopping up isolated points of resistance.

"An enemy patrol, by means of a ruse, succeeded in capturing the guards and freeing the prisoners, who had begun preparations to attack Company C from the rear, when Sergeant Funk walked around the building into their midst. He was ordered to surrender by a German officer who pushed a machine pistol into his stomach.

"Although overwhelmingly outnumbered and facing almost certain death, Sergeant Funk, pretending to comply with the order, began slowly to unsling his submachine gun from his shoulder, then with lightning motion brought the muzzle into line and riddled the German officer. He turned upon the other Germans, firing and shouting to the Americans to seize the enemy's weapons. In the ensuing fight, 21 Germans were killed, many wounded and the remainder recaptured. Sergeant Funk's bold action and heroic disregard for his own safety were directly responsible for the recapture of a vastly superior enemy force, which if allowed to remain free could have taken the widespread units of Company C by surprise and endangered the entire attack plan." Signed, Harry Truman.

Had you trained with Sergeant Funk?

Pete De Vries: No, he was in a different company, but I knew him well. He was quite a guy; we were both in the 508, but in different companies. He just passed away a couple of years ago. And he was the most decorated paratrooper in World War II. He got the Congressional Medal of Honor, Distinguished Service Cross, the Silver Star, the Bronze Star, Purple Heart. Then he got the highest award from the Belgian government.

Aaron Elson: Now, this is the citation for the Silver Star that was just upgraded to the Distinguished Service Cross? Can I read it into the tape recorder? "Sergeant Peter S. De Vries, 508 P.I.R., 82nd Airborne Division, United States Army, for extraordinary heroism in connection with military operations against an armed enemy at Nijmegen, Holland, on 17 September 1944.

"Though wounded upon landing, Sergeant De Vries advanced forward and singlehandedly wiped out two machine gun emplacements, killing approximately six German soldiers. Sergeant De Vries then led his men in clearing snipers from several houses. At one point he attacked a building singlehandedly, killing two Germans manning a machine gun, while another group cleared a building across the street.

"After the company had advanced further into the city, at least two German machine guns began firing into the column, pinning down the entire company. Sergeant De Vries maneuvered his point from the line of enemy fire to establish a base to cover the German positions, and without other assistance assaulted one position with a submachine gun and grenades, destroying the position. He succeeded in diverting fire of the enemy upon himself and permitted his company to neutralize the position.

"The outstanding bravery of Sergeant De Vries and his willingness to close with the enemy contributed in large measure to the success of his company's attack and rendered a distinguished service in the accomplishment of his company and battalion's mission, were in keeping with the highest tradition of the military service and reflect the utmost credit upon himself, the 82nd Airborne Division and the United States Army." Signed, Robert L. Meisenheimer, chief records reconstruction branch.

Now, were you evacuated after that, or did you serve further in Holland?

Pete De Vries: No, I was put in a field hospital. And then we went back to France. That's when the Bulge broke out.

Aaron Elson: You were in the field hospital when the Bulge broke out?

Pete De Vries: Yeah. What happened is they were getting everybody ready, the trucks and everything, and there were a few of us that were in the hospital. When we heard everybody was moving out, we got dressed and we went AWOL from the hospital. We wanted to be with our outfit.

Aaron Elson: You didn't leave the hospital officially?

Pete De Vries: No, we just went. We put on whatever we had, and it was fortunate enough that we were able to get some winter clothes, because as you know, it was a hell of a cold winter there. Both the 82nd and the 101st were supposed to go to Bastogne. But what happened is, I think his name is Feiffer.

Aaron Elson: Peiper.

Pete De Vries: Peiper. His unit was gonna try to go into Belgium; they were headed for Antwerp. So when the word came, General Ridgway was supposed to be in charge, and he was pissed off that the two units weren't together. But when this happened, they just cut us off at a fork in the road. Then the 101st went into Bastogne and we headed towards Werbemont.

Aaron Elson: Were you wounded in Normandy as well?

Pete De Vries: Yeah, I was wounded all over. Everyplace I went. It's like a friend of ours that was with the unit in France, Holland, and also in Belgium he was taken prisoner. But each time he got away. I think he was captured twice in Holland, and he got away both times. I remember we met up with him when we were going into Belgium, and we asked him, "Who the hell are you gonna be with today?"

Aaron Elson: Was that like a jinx?

Pete De Vries: No. But you know, the thing is, he never was sent to any POW camp. He always got away.

Aaron Elson: What's this picture here?

Pete De Vries: This is at the Wall. And if you notice, on these different things, that the leg is light, part of the weapon is missing. Each one of these things means something. And this is when we were in Cherry Hill. We had a big service there for the MIAs, so they put our pictures in the paper.

Aaron Elson: How long were you in Vietnam?

Pete De Vries: I can't talk about that.

Aaron Elson: I noticed that the incident in the Battle of the Bulge took place on December 19. How did you spend Christmas?

Pete De Vries: Freezing my ass off. What we did is we took hand grenades and hung them on trees for Christmas balls. As a matter of fact I think it was on the 25th if I'm not mistaken. I think that's when Patton's units raced into Belgium, and like I say, we already had got rid of what we had to do. And that was it for me. I went back to England, and I stayed in the hospital there for a while.

Aaron Elson: What part of your body were you wounded on there?

Pete De Vries: I was hit in my leg. And we went back to England. Then when they were getting ready for the units to come home, I was in the hospital yet, and the 508 stayed in Germany as America's guard of honor. So instead of going home, I went back to Germany with my unit, while the rest of the division came home to march down Fifth Avenue. Well, that was all right, because I wanted to be with the unit, although some of the guys from the 508 did come home. And as far as it goes with points, even if I wanted to come out at that time, even with as many points as I may have had, I couldn't have gotten out anyway because I enlisted for the duration of the war plus six months. So the six months was up in September 1946. In other words they told you when the six months was up. I enjoyed myself. I stayed over there for a while.

Aaron Elson: Now, you enlisted because your cousin, Peter De Vries...

Pete De Vries: Yeah, he was killed in Pearl Harbor.

Aaron Elson: Had he been a role model for you?

Pete De Vries: Not really. I didn't see that much of him, just once in a while when the family got together. He and my brother both went into the service in peacetime. So he was in Hawaii. He was here and there, and my brother was the same way. When my cousin got killed in Pearl Harbor, my brother was on Hickam Field. He got hit and he lost a couple of fingers. Then he went with some Air Force unit; he went hopping along the Pacific.

Aaron Elson: Even though he'd lost a couple of fingers?

Pete De Vries: He stayed in. I guess that's all he knew. As soon as he got out of school he went into the service. Then I had other cousins; as a matter of fact I had an uncle that served with Chesty Puller. He was with Chesty Puller in Nicaragua when he got one of his Navy crosses; he was with the Marine Corps. But they decided to stay in. That's all they knew, what the heck.

Aaron Elson: And your brother was killed in Guadalcanal?

Pete De Vries: Well, he was more like a stepbrother. He wasn't really a brother, but he was still considered like a brother. That's why I always say my brother.

Aaron Elson: How far back does your family go here? Have you been in this area a long time?

Pete De Vries: Oh yeah, a lot of my family was here. They lived in Lodi. As a matter of fact, my father was born in Lodi. It was his parents who came from the other side.

Aaron Elson: They came from Holland?

Pete De Vries: Yeah.

Aaron Elson: How did you learn to sing Irish tenor?

Pete De Vries: My mother was Irish. Matter of fact, she was related to Chancy Olcott, the great Irish tenor. I think he was from the 1800s. I think he may have even been before John McCormick. So that's why I always liked the Irish songs. When we had family get-togethers, most of my family played western music, because I had an uncle who was a Texas Ranger. After he got out of there he went doing rope tricks and all with the rodeos, so I guess we got in the habit of that with the western music. We had a band in the family. Even though we did that most of the time I would do all the Irish songs.

Aaron Elson: And what are these pistols here?

Pete De Vries: These are like the old .45s. This is what they just sent us, over here, because part of the 5th Special Forces, they were the first Special Forces regiment. And this is when I retired, that plaque there. They sent me that, or gave that to me.

Aaron Elson: So you were 82nd Airborne...

Pete De Vries: Second Ranger Battalion, and Special Forces, and then for a couple of days in France I was in the 101st.

Aaron Elson: Really?

Pete De Vries: Yeah, well, we didn't hit our drop zone, and we wound up with guys from the 101st Airborne. That's when I ran into these guys from the 101st, and one of the officers ...I still can't say his name right, Miklis, he was a colonel ... he says to me, "What unit are you with?"
I said, "Company B, 508 Parachute Infantry Regiment, 82nd Airborne."
So he says, "Like hell you are. You're with the 502nd, 101st Airborne Division." So I was with them I think for about three days.

Aaron Elson: Those must have been some three days.

Pete De Vries: Yeah, well, like I say, they were great guys.

Aaron Elson: Now these are. ...You don't have a chest big enough for all these medals.

Pete De Vries: No, well, that's because there's a couple, you know, like the Silver Star here, all these, the Legion of Merit.

Aaron Elson: The ones you said you wear, you said for a long time you didn't wear any except...

Pete De Vries: I don't wear nothing. The only thing I ever wore was my jump wings and the combat infantry badge. That's all I ever wore. But then one time I was on the Rutherford VFW, and I knew Eddie Smith from the Ranger battalions in World War II, and he happened to be the commander down there. He asked me about joining the color guard. I was unsure from the beginning. Then I said, ahh, what the hell. Matter of fact, I was the only man ever to get on the color guard that was not a member of the post. That was an honor, because they had a very outstanding color guard. And that was the time, well, Eddie, he told the guys this and that. As matter of fact, Bill DePugh took over as head of the color guard unit. So they had a dinner, and at the dinner they were announcing the guys from the color guard. When he called for me, I stood up, and then he mentioned my name and everything. And he says, "When the United States ran out of medals to give him he was decorated by three foreign countries."
So everybody looked around and all they saw was a pair of wings and a combat infantry badge. So they said how come you don't have any ribbons or anything?
I said, "I just don't wear them."
Then they all got together and said, "From now on you're gonna be wearing

them." So after that, I started wearing them.

Aaron Elson: Which are these here?

Pete De Vries: This is the New Jersey Distinguished Service. That's the one that we just got. These are from Korea. And this was the medal that I got from New York. I belong to the American members of the Croix de Guerre.

Aaron Elson: What are the two from Korea if you were wounded before you ever got to the front?

Pete De Vries: Well, this is the UN medal for the Korea service, and then, you know, the service. ...

Aaron Elson: How long were you in Korea?

Pete De Vries: I was there maybe a month. I just got there, and I came right home.

Aaron Elson: With the 82nd?

Pete De Vries: No, I was going in as a replacement with the 8th Ranger Company. But the funny part about it was, they were reading on the service record, the 2nd Ranger Battalion. At that time in Korea they were companies, and they were assigned to different units. So they had the 2nd Ranger Company, which they were gonna send me up to for the jump in Monsiny, but they never realized that the 2nd Ranger Company was the black Ranger company. They did Monsiny and then Sakto, and they did the combat jump with the 187th in Korea. But they were going to send me in with the 2nd Ranger Company because they saw 2nd Rangers [on my service record], but I was supposed to get assigned to the 8th Ranger Company. They were going to send me in for the Monsiny jump. And when I got in the jeep to go there, the goddamn jeep got hit. Threw me out of the jeep; I hurt my back. They grabbed a stretcher and put me inside of one of these small ambulances. I guess the ambulance must have went a half a block and that got hit, and I flew right out of the back. So they packed me up and sent me home. They said that's enough for this little bastard. You know, I could have come out and said to people, "Oh, I did this over there, I did that," but I didn't do it.

Aaron Elson: From what I understand, the Rangers really took an awful pounding in Korea.

Pete De Vries: Well, see, the Ranger companies were sent out to do all the scouting. I'd say one Ranger company was attached, say, to the 24th Division. So they would go out and do all the scouting, for artillery fire, whatever. In other words, it's like in Vietnam later on; they called them the Lerps, the Long Range Reconnaissance. This is basically the same thing. They would go out and find the different positions, or get behind the enemy and silence them. And this is what the Rangers were supposed to do. And that's why, when they used the Rangers in the Casserine Pass, they used them as regular infantry; that's how the First Ranger Battalion got wiped out. They didn't use them for what they were supposed to be used for; for reconnaissance, to get behind the enemy lines.

Aaron Elson: Who's this boxer here?

Pete De Vries: That's me.

Aaron Elson: You boxed, too? Was that after you were in the service, or before?

Pete De Vries: Well, this picture here was taken in 1946, because I went over to Ohio, and I went to see a buddy of mine, we were in the service together when I first came out. I was on the boxing team in the service. So I went over and I said what the hell, I need a couple of extra bucks because I stayed for a while, so I started fighting over there.

Aaron Elson: How did you do? Did you win?

Pete De Vries: Yeah, I won 11 out of 13.

Aaron Elson: What class?

Pete De Vries: Welterweight.

Aaron Elson: What do you weigh?

Pete De Vries: Well, at that time I weighed about 147. ... This is in 1943.

Aaron Elson: And at what point did you make sergeant major?

Pete De Vries: This was late, because I went back in the service again. I came out in '46, and I went to Ohio for a while. Then I said, hell, this is not for me, because I had a year to [go back in].

Aaron Elson: So you first enlisted...

Pete De Vries: In 1943.

Aaron Elson: And you were 17?

Pete De Vries: Yeah.

Aaron Elson: And your first combat was in Normandy?

Pete De Vries: Yeah, it was a couple of months into my 18th birthday.

Aaron Elson: You trained with the Rangers in England?

Pete De Vries: Yeah.

Aaron Elson: And you got hurt there?

Pete De Vries: I got hurt. I went into the hospital. In the meantime, they were getting trained for certain things that they were supposed to do. While I was in the hospital, I met one of the guys [who was in the 82nd Airborne]. He had gone on one of the jumps. I don't know if it was Sicily, I don't remember, it's been so many years ago. We happened to be talking, and I told him, "Before I went to the Rangers, I went through jump school and everything."

Then he says to me, "We just came over with the 508th. We went into Nottingham."

Then they told me my outfit moved out, because they went over to Scotland. So I told him, check it out for me. He talked to his C.O., and the C.O. says, "Yeah, he can transfer over." So I transferred over to the 82nd. At that time, when we were going over for the invasion, when we were flying over, as a matter of fact, I was thinking of the other guys. I said, they're making Pointe du Hoc and all. But with the injury I got – as a matter of fact I'd hurt my back a couple of times – it would have been rough to do the climbing. I'm not sorry.

Aaron Elson: You hurt your back during a jump?

Pete De Vries: I hurt my back three times on the jumps. As a matter of fact, on my fourth jump in training at Fort Benning, we did a night jump, and I landed in a hole. One leg was on the top of the hole and the other one went in the hole, so I got all the pressure on my one leg. My knee swelled up, and we were supposed to make the next jump which would be the qualifying jump. When I went to the dispensary, they said, "You aren't gonna be able to jump." The knee started swelling. So I had all my buddies there. They grabbed ahold of me and they put me in a whirlpool. I thought my leg was gonna shrink. They had me in there almost all night, with the treatment there. They were rubbing it and everything. And they put a tight bandage on it, and I made my fifth jump, and finished. Otherwise I would have had to wait till the next school came. But any airborne guy is bound to get trouble with the back, because of the way you land. Even though you're relaxing your legs, it's a shock when you jump, you feel it up here. Every airborne guy who's made enough jumps, they all have got back trouble.

Aaron Elson: And where did you make your combat jumps?

Pete De Vries: France, Holland. That's it. Because there were no jumps in Belgium. The only ones were a few paratroopers who came in when they dropped the supplies.

Pete De Vries: When I worked with the Grand Union in Carlstadt, they had a guy there who served in the German army, and they were always talking about the war and all. I overheard him one time telling these guys how he shot the American paratroopers as they were coming down in their chutes. And I got a little peed off at him, and I just told him where to get off at. You get a lot of these guys. We had a guy when I was with the county; he was with the Italian army, and he's another guy, talking about the war, the war, the war. He happened to be in the same area I was in. And he was serving as part of the German army. Well, it was a stupid statement to start off with, but he says to me, "How come I never seen you over there?" You know, it's stupid. You're not gonna meet and start talking. But as soon as he said that I said, "Well, let's put it this way. If you met me over there, you wouldn't be here now." And he just shut his mouth, he didn't know what to say. But it was a stupid statement, "How come I didn't see you over there?" What the hell. What do we say, Hiya, buddy?

Aaron Elson: What did you do for Grand Union?

Pete De Vries: I worked recouping. In other words if there were broken packages I salvaged what was inside. When the supplies came in, we ripped them up and put them on the shelves. But the old back injury came back to haunt me, and they had to terminate my job because I couldn't do it. So I was there only for a couple of years.

Aaron Elson: Did you work for the borough?

Pete De Vries: I worked in town here under the CETA program for a couple of years. Then I worked for the Bergen County Road Department for ten years. Then I retired in 1991 or '92.

Aaron Elson: What led you to retire from the Special Forces?

Pete De Vries: The injuries came back to haunt me. I went out in '70.

Aaron Elson: Why is it that you don't tell war stories?

Pete De Vries: Because I don't believe in it. Too many men lost their lives and they're the ones that you should tell stories about.

"I go to sit down ...forget it! I made a mistake. I crushed the six eggs in my pockets."

Hors d'oeuvres de combat

Tony D'Arpino, Ruby Goldstein
712th Tank Battalion
Milton, Mass., Nov. 28, 1992

Ruby Goldstein: I went to gunnery school at Fort Knox. I was in Fort Benning at the time. So they had to pick different people to go to gunnery school. Everybody lined up in the morning, that's it. They'd call out your name, you didn't volunteer nothing.

So we go to gunnery school, and everything is fine. We get on a tank. The radio is not on. I'm up in the turret, the driver's down below, just us two in the tank. We're going to the firing range. We're going cross-country. We're going like this [motioning up and down], and I have my gloves on. I'm in the turret, standing on a little folding seat.

The turret hatch is round, it opens up in a half, and there's a pin that locks it in place.

But we're going up this hill, and as we hit a bump, the pin breaks off and the hatch comes down on my left side, and I'm holding on to brace myself, and the hatch comes down on my hand, right across the center, and it bounced. Thank god it bounced, because this half would have been broken off.

This white mark, it was like a bubble. It burst, and the blood started to come out. So I grabbed my handkerchief and I tied it around, and I stuck it in my jacket, and I'm hollering at the driver. We don't have any radio on. How is he gonna hear me with all that noise?

We finally get to the firing range. I climb up. I jump down onto the ground. They get me in a jeep, back to the post, to the hospital. We get in the emergency part there, and they say, "We'll be right with you." I sat there for two hours. Then a nurse came out, and I told her what happened. She looked at my hand, took me into a room, put it over a sink, washed all the blood off, and threw the handkerchief away. It didn't need any stitches because it was thin skin. And then she put a roll bandage over my hand, rolled it right up, and gave me a sling. "Okay, you're all set."

I go back. I can't dress. I can't undress. I'm not used to doing it with one hand. So the fellows would help me untie my shoelaces. At that time we didn't have boots, we just had the midcalf shoe. So they helped me, on and off, and meanwhile I'm still climbing up and down the tanks with one hand, and trying to disassemble things. You have to do it blindfolded, taking a machine gun apart and all that stuff. It was hard with one hand, but what are you gonna do? I did the best I could.

We graduate. I get back to Fort Benning. They send me to the hospital. Now they put a cast on, [all the way up to the elbow]. And I was still going out every day with everybody.

I got a furlough out of it, after I took the cast off, which was all right. I didn't mind that. And it didn't hurt. It just shows you how things can happen.

Tony D'Arpino: We had a guy who had two million-dollar wounds, and one was caused by something as silly as that. A gunner in the second platoon, his name was Sinclair. He was from West Virginia. And they were in combat. They were going through some brush. He had the gun traversed. He was going to shoot something to his right, and the gun traversed to his right and hit a small tree. It snapped the lock and spun the turret around and broke his arm. He went to the hospital. He was gone I don't know how long. He comes back, he wasn't back two days, and he's in the turret of the tank again as a gunner. He had his helmet off, and a mortar shell hit about two miles away, so a piece of shrapnel comes flying. He gets a three-stitch cut in his scalp. They brought him back to the hospital again. Two million-dollar wounds.

Ruby Goldstein: We had a driver in my platoon, Duane Miner. He was from Minneapolis, I think. Tall, handsome looking kid, just married. In back of the driver, up above, in the turret, you've got your 75-millimeter, you've got your gunner, tank commander, and your loader, on this side, which is in back of the driver.

The gun was so hot from firing, the machine gun, he didn't open up the cover. You pull it back and open up the cover. If you leave it on, she's gonna keep firing. And he's sitting up there, Miner is down below, he opens up the hatch, he gets up, it fired. It killed him. That's how accidents happen.

We had another kid, at the Falaise Gap. Remember when we encircled them all? That's the first time they ever caught 40,000 prisoners at one time. We were closing the gap. And everything was quiet. In the distance was the woods out there. Everything was quiet. We didn't know what was in the woods. But we knew that it was our job to encircle and we had to close this gap. And we got out, took a little bunsen burner we had, you remember? Put it in back of the tank, light it up, take your cup, put some water in it, heat it up for coffee. A mortar shell lands, beeko, he's gone. Just for nothing. Out of the blue. That was the only one that landed at that time, the first one. And then after we jumped back in the tank, all hell broke loose. That's when I caught shrapnel in the neck.

Tony D'Arpino: This was the Falaise Gap [pointing to a section of the battalion's unit history], the pocket there. The battalion knocked out 620 vehicles and [was credited with] the surrender of 1,100 Germans.

We were all lined up there together, as I recall it, and in C Company everybody took turns firing the guns.

Ruby Goldstein: We just went to close the gap, and as soon as they started firing all hell broke loose. The next thing you know, the mortars started to come down, and I caught [shrapnel] in the neck. It started to bleed. I took out my handkerchief, and I held it up against my neck. I jumped down, and a jeep came by. They had a stretcher with a fellow on it, and one in the back seat, and the driver. I got in the front, and we went to a first aid hospital. It was in back of a huge building, like a castle. But we went around the back, to the cellar, and they had all the guys who were wounded, everybody in line, waiting their turn to get treated. It was 2 o'clock in the morning, something like that. Finally, I was next. I get on a white porcelain table like a kitchen table, strip to the waist, lay down. The doctor's got a flashlight. He's looking at it, and he says, "Oh, that's nothing. A little bit more and I wouldn't even have to do this."

I said, "Thanks."

He had a pail there, and he dug a knife, scalpel, who knows what the heck he had. He went in and dug it out and I hear, "Clunk." I said, "What was that?"

He said, "Ah, you don't want to see it." But I looked. It had flesh on it, and it was bloody, with dirt on it. He dug out another piece, and that was it. He couldn't get it all, because it had already gone in. I still have it in my back, small pieces. And then somebody put sulfanilamide, then they bandaged my neck, that's it.

Then I went to a replacement depot, and from there they sent me to another replacement depot in the woods, and I rode in a truck all day long to catch up with the outfit. And when I left, they don't know what happened to me, nobody does. They don't know if you're alive or dead, you disappear. If somebody close to you knows that you got hurt, that's all they know.

They put me in a replacement depot, and I rode in a truck. It was one of these open trucks, and with the dust and the dirt, I caught a cold. We got into the woods, and I didn't know where they were taking us, none of us knew. We got off the truck. I climbed in the cab of the truck. I lay down on the front seat, and I felt like I was dying. I was sick as a dog.

"Everybody off! Everybody off! Line up!"

I go to line up, and there's a truck with the tailgate open, and a fellow hands me a canteen cup, and what do you think they're doing? Everybody get in line, they're filling it up with cognac. This commanding officer, this lieutenant colonel of this replacement depot, was a sergeant in World War I. He was a tough egg. And they filled up my cup with cognac. Straight. And I'm sipping it, and sipping it. Then you've got to put out your hand, and some fellow was there; one guy takes you by the hand and he has a tent all ready, and he has two blankets. And you go with him. You sleep in the tent, you on one side and him on the other. I drank that whole cup. When I woke up, I didn't have a cold. It must have knocked me right out.

I woke up, and all I had on was what I was wearing, the clothes. Shirt, shorts, the pants, socks and shoes, that was it.

So we line up, and now we're gonna get chow. I have a cup. One guy gives me the cover of his mess kit, and another one gives me a fork. And you lined up and they dished out the food, and this is what you ate. But what the heck are you gonna do there all day? There's nothing you can do. So we had to line up, and a colonel comes around. He's looking everybody over. He says, "Did you shave?"

I said, "No, sir."

He says, "Why not?"

I said, "I just got out of the hospital and was brought here. I don't have any gear."

"That's no excuse. See my orderly. My tent is over there."

I go down to his tent. There's an orderly in there. He gives me the colonel's stuff, and I took a shave. Then, after I get out, what are we gonna do there all day? So we're getting hungry, it's getting close to noontime. We take a walk, and we get to a farmhouse. We get some eggs. But we bought them. The Germans wouldn't buy them. They'd take what they want. I had some francs in my pocket. I said, "Give me six eggs."

I put them in my field jacket, three in one pocket, three in another. We go along, go into another farmhouse, and I want some eggs.

She went out to get the eggs, and I go to sit down. Forget it! I made a mistake. I crushed the six eggs in my pockets. What a mess I had.

And I got the other six eggs. I cleaned up as best I could. I cleaned out my pockets. She gave me the six eggs. Then I said if she had a rabbit we could buy a rabbit. So it cost me, I think it was ten francs, and it's two cents a franc. Twenty cents, and I got a rabbit. It was a nice big, fat one.

We get back to camp. We said, how the hell are we gonna kill this and cook it? So this one kid from down South says, "I'll show you how we do it."

He takes the rabbit by the hind legs, and on the tree, Bam! Hits the head right on the tree, holds the hind legs, puts the rabbit on the ground, puts his foot under the neck, and pulls his head right off. Then takes a knife and guts it.

So we got a couple of branches from a tree, and two forks, put another branch in here, cleaned it off, dug a little pit, started a fire, and I got some salt from a guy, and we poured it all inside of the rabbit to clean it out. We didn't have any water. We poured all the salt, and we're scraping it with knives to clean it out, and everybody, their mouths were getting full of saliva. We're gonna have something to eat.

We're turning that thing, and turning it and turning. It should be done by now. We break a piece off and go to eat it. Did you ever eat shoe leather? You started chewing. You figured look, it's better than nothing. You spit it out; you couldn't eat it.

Tony D'Arpino: In C Company, I can't remember who thought of the idea first, but you get an empty five-gallon can, with a handle on it, something like painters use.

Ruby Goldstein: Yup. I know what you're going to say, because we did it.

Tony D'Arpino: You put gravel on the bottom, about six inches, and then you put some potatoes. Then you put about six more inches of gravel on top.

And you tie it underneath. The tank had two exhausts coming out, and you tie it to that. And after the tank has been running all day long, the potatoes are baked. And we put the gravel on it so we don't get the smell. We used to have baked potatoes all the time.

Ruby Goldstein: We did something similar. We didn't have the kitchen trucks very often, remember? So whatever you could scrounge you scrounged, wherever you happened to be. So one of the fellows says, "We're gonna cook up some stuff."

We got some cans from the kitchen, these big cans, put a little hole, then put a piece of wire through each hole on the top. And we built a fire. We put dirt in the bottom, made holes in the bottom, put some gasoline on it, and put a smaller can on top of it, with a little bit of water. Then we went scrounging for vegetables. And we hit a potato field. So if you hold your lever and you gun it, the tank turns. This tread's stopped and you're turning. And what are you digging up? Potatoes.

So we peel the potatoes, chunk them up, throw them in. We had cans, if you remember, of English style stew.

Tony D'Arpino: I can still smell it!

Ruby Goldstein: And we'd throw it in, whatever vegetables we could find, the potatoes. And I made a pot, I mean a big can full of it. And everybody had it. And you know something? It was the best thing you ever tasted in your life. It was delicious.

Tony D'Arpino: Some of the rations we used to get had bouillion powder. Everybody would throw it away. I'd pick them up and save them. I had a gallon can too, a big empty can. I'd fill it half full of water, and put about a dozen packages of that bouillion powder in there. Then I'd scrounge around and find a carrot here, a root there. Best goddamn stew you ever had.

Aaron Elson: What were the rations like?

Tony D'Arpino: When we first went over there we had the cans, right? There were three different kinds. There was meat and vegetable stew, meat and beans, and hash. You had to have one of them for breakfast.

Ruby Goldstein: Yeah, but then we had another can, with the crackers.

Tony D'Arpino: That was the box.

Ruby Goldstein: Not the C rations.

Tony D'Arpino: Yeah, the small cans of crackers, the round crackers. There were ten crackers in them.

Ruby Goldstein: You had peanut butter.

Tony D'Arpino: Peanut butter.

Ruby Goldstein: Because that's what I ate when I got hurt one time.

Tony D'Arpino: And there were little containers of butter. You couldn't even melt it. You put it in a frying pan.

Ruby Goldstein: We used to bitch a lot, and why? Because those in the back, like maintenance, service, headquarters company, they couldn't keep up with us. There's no way, because they're not protected like we were with our armor. So their rations were good. We had to scrounge. Whatever you had with you, that was it. You couldn't say, "Well, let's send somebody back and get some stuff to eat." Uh-uh. But we survived.

Tony D'Arpino: Once it was wintertime, and we took this small town, there was a farm, and they must have just killed a cow, because they had a hind quarter hanging up. Some stupid guy name of Klapkowski, he took it and put in the back outside of the tank. The goddamn thing froze solid. I said to him, "What good is that?"

He says, "Why, we've got an axe on here, we just chop off a piece."

It was just as hard as this table.

But the Germans, once we got into Germany, they used to can everything. I don't know if you ever came across it, but the sausages, they put them in jars. And they were all cooked. And they put the white lard, pure lard, white as snow, there'd probably be a dozen sausages in there. And pork chops. All cooked. We used to love to find them. You know, find a skillet someplace, start a fire, and just heat 'em up.

And cherries. Jars of cherries. They could have poisoned us. We'd eat more of their food when we went in these small towns than we did our own, because we never got any.

But then toward the end we got 10-in-1 rations, they weren't bad. They had cans of bacon, sausage meat, and even a fruit cocktail.

Ruby Goldstein: Spam. How can you forget Spam?

Tony D'Arpino: And crackers, and little bars of chocolate.

Aaron Elson: How did you make coffee?

Ruby Goldstein: We had a little bunsen burner. You opened it up, put gasoline in it, and started a fire. And a wick. And you'd put a can on it, or your canteen cup, you'd heat it up. It was instant. You couldn't get any real coffee. Where could you steal that?

Tony D'Arpino: And what if you ever did find it? We did come across some coffee grounds, I don't know, from a house or what. They put it in this can I had, right, start a fire, boil water, put the grounds right in it. And then you get some cold water and put it on top, and all the grounds would go down to the bottom.

Ruby Goldstein: That was living it up.

Aaron Elson: You said that one time when you were hurt, you ate peanut butter?

Ruby Goldstein: They had to get rid of [the sergeant in] No. 4 tank. I was No. 5. I forgot his name right offhand. But anyway, when we got called on for the airborne troops – we were attached to the 82nd if you recall in the beginning, and they called up some tanks to help them. And when you're going somewhere, you're going blind. They tell you, "Go down the road," and that's it. But you're wary, you don't know where you're going, you don't know what you're gonna meet.

I come down a country road, and there are hedgerows here, there's a field over there. I come across and reach a dead end, and I've got to take a right. As soon as I take a right, "Baanng!" We get it. What is it? An antitank gun. Breaks my track. And when you break your track, you're stuck.

Tony D'Arpino: You can take the broken track and you put it on the big front sprocket, and by pushing the magnetos together, it kind of brings the track into place.

Ruby Goldstein: We carried extra blocks with us. That's if you were fortunate enough that you didn't get them shot.

Tony D'Arpino: But in real combat, we used to destroy the tank before you'd try doing something like that. If you had to ditch a tank, you didn't want to take a chance of the Germans taking the tank over, so you'd destroy it.

Ruby Goldstein: So when they broke my track, I had Charlie Bahrke – he was my gunner, and the 75 was loaded – I just hit him right in the back, and when I hit him in the back, he knew, Bingo, let it go. And that 75, just like in a bowling alley, with pins, it went right down where the antitank gun was. A little "pfft." Machine gun nest, anti-tank gun, everything flew.

All of a sudden I hear firing. We're on the road here, and there's bushes here, and they're firing in the field. But there's an opening over here, and there was an opening further back.

So I was [in the No. 5 tank]. The No. 4 tank was way back there, before the other opening. When I started to hear the machine gun fire, do you remember … we had flare guns?

Tony D'Arpino: They were used for smoke, too.

Ruby Goldstein: It was wired to the inside of my basket in the turret. So I undid the wire, took the flare gun, loaded it up, and from my turret, I lobbed it right over the hedgerow, right toward [where the firing came from]. It couldn't harm them, but it must have scared the heck out of them. Then I jumped out and I said to the fellows, "I'll be right back."

From where the tank was, I come around and go over [to the hedgerow]; now there's an opening here. A paratrooper's there. I said, "Stay where you are, because there's a machine gun nest in there."

So I said, "If you're gonna come over, make like a snake." He didn't, though. He was crawling. We were taught not to crawl. And all of a sudden, "Zzzzooop!" He was hit. I lay on my stomach and I grabbed ahold of his jacket, and I pulled him over to this side. He was dead.

Then I went back to the tank and threw some more shots from the flare gun over.

Now, all of a sudden, I hear a big gun going off.

I run over. Charlie Fowler [in the No. 4 tank] had gone into that other opening, and I'm trying to tell him I saw where the shots up on the hillside were coming from. That's not a machine gun firing up there. It's shells.

So he's buttoned up. I take out my .45, and I'm banging on the tank, and I'm hollering, "Open up! I want to tell you where to" fire his gun. I couldn't do it where I was. My tank wasn't moving. But he had a perfect place for it.

He was the No. 4 tank. I was 5. I went in first, and he stayed back. He's supposed to go first, he's supposed to be in front of me, but he didn't. But I think they got rid of him because he did something bad afterwards.

And he wouldn't unbutton. Don't tell me you can't hear the butt of a .45 hitting the turret of your tank, and I was banging on that. But then again, you can't blame him. They could do this if you unbutton: "Pfft," throw in a hand grenade. Kills everybody in there. That's all they have to do. Or if your gun barrel is not elevated too high and your block is open without a round in it, that's what they do. Throw a grenade right down into your barrel, kill the crew.

Anyway, he wouldn't unbutton. But they saw him, because they fired. And when they fired, here's the hedgerow, and me right here in this opening, and I'm banging on this tank and hollering, but no response.

They hit on this side of the hedgerow and I'm on [the other] side. And the force was so great of this shell landing here, it picked me up off the ground. Bodily. Picked me up and I fell down.

I get up, and I start to bang again, and I'm screaming.

Now another one hit. When it did, it picked me up, only this time I don't get up. This time, my head is a balloon, and it's growing bigger, bigger, I'm gonna burst, that's how it felt. I said, "I bought it." And I stayed there for maybe a minute. I crawled on my hands and knees across the road. I got up on the other side of the hedgerow, and I lay in the bushes for two hours. And I felt like that was it, I'd had it. But everything subsided. I was okay. I had a can. I opened the can, had some crackers and peanut butter and a drink of water. And everything was fine. I got back [to my tank], and they were good, they didn't come out. They stayed in the tank and they kept their eyes open, for anything that was coming.

Then we got word [back to headquarters], and they came up and fixed my track. But before they came back, two men come down the road. Everything is quiet now, and I don't know who they are – I mean, they're Americans. One is an aide and one is a general, but a one-star. Dirty. They have to be dirty, because that's the first thing the enemy will go for, if they see any identification of any kind that there's an officer.

So I told him what happened. He asked my name, rank, serial number. And he says, "Have you got anything to drink?" But I had dumped my canteen of water out, and there was a hut in the back there, and they had big cider barrels. We'd dumped our water out of our five-gallon can, and we'd filled it with cider. It was apple cider. It wasn't to get drunk on, but it was better to drink than just plain warm water.

Then I said yes. So I take out my canteen, and my cup, and I give it to him. He says, "What is it?" It didn't look like water. I said it was apple cider. And you know, you have to use your head, but you don't think. When I first went to get the apple cider, they could have had that [boobytrapped].

I gave him a drink. He says, "It's not bad." And he gave his aide some. Then I told you, he had my name, rank and serial number. I never saw him again.

But they got through, on account of us blocking the road. But you see, the Germans didn't play nice. If they captured somebody, where are they gonna take him back, to their quarters? They kill him. Our soldiers. So what do we do? We retaliate. If you capture a prisoner, what are you gonna do with him? You're supposed to go with the rest of your men somewhere, you had some destination, so what are you gonna do? Are you gonna drag him with you?

So they caught some. And I said to one of the paratroopers, "You have to turn them in." They're gonna interrogate them, get whatever information they can out of them, and that was it.

Tony D'Arpino: We captured a couple of Germans. Klapkowski. …

Ruby Goldstein: They didn't do that. They disappeared, and I'm hanging around my tank waiting for them to come up to fix my track. "Brrrrrrrrp." That's it. No more [prisoners]. But the word came down: Keep the prisoners alive. They couldn't get any information. Why? They were knocking them off. But they were knocking ours off, too. If they caught us, they'd frisk you, they'd take whatever they wanted away from you. They weren't gonna leave you and say, "G'bye now."

Tony D'Arpino: Klapkowski caught a couple of prisoners. He took one of their wallets, and he's looking for pictures or something, right, and there was a picture in there of a German soldier, and they had this girl on the table. There were two soldiers, one holding each leg apart, and the one that he captured was there, ready to … you know … Klapkowski turned around and "Wham!" He hit him. Now they radioed ahead and told them we had two prisoners that we wanted picked up. So we're waiting for them. Now this guy, he's got to go to the bathroom bad. And Klapkowski says to me, "That sonofabitch is gonna shit his pants. I ain't gonna let him pull his pants down." I can see this stupid bastard; we're gonna stand here and smell it. He did, he made that guy mess his pants. Then they finally came and took the prisoners. Those were the only two closeup prisoners I ever got.

Ruby Goldstein: When you went into the service, you had to line up and get your clothes issued, do you remember? We went out on a platform, this is in January. It's cooold out there. And you're not supposed to bring anything – only the civilian clothes that you're wearing, a little bag with some stuff, that's it. And we had to disrobe right on the platform. Put on long johns, and put on your uniform. They'd just look at you and whatever they gave you, that was it. Too big, too small, you got it. We dressed fast, because it was too cold out there. Then when we got back inside the building, it was like a huge hangar in there. Then from there, they put us on the train, and we wound up going to Fort Riley,

Kansas.

They'd ask you, "What do you want, mechanized or horse cavalry?" I liked horses, so I picked horses. And when we got to Fort Riley, wherever you were told to go, that's where you went. I wound up in a barracks on this side of the field where the horse cavalry is. And way the heck on the other side was mechanized cavalry, and you went through your basic training.

Tony D'Arpino: They worked it a little bit different with us. We went into a big hangar like, too, and they had a clothes and supply room. They took your civilian clothes, and they had boxes. They sent them home. And then you'd go up to a guy, and he'd put his hand around your neck. "Sixteen and a half. Give him three." Put one on you, two in the duffel bag. You come through there, and you're looking like Sad Sack. The shoes are so goddamn big you could turn around inside of them. They don't even give you a chance to lace them up. All the tags are on the pants, which are about six inches too long, then the overcoat. That's how you got your clothes.

Ruby Goldstein: Take a look (displaying a photo). Remember I told you about the guy that got shot with the machine gun? There he is with me; I'm holding my canteen cup, and there he is beside me. That's Duane Miner. That's me with the cigar in my mouth. I always had a cigar.

And there's my gunner, Steve Krysko; my driver, and myself sitting down, and Charlie Fowler in the back.

Aaron Elson: You said Charlie Fowler had done something bad.

Ruby Goldstein: Not with me. On his own vehicle. Some of the fellows know the whole story, but from what I gather, he put a piece of a branch or wood in the turret ring, and if you put it in the turret ring, you can't traverse. So what does that mean? You can't use your 75. Somebody found out, and they claimed he did it.

Aaron Elson: Why would he do something like that?

Ruby Goldstein: It wasn't talked about.

Tony D'Arpino: There's a lot of little things eating at you that you hear about, but you don't always know the whole story. Like myself. I know that Lieutenant Flowers' platoon, he had the first platoon, and he lost a lot of men on that Hill 122.

One of the drivers in that platoon was a guy named Paul Farrell. He came from Haverill, Mass. A handsome guy; he had red hair, and he was married. We were very friendly because we came from the Boston area. When we were at Fort Benning we used to go to the bars together.

Farrell was in the first platoon, and I was in the third platoon, so we didn't get to see each other that often once we went into combat.

Our platoons came together one day, and I asked for Farrell. One of the guys says, "He's sitting in the tank, he won't get out." So I go over, I drop myself down into the assistant driver's seat, and he says, "Hi."

I said, "What's the matter?"

He says, "We aren't gonna get out of this alive."

I said, "You really believe that?"

He said, "Yeah."

I said, "If I thought that, I'd get up, take off. Go back. Over the hill." I said, "You're gonna get out of it alive, don't worry about it."

"Nooo," he says.

That was the last time I ever saw him. His tank got knocked out. And that guy – when you had company guard, and you go to guard mount, they always used to give a 24-hour pass to the best-dressed. Farrell got it every time. He was just made for a uniform. He had the build. The shirt fit just perfectly, like a model.

I can remember, we had a young kid – young kid, we were all young kids – but the loader on our tank was Luigi Gramari. He came from Utica, New York, and he was probably a year and a half younger than I was. And we had the honor to go back up Hill 122 after Flowers got knocked out. We were gonna go up there and take it. We were in Lieutenant Lombardi's tank, and Gramari threw a tirade. "You stupid sonofabitch!" he's saying to the lieutenant. Now this Gramari, he weighed about 110 pounds. He says, "All the goddamn first platoon just got killed and you're gonna go up there?"

I grabbed him. I said, "Get in the tank, will you, and be quiet." And one thing led to another, and we finally made out all right, but he was going on because he'd heard about all these guys that got killed, and now we're going to go do the same thing? How crazy can you be? He was telling Lombardi, but Lombardi was taking his orders from the infantry.

It was getting dark, and he thought we were going to go right then and there, but we waited until the next morning. By the next morning we made out all right.

Aaron Elson: Ed Spahr told me that once you were driving through a woods, and there was somebody in the tank who said, "We're not gonna make it out of the woods."

Tony D'Arpino: That was Klapkowski. Klapkowski, the same guy, to Gramari. He's the one who got Gramari in this condition. I finally told Klapkowski off. Klapkowski was the gunner, Gramari was the loader. And Lombardi was the tank commander. And Klapkowski would say to Gramari, "We ain't gonna make it. You know what's gonna happen? Someday," he says, "the tank's gonna get hit." And he says, "Lombardi's gonna go to get out, he's gonna get shot and he's gonna come down inside on top of me, on top of you, and you ain't gonna make it, and the tank's gonna be on fire." And I, I just blew up. I told him, "Stop talking that way." Because he's making me scared.

He liked to talk, Klapkowski. I told you this before, I used to tell him, "Make sure," I said, "when the tank gets knocked out that that gun is in the middle. And if it ain't, so help me God, I'll haunt you. I'll pull the sheets right off the bed."

Ruby Goldstein: If you have that gun over the cover for the driver or the assistant driver to get out, how's he going to open it? So he's got to go through the escape hatch underneath.

Tony D'Arpino: He had Gramari so scared, here's how bad it got, and I ain't kidding. I shouldn't even say this because you've got a tape on. If we were in combat and we were getting fired at, and Gramari had to go to the bathroom, we used to keep the empty boxes from the .30-caliber machine guns, and he'd piss in them. And then he'd reach down where that opening you were talking about was, and he'd hand it to me, the driver, to throw out the hatch.

I finally said, "Hey, Gramari, when I have to go, I go outside. You do the same thing." I was trying to get him so he wouldn't be so scared.

Klapkowski was one of the best gunners that the company, that the battalion had. But he was also...after you hear this, you can either leave it out or do what you want. ...

They had five syringes of morphine, one for each man in the tank. Now, in our platoon, third platoon, Lombardi wouldn't let each guy keep his own. He was afraid they'd lose them. He figured one man should have them all. So he gave them to the gunner, and they Scotch-taped them inside the helmet lining of the gunner. That's the last we ever saw of the morphine unless we needed it.

Klapkowski's gone back to the States now on a 30-day furlough because he's got the Silver Star and all this other bullshit. He and Lombardi both had gone back to the States on a 30-day furlough. Gifford takes over that tank. When we had it knocked out, we had to destroy the radio. When I destroyed the radio, I found the five empty syringes. This is what Klap was taking. He had a very nervous habit, he kept taking his handkerchief and wiping his face, a thousand times a day.

Everybody else was going around getting souvenirs, guns, daggers, medals. Klapkowski: perfume, nylons, anything for the ladies, and he made out like a bandit.

I told you the story about the paratroopers in Fort Benning. I used to go to Mass with Klapkowski every Sunday morning. I never went in town with him, because I knew he was crazy. I hung around with the guys from Massachusetts, and that was it. But one Sunday morning I wake up Klap, and the blanket's over his head. I'm shaking him, and he isn't waking up. So I pull the covers down. I didn't recognize him. His eyes were closed. His face was twice as big as it usually was. It scared me. So I went and got the motor sergeant, who used to have his room right in the barracks, and we took Klapkowski to the medics.

He had gone in town the night before, and he saw this paratrooper who reminded him of something, and he picked a fight with him. He said there were three or four of them who jumped him. He was in the hospital for a week.

Ruby Goldstein: I had a similar incident. My driver, George Bussell, he was so stocky. When we went through basic training, they had a ditch. In order to help somebody who got hurt, you had to carry them. So you'd have to get on your back, and you'd have to crawl with him. I'm a hundred and fifty pounds, and this guy's two-fifty. It's like putting an automobile on you. How are you gonna carry him? But I carried him. That's how heavy he was.

We go into town. We go to Phenix City, right over the little bridge from Columbus.

Tony D'Arpino: That was off limits, yeah.

Ruby Goldstein: And they've got a barroom here, a barroom there. No matter which one you go to, there's girls with the dice to sucker in the soldiers. So we go in one of them, and we stand at the bar, George and I. We have a drink. And we hear this music; there's another room over here. We go into the room, and there's a couple of civilians sitting there with a couple of girls. I go to the bar, and finish my drink. George asks one of the girls to dance. She accepts. He's on the dance floor with her. Then all of a sudden I hear a commotion. I don't know what it is.

So I go in there. George is on the floor, the girl is on the side, and this guy's got a chair and he's whacking at him. He objected, the Southerners objected to him dancing with one of their girls. He's gonna lift the chair up to hit him with it. I grabbed him, and I suckered him one. A guy got up from the table, grabbed me and suckered me one. Now we're all on the floor.

I got up, I went crazy. And George was banged up real bad. Now I've got to get him out of there, because I know the two of us are not gonna last too long.

I got ahold of him, we got him out, and I know damn well the MPs, if they grabbed us, we're locked up, forget it. I got him back to camp, and his face was so beat up, just like what you were talking about. And why? He had a few drinks. He had no business asking the girl to dance. And this is what happened.

Now this same George Bussell is alive. He's never corresponded with anybody. He's never attended a reunion. And he lives in Indianapolis. He's in the book. And they tried to contact him. He won't have anything to do with anything.

Tony D'Arpino: What I was saying about being sensitive about things. We were at one of the reunions, I forget which one it was now, and Jim Flowers was talking to me. He likes me. He always says, "Always glad to see you." He knew me a long time, because he came from B Company to C Company, he was very nice.

I said, "You know, I remember you, and this lieutenant we used to have named O'Grady. He stayed with the 10th Armored Division. And I said, "That DuVal was a no good bastard." He was in the second platoon. Flowers says, "Yeah, I knew him." He said even the officers didn't like him.

Then I said I remember the sergeants we had, the first sergeants. We were among the first recruits down in Fort Benning, and I remember Sergeant Ellis. Then I said Sergeant Montoya. And he says, "Don't ever mention that goddamn name." Now, I never knew nothing between those two guys. "Don't you ever mention that sonofabitchin' yellow bastard's name in front of me again." He was jumping all over him. I didn't say anything more. So, you know Burl Rudd, Sergeant Rudd. He hasn't come to the last few reunions because he was [injured] in a fire. So I grabbed him, because he's very friendly with Flowers. I said, "I'm shocked. I just mentioned Montoya's name to Lieutenant Flowers."

"Oh, Jesus Christ," and he told me the whole story. I used to be in a different platoon. I never knew this thing happened. He evidently got yellow when Flowers needed him and left him in a bind. [Editor's note: Don Knapp, a crew member in Sergeant William Montoya's tank, and Jake Driskill, the maintenance sergeant who worked on it, have both confirmed that there was a problem with the transmission of Sergeant William Montoya's tank that caused him to stay behind when Lieutenant Jim Flowers went on a mission on Hill 122 in Normandy, on July 10, 1944. Four tanks were destroyed and nine crew members killed. Montoya, who passed away several years ago, remained with the battalion and performed well in combat. He was wounded in November.]

This is one thing about the tanks. You're dependent on one another. I mean, when you have five guys in a tank, and they put you on guard duty at night in enemy territory, they've got to depend on you being awake and not asleep because they might wake up dead. So you had to depend on one another.

I always said, the Air Force had it rough, but when they got through with their mission they went back to a nice barracks, hot meals, showers and everything else. The Navy, the same way. They're on the ship. They have their battles and then they've got a bunk to sleep in. They've got cooks cooking for them.

Us guys, we had no heat in the tanks in the goddamn winter. I remember digging out snow, putting branches down on a blanket, and a blanket on me; when I woke up in the morning I had about twelve inches of snow on me because the wind was blowing.

We had a rotation plan in our tank. The engine compartment stayed hot almost all night. We used to take turns, one night apiece, sleeping on the engine compartment.

You just can imagine. It's raining, you're soaking wet and you get cold, in that goddamn piece of steel. There was no fan even.

Ruby Goldstein: You know what they had to do? We had a gun port on the loader's side. See, here's your 75, you had your gunner, tank commander, your loader on this side, where he would throw a shell in the breach. On the left, right up here in the turret, there was a porthole, you open it up, push it out. You could get air.

But what was happening in North Africa, they find out, at night, the Germans used to come up. It's hot, you've got it open for air, they even dropped the hatch on the bottom to get some air. They're scared to open up on the top. And they can't throw a grenade if you had your 75 barrel elevated high enough. It's not easy to put a grenade in. But if that porthole was open, the pistol port, they'd throw a grenade in, everybody's lost. So the only way they could do it is tell them not to open it. Didn't help. So they welded them shut. Because too many men were getting killed.

Tony D'Arpino: When they fired the big gun, the 75-millimeter, there was smoke and everything else. You've got nothing to suck that out. Today everything is different, but they didn't have none of that stuff. And those tanks were cold.

Ruby Goldstein: I had a pair of green knit gloves. And a leather glove over it. When I'd post the guard outside on the tanks, and it was cold, it was freezing.

I had my boots and overshoes on top of the boots. It was so cold I used to take my gloves off and suck my fingers. I'd have the fingers in my mouth and suck them so that I wouldn't freeze. That's how cold it was.

And you didn't stand. You were scared, you didn't know what to do. You know, as you stand still, you're not moving. You're not circulating. And you didn't know whether you should move or not, because your ears have got to be wide open to hear things. And if you were having perimeter, you have a section, and you stay there. You don't go traveling because you're gonna get killed, whether it was by friendly fire or enemy fire. So you stayed in that area. But it was cold.

Tony D'Arpino: I used to have a ritual when I was on guard duty. You're scared, I don't give a goddamn what anybody says. I mean, it's one thing being scared and another being yellow. And you're scared.

And I used to have a ritual. I'd be alert, but it kind of occupied my mind. I'm the only boy in my family; I have five sisters. When I was on guard duty, I'd start with my oldest sister, and picture her in my mind, her name and everything else. Then I'd go down to the next one, and the next one, and the next one, and the next one. And this kept me going. Then my mother and father. Then I'd think of my uncles. And by the time the two hours was up, you went through the whole family. But it kept your senses. It just helped me, that's all I know.

Aaron Elson: Did you ever get frostbite?

Ruby Goldstein: A lot of guys did. I was lucky. When I was in the hospital, they had amputees, their toes, their feet, their fingers, their hands. All from frostbite. They turned green with gangrene. If you looked at it, it was sick looking; you wouldn't believe it.

Tony D'Arpino: Then they gave us boots. Remember those boots? We had them and the goddamn weather was getting hot and we still had boots. I took the goddamn things off once in a while, and the smell on my feet, I couldn't stand it. I think I had two showers all the time I was over there.

Ruby Goldstein: Do you remember the time when we were in Normandy and we kept on going further and further? We had the same clothes; you didn't take them off and you couldn't wash. How did you shave? You shaved out of your helmet.

Tony D'Arpino: Your duffel bag was stored. You just had a few things in your Musette bag.

LST 289, which made it back to port after being torpedoed during Exercise Tiger.

LST 507 leaving Brixham, England, on April 27, 1944.

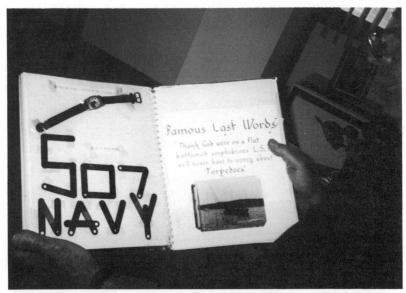

In his memorabilia book, Angelo Crapanzano has the watch he was wearing when the torpedo struck LST 507 at 2:03 a.m. – smashing the watch's face – on April 28, 1944, and a set of feeler gauges he had been carrying in his pocket. The page on the right says: "Famous Last Words: Thank God we're on a flat bottomed amphibious LST. We'll never have to worry about torpedoes."

Carmine Galasso/The Bergen Record

Exercise Tiger survivor Angelo Crapanzano in 1994. Below, a group of German E-boats setting out to hunt for prey in the English Channel.

Beth Balbierz/The Bergen Record
Former paratrooper Ed Boccafogli at his home in Clifton, N.J., in 1994.

Don Smith/The Bergen Record

Pete De Vries in his "Airborne Room." Below, De Vries' medal case.

Don Smith/The Bergen Record

Pete De Vries enlisted at age 17, after a cousin was killed at Pearl Harbor.

Don Smith/The Bergen Record

Pete De Vries in 1997, taking part in a Memorial Day parade.

Doug Coleman, left, and his father, Cleo. Doug fought in Vietnam with the 1st Air Cavalry Division, and Cleo served in World War II with the 712th Tank Battalion.

Four members of Cleo Coleman's five-man crew in Normandy, from left: Coleman, Roy "Rip" Bardo, Leslie Vink, and Louis Gruntz.

Carmine Galasso/The Bergen Record

Clockwise from top: Lou Putnoky aboard the USS Bayfield, which served as the flagship of the Utah Beach invasion fleet; Putnoky in 1994; Putnoky – bending over, in foreground – helping to load wounded GIs onto a landing craft on D-Day.

Above, a Coast Guard photo of the Allied invasion fleet firing on German aircraft in the pre-dawn darkness of D-Day. At left, the USS Bayfield.

Shipboard services on the Bayfield before the invasion of Okinawa.

Wes and Angie Boyer at their home in Mt. Bethel, Pa., in 1997. At right, Wes – who served in World War II, Korea and Vietnam – in uniform during World War II.

Ruby Goldstein of the 712th Tank Battalion. At right, retired Col. Clifford Merrill.

George Bussell, right, trained on a tank with twin turrets at Pine Camp, N.Y. The tank was known as a Mae West. At left, the real McCoy.

Sue Goldstein, left, and Jan Merrill. The two women, whose husbands served in the 712th Tank Battalion, know it is better for their husbands to talk about the war over a meal than to not talk about it at all.

Mickey Cohen, left, and Frank Miller at the 1997 "Nuts" dinner at West Point. As members of the 101st Airborne Division, the two veterans were encircled during the siege of Bastogne.

"I always wanted to shoot the clock out of a bell tower," says George Bussell of the 712th Tank Battalion. At left, the bell tower of a church in Amberg, Germany, where the 712th was stationed after the end of the war in Europe. Below, two light tanks of the 712th's D Company that were knocked out. The 712th spent 310 days in combat, 298 of them in active contact with the enemy, according to the battalion's unit history.

From the collection of Paul Wannemacher

Photo by Jack Roland/From the collection of Paul Wannemacher

Prisoners being rounded up by the 90th Infantry Division in the Falaise Gap during August 1944. Much German equipment in the Gap was horsedrawn.

The railroad tracks at Heimboldshausen, Germany, after an explosion on April 3, 1944, in which Lieutenant Ed Forrest of the 712th Tank Battalion was killed. The explosion was caused when a lone German fighter plane attacked empty, fume-filled tanker cars shortly after Forrest's company had set up its headquarters in a building across from the tracks. Below, the same spot in Heimboldshausen in 1997.

From the collection of Paul Wannemacher

The crematoria at the Flossenburg concentration camp, which was liberated by the 90th Infantry Division and the 712th Tank Battalion. Below, a pile of shoes at the camp, visible on the right side of the photo above.

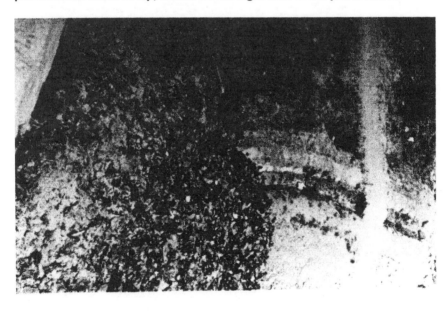

President Harry S. Truman awarding the Congressional Medal of Honor to John Hawk. At right, Hawk in 1997.

At left, Les O'Riley and Jim Cary, at podium, during an annual ceremony in which the names of 712th Tank Battalion veterans who've passed away are placed in a brazier and burned. Flags are also placed in a Styrofoam cross and Star of David.

Ruby Goldstein: Whatever you had with you. And when we finally got clothes, you had to disrobe, and if you were near water of any kind, you'd wash yourself, and take your clothes, take the shovel, dig a hole and bury them. You'd get new clothes, but the old ones were so rotten, you could die from the odor. Listen, how long can you wear something? You know what I mean?

Tony D'Arpino: We had these knit hats in the winter. Your hair, it hurt just to touch it. The guys used to joke, "Well, I guess I'll comb my hair," and they'd take the hat and screw it around a couple of times, and it looked like they'd stuck their finger in a socket.

Tony D'Arpino: At Fort Jackson, South Carolina, when we were getting ready to go overseas, I had to go to the stockade every morning and pick up this kid named Durr. He was from Mississippi, couldn't read or write, and he had gone AWOL on furlough, stayed AWOL, and he went to this big city in Mississippi. He used to go there quite often I guess, in uniform, and the MPs around there stopped him one time and said, "When is your furlough up?"

And Durr said, "I think it's just about up."

They court-martialed him, and put him in the stockade at Jackson. And my duty in the morning was to go down and take him out so he could come with his tank crew and do the firing. And then I'd bring him back to the stockade, go back up and help clean guns and everything else, and then we'd eat. I said to Lieutenant Lombardi, "Who the hell's getting punished around here? All he does is get escorted up to the tank with us and does his firing, and then he goes back into his nice warm cell, and we've got to go back up there and clean these guns and then eat. Who's getting punished?"

Ruby Goldstein: We had a fellow one time, I can't remember his name, but we were lined up at Fort Jackson and Clifford Merrill said something to us. This guy opened his mouth, and everybody is looking straight ahead. And Merrill looked around and said, "Did you open your mouth?" He looked him right in the eye and he didn't answer.

Merrill had him dig, between the barracks, a six by six by six. He was a short guy. And he kept digging that hole, and digging that hole. If you ever try that, you'll see how difficult it is. He dug that hole there, and he couldn't get out. He was a sick puppy. Just for opening his mouth. See, you're not supposed to be a smart ass. You listen. Keep your mouth shut. You're told to do something, no backtalk, you do it, right or wrong, whether you like it or not. Those are orders.

Because if you don't obey orders, you have a big problem.

Tony D'Arpino: In our company, we had two kinds of punishment. One was to dig a six by six by six, and then the sergeant would throw a cigarette butt down there and say, "Now fill it in." That's if the weather was cool. If the weather was real hot, they'd make you go in and put on your Class A uniform and your overcoat, and your full field pack, and walk around the goddamn company area for two hours at a time, a ten minute break and then two more hours.

Aaron Elson: What was the transition like from training to combat?

Tony D'Arpino: When we went to England, we went to camp in Chiseldon. It was quonset huts. And we get there, the bunks were all wood, handmade, upper and lower. Potbellied stove. And there was a mattress cover on each bunk. And they said, "Your mattress is out back, just take the cover out and fill it up." And you go out back, and there's a goddamn mountain of hay there; that was your mattress.

We were only there a short time, and then they wanted to make a hospital out of that. So they moved us out in the field, on Sunday morning. They put us in trucks, and out in this field, there were these big cow turds. And the guy had the azimuth, the aiming circle, whatever the hell they call it, and we pitched tents. And that's where we stayed, until we went across the channel.

You were talking about the first day in action. I remember that day, because I was trying to make a little joke about it, all this training you had and everything else. I was the assistant driver, and an assistant driver in the States, his job was, before the tank driver started the tank, you had to go back and open up the engine compartment and stand there with a fire extinguisher. So the first thing I said, that first day in action, "You want me to open the engine compartment?"

Lieutenant Lombardi says, "Forget all that shit."

So now, we aren't in action, I don't know, three hours, and we hear Sergeant Schmidt in the second platoon, the tank commander's killed. They told him, "Don't ride the turret." And he was sitting on top of the turret. Sniped right between the eyes. He was the first casualty in the company.

I don't know if it was the next day or the day after. Captain Cary, who was our company commander, he used to tell us, "Watch out for booby traps." He opened a gate or something, and it was boobytrapped and hit him in the ass, he got wounded, and he went off.

But I remember that first day of action. Then you start saying, "Hey, they're playing for real, this is no more games now." And you're saying to yourself, "I wonder who the hell is gonna be next." And you look around, and you're saying, "It could be any one of us. Who knows?"

I never got wounded. The only thing I had, the first tank I was in hit mines. Just before we were going across, they had a little cow path, a dirt road there, and it was mined. The night before they shot everything they had at us. That meant either they were counterattacking or they were moving and they didn't want to take all this ammunition with them. They just shot off the ammunition and took off.

So we knew the area was mined. And I can still see like a cow pasture, with a gate, and it was open. Lombardi figured we can go through that gate. I was the assistant driver, and this guy named Cardis Sawyer from Texas was the driver. Klapkowski was the gunner, and Grayson LaMar was the loader. I don't know what made him do it, but just before we got to the gate, Lombardi told Sawyer to stop, and he said, "Open hatches." And we all opened our hatches. Then he said, "Proceed through the gate."

That's the last thing I remember for a while, because, "Boom!" Shit was flying all over the place. My helmet was gone. I could feel something hot running down my left leg. I thought my leg was blown off.

The three guys in the turret, they got right out. Sawyer and I stayed in the tank, and I was stone deaf. When the stuff cleared and I looked down, the transmission had a crack in it, and the hot oil was running down my pant leg and inside my shoe, and that's what I was feeling.

There was an aid station just down the road. So Sawyer and I went down there. Sawyer went in first. I heard him scream. I said, "The hell with this!" I went back to the tank. I never saw Sawyer again.

Then I had this constant ringing in my ears. [With Sawyer gone], they made me a driver. I told Lombardi, "You know, you ought to keep me out of that driver's seat." I said, "I want to stay in the tank, but give me another job, because I can't hear. You might tell me to stop and I'll keep on going, and get everybody killed."

"No matter where you go on any ship, you always end up with some rebel who plays the guitar and keeps playing 'You Are My Sunshine' over and over."

Tiger burning

Angelo Crapanzano
LST 507, U.S. Navy
West New York, N.J., May 2, 1994

Angelo Crapanzano: There were something like 20,000 guys involved in Tiger. They started in January having these dress rehearsals [for D-Day]. There were two or three before us. One was Beaver; I forgot the other names.

Then we come along. One of the reasons that the earlier exercises had no problems was because the English Channel was pretty rough. Rough water's not good for E-boats. They want calm water. So what happens, when it's time for Tiger, the water was like a lake.

Aaron Elson: I interviewed an antiaircraft gunner who was on the beach; he was in the first wave and said it was the most beautiful day he'd seen in a long time.

Angelo Crapanzano: You know, the English Channel can be like a lake, and when it whips up it can be rougher and nastier than the Atlantic Ocean. You can go from one extreme to the other. A lot of people don't realize how rough the English Channel can get.

So what happened, there were eight LSTs; the first five came out of another port, and they went out into the Channel and waited. Now, around dusk on the 27th, the three LSTs – the 507 that I was on, the 531 ... I'm not sure about the third – when it came time for us to go out and rendezvous with them, we had two British corvettes to escort us out. When we got out there and lined up, the corvettes turned around and went back to England. A lot of us were wondering why these ships were going back; where the hell is our escort?

We ended up with one escort ship. It was about a mile in front of the lead ship, so the sides are wide open in effect. The 507 is the last ship in line, which is uh-uh, bad. That's how they hit them. But the thing you've got to remember is this: Nobody ever even suspected that a thing like this would happen. The element of surprise was devastating. Plus, what made it bad is that it was 2 o'clock in the morning, and it was dark.

Oh – the day before this operation, I received a tetanus shot. A few of the other fellows did, too – not everybody; they go according to your chart. The last time I'd had a tetanus shot was in boot camp. That was the first time I ever had a tetanus shot, and I ended up with a 104 fever. So they gave me this booster shot, and the next day, as we're approaching this convoy, I started to feel funny. I thought, "Don't tell me I'm gonna get sick again."

I was concerned, because I had the midnight to 4 in the morning watch in the main engine room. I was a motor machinist's mate first class, diesel engines.

It was approaching midnight, so I went down in the engine room. My engineering officer was down there, and I told him that – well, I didn't tell him, you can't – when you've got two big 12-cylinder diesel engines running full speed they scream. You have to wear cotton in your ears, and you can't talk. You either read lips or motion. I told him, "I don't feel good. I feel like I've got a fever." So he said, "Go up to the pharmacist's mate."

I go up to the pharmacist's mate, and he takes my temperature. Sure enough, 104. So he says, "What are you doing out of your bunk?"

I said, "I've got the 12 to 4 watch."

He said, "Go down and tell the engine room officer I told you that you should go to your bunk."

I go back down to the engine room, and I tell him. So he says, "All right, I'll cover you." So I go up to the crew's quarters – now this is odd ... I got this weird feeling ... I thought, "Where the hell is my Mae West?" My life jacket. I never had a feeling like that before, and we'd had plenty of general quarters drills. When you have a general quarters drill it's mandatory you wear your life jacket, and if you're topside you've got to wear your helmet. And I start looking for my life jacket. They're thrown all over the place – on top of the lockers, under the lockers – and I'm looking, I'm looking, and I find it; it's all full of dust. My name, "Crappy," was on it, because everybody called me Crappy. They've been calling me Crappy since grammar school, for Chrissake. So I grab my life jacket, I take it over to my bunk, and I lay it right on my bunk. And I lay down.

I must have gone to sleep. I don't know how long I was sleeping, but all of a sudden general quarters was sounded. So I jumped up, and without even hesitating I grabbed my life jacket and started running for the engine room. I'm lacing it up, and as I'm going down the ladder I hear 40-millimeter guns going boom-boom-boom. I thought, "What the hell is this?"

But I figured, well, it's an exercise. When I got down to the engine room I said to the engineer, "What's going on?"

Aaron Elson: You went to the engine room?

Angelo Crapanzano: Oh yeah, I had to. When they sound general quarters, you've got to be dead not to go. So now it's about twenty minutes to two.

My job in general quarters was up in the front of the engine room where they have the annunciators for the wheelhouse. When they changed the speed, it was my job to note the change of speed and then record it in a log. That log is very important in the Navy, in case two ships have an accident. The first thing they want to see is the log and the speeds. I'm getting all these changes of speed and thinking, "What's going on?" Full speed. Half-speed. Stop. Quarter speed. I'm writing all these things, and the last thing I remember writing – I know exactly when we got hit – is 2:03. Everything went black. There was this terrific roar, and I got this sensation of flying up, back, and when I came down I must have bumped my head, and must have been out for a few seconds. When I came to, I felt cold on my legs. And it was pitch black. The torpedo went in the auxiliary engine room, which is just forward of the main engine room, and the only thing between the auxiliary and the main is a steel bulkhead about an inch thick. The six guys in the auxiliary engine room were instantly killed.

I knew the engine room like the palm of my hand. I knew I had to go forward and to either corner, and there was an escape ladder on either side. I ran to the ladder and I went up. When I got topside, I couldn't believe what I saw: The ship was split in half and burning. Fire went from the bow all the way back to the wheelhouse. The only thing that wasn't burning was the stern. And the water all around the ship was burning, because the fuel tanks ruptured, and the oil went into the water. On the tank deck we had fifteen Army ducks [amphibious vehicles], and every Army duck had cans of gasoline on them, and all that was going into the water. It was an inferno.

The soldiers were panicking. You couldn't blame them because they're not trained for disasters at sea. They're trained for land fighting. A lot of them jumped over the side immediately, without even waiting for the captain to say "Abandon ship." The ship was crowded with personnel. Every LST had two or three hundred Army personnel, with all the vehicles; this was a real dress rehearsal. They had to do this for the guys to get used to the ships, where the heads were, how to go to eat. Also, how to dog down their equipment so it wouldn't roll and slip.

It was so crowded that a lot of the soldiers were sleeping topside on their vehicles. When the torpedo hit, a lot of these guys got blown right into the water. There were even small jeeps that got blown into the water. It was an inferno, and the only place that wasn't burning was the stern. So I ran back there.

Now, there's a bunch of guys back there, and everybody's wondering what happened, what the hell's going on? In the meantime, while we're standing there, the 531 is hit by two torpedoes, and it goes down in about ten minutes. They claim that maybe ten or twelve guys got off of that ship.

The captain yells to the gunnery officer, "Empty the magazines" of all the 40-millimeter shells. He was worried that it was gonna get so hot it would blow the whole thing. So we formed a line and they were passing the cans with the shells, and we were throwing them over the side. That lasted about ten minutes. Then he said, "Abandon ship!"

This is tough, because a thousand things are running through your mind at one time. Oh – wait a minute – while we're standing there, the gunnery officer says, "Here comes another torpedo!" And we look over, and there's this thing coming right toward the ass end of the ship. It missed us by no more than 12 feet. You know what kind of feeling that is? Your blood freezes.

Aaron Elson: Do you remember what went through your mind? Was it terror?

Angelo Crapanzano: No. Your mind goes blank. Because you're almost saying to yourself, "What's this going to feel like when it hits? I'm dead."

Now we've got to go into the water, because the fire is getting worse. There were a lot of guys on the front end of the ship, and the tank deck was burning right under them. I had guys telling me that they hesitated; a lot of guys didn't want to jump in the water right away. I didn't want to either. It got so hot on the deck that their shoes started smoking, because the tank deck was burning fiercely, and that's all metal. It's just like a gas jet stove, and all the heat's going up to the top deck.

All right, so you've got to jump. I run to the railing, and I look down, and I see all these guys in the water already. Now I say, "What am I gonna do? I'm gonna jump and I'm gonna hit somebody."

Then I'm saying – this is all in a split second – when I jump in the water, is somebody gonna jump on top of me? How deep down will I go before I come up?

The thing I didn't realize is this: I knew – because the seawater cools the engines – that the reading on the water coming in was 43 degrees. What I didn't know was what 43 degrees felt like. When I hit the water, it took my breath away, that's how cold it was. It was frigid.

But I wasn't thinking too much about the cold. I was thinking, how do I save my ass? So I swam for the back of the ship. Everybody was going to the back, because that was the only part of the water that wasn't burning yet.

Aaron Elson: When you hit the water, how deep did you go?

Angelo Crapanzano: I must have gone down a good six, eight feet. Because this is a 40-foot jump. You had to climb up over the railing and then jump. But it's feet first; you get down nice and clean. But like I said, I was worried, you're looking, and it's dark, and you say, "I hope I don't hit somebody."

So I come up. Then I was worried about the flames in the water, but they were further up; the whole back end was good yet. So we're all back there, a bunch of soldiers and all the sailors. And next to me was my shipmate, John McGarigal. He was a storekeeper, and he was in the wheelhouse when this happened. I met him over this past weekend, and I asked him – because I knew that all the guys topside had to wear helmets, and I knew that he had a gash in his forehead and he was bleeding badly – I said, "Didn't you have your helmet on when the torpedo hit?"

He told me he had removed his helmet to wipe his brow, because he was sweating – and that's when the torpedo hit. The concussion blew him from one side of the wheelhouse to the other, and he banged his head.

And the other thing I learned – this is odd – is that, guess who was sending the speeds down from the wheelhouse to me? Him. Fifty years I never knew it.

So we're all back there in the water; what the hell do we do now? And what the hell is going on? Who hit us? What was it? We didn't know.

Then we see this large oval life raft. Every LST carries about 12 of them around the outer rim of the ship. In an abandon ship, the chief boatswain's mate is supposed to go around and cut them loose, and they slide right down in the water. But it didn't happen that way. Out of the 12 life rafts that we had, only two or three got released. And we were lucky; we got one of them. We saw this life raft drifting towards us. It had gone through all the flames in the water, and the whole center was gone. These life rafts are big, and very wide, and the outer rim is about a foot around. In the center is a wooden platform; it has water, fish hooks, all this crap for survival. That was all burned away, and the outer rim was all charred. But it was buoyant, and was floating. So when I saw it coming towards us I said, "Let's grab this!" I grabbed on, and McGarigal next to me, and nine soldiers got on it. There were eleven in all when we started.

I said, "We've got to kick like hell, get the hell away from the ship," because when it goes down, it's gonna suck us down with it. And we've got to get through all this water that's burning. So by kicking a lot, and splashing, we finally, little by little, got to the outside of the flames. It was a matter of hanging on and surviving, and little by little we drifted away from the ship. And I watched – I could see my ship burning, and little by little going down.

Meanwhile, the water was full of bodies. I saw things that I couldn't believe. I saw bodies that were – what's the right word? They were stuck all together and charred; they were fused together and all black. They had gone into the fire, and never got out.

What killed the majority of the soldiers was the cold water, hypothermia. The other fact was that 95 percent of them had their life jackets on wrong. They had them around their waist instead of under their armpits. A lot of them jumped in with their packs on their backs – with their rifles – I don't know what the hell they were thinking. But it was a complete panic. They wanted to get the hell away from the ship.

I saw bodies with arms off, heads off, heads split open, it's unbelievable. A lot of them were literally blown into the water. I understand that some soldiers got out of the tank deck through an opening in the side. The opening couldn't have been made by the torpedo, but it could have been made by the concussion. I don't know how many but some of the soldiers got out of the tank deck through this opening and they were burned before they even got into the water, because the tank deck was an inferno.

Here's another thing, to show you how cold the water was. After I was in the water no more than an hour, I couldn't feel my legs anymore. It was like there was nothing there. Then I was starting to really worry, because I used to read these stories about the Murmansk Run in the North Atlantic. The water's even colder up there, but when a ship would get hit, if the guys were in the water any length of time, they would have to amputate their legs. This is what kept going through my mind, for four and a half hours in the icy water.

Aaron Elson: I've heard of the Murmansk Run, but don't know much about it.

Angelo Crapanzano: That was the North Atlantic run that they took to deliver all the goods from here to Russia. We were supplying them with tons and tons of stuff. And the German U-boats, the wolfpacks, had a picnic up there. And the water up there has got to be in the thirties; you can't survive in that too long. And if they do get you out, who the hell wants to live with no legs?

Aaron Elson: So you had some knowledge of what was going on?

Angelo Crapanzano: A lot of it is just common sense. I knew about hypothermia. When I started to feel the sensation of sleeping, I told the nine soldiers on the raft, and I kept repeating to them, "Don't fall asleep, whatever you do. If you fall asleep you're dead. Keep kicking your legs. Sing. Talk. Do anything, but don't fall asleep." And little by little, they were kicking, there was conversation, but then, after a while it changed into a lot of praying, and yelling, and begging for mercy. I heard it going on all around me, guys screaming and crying, and dying.

Aaron Elson: Would people try to keep each other's spirits up?

Angelo Crapanzano: Yeah, but then the mood changed, because we started to realize that, hey, we're gonna be here a long time. Is anybody coming back? Then I started to worry about whether these E-boats would come around and take us as prisoners of war. All these things go through your mind.

After about two hours, three soldiers said, "We're gonna make a swim for it." I said, "You're crazy. What do you mean, make a swim for it? You don't even know where you are. You don't know what direction you're gonna go. Suppose you go in the wrong direction."

They went, and that's it. Those three, gone.

And then a little while later, I had an Army lieutenant on my raft who went completely berserk. Yelling and screaming. And he lets go, and he's gone.

Now there's five soldiers left. And little by little, time went on and on and on. In the course of the next period of time, after the lieutenant went, every half hour or three quarters of an hour, one of the other guys would just fall asleep and slip off. I watched the nine soldiers die, and couldn't do a thing to help them.

You've got to understand that as time goes on, I'm not feeling so great either. I'm losing a lot of my strength. You lose a lot of your ability to think straight, too. And little by little, all the soldiers went. That was it. They were gone. It was just John and me who were left.

Now it's got to be close to dawn. It's still dark. I'm in bad shape, and McGarigal's been unconscious for two and a half or three hours, because he's lost a lot of blood. He had an ugly gash in his forehead. I was holding myself to the life raft with my left hand, and I was holding onto McGarigal with my right hand. And then it got to a point where I must have went in and out of consciousness myself.

Now it's four and a half hours I'm in the water, and I'd just about had it. I figured I wasn't gonna make it. And all of a sudden – I'm looking in the distance, it's still dark – I see this light. It's bobbing up and down, and it seems to be getting bigger. So when I see this, I immediately assume that help is coming. And I passed out.

Angelo Crapanzano: For 40 years after the war, Exercise Tiger was a complete secret. The only guys that knew about it were the survivors, and not even their families. I didn't tell my wife about this, or my kids. They knew I lost a ship, and they knew I got the Bronze Star, and that's where the story ended.

In 1982, I joined the VFW in North Bergen. I used to go religiously; never missed a meeting. On the night that the "20/20" show was on, I didn't know about it. We were eating supper, and I said to my wife, "You know, I don't feel like going to the meeting tonight. I think I'll just stay home and watch TV." So I get up from the table, go into the living room, and open the paper. I'm looking down the schedule. I didn't usually stay up till 10, and the "20/20" came on at 10. So I look all the way down, and it says, "20/20. The mystery surrounding the killing of 750 GIs in a D-Day rehearsal." I couldn't believe it. This is 40 years later. Holy Christ, don't tell me that this is about Tiger. I jumped on the phone because my son-in-law at that time and my daughter lived in Iselin, he had a Beta – in 1984 there was no VCR, there was just Beta – and he had just gotten it maybe six months before. So I got ahold of my daughter and I said, "Tell Russell to tape the whole '20/20' show. It's on from 10 to 11."

Then I got ready to watch it. I sit in the chair, put it on, and sonofabitch, they show you the ass end of the third ship that got hit. They blew the back end of it; that's the 289. When I saw that, I said, "Oh my God, it is!" I watched the whole thing. I was dumbfounded. I wept.

Aaron Elson: Up to this point, had you talked about it with anyone?

Angelo Crapanzano: No.

Aaron Elson: When you were were hit with your depression (in 1968), did you tell the psychiatrist anything about it?

Angelo Crapanzano: No, I never went into any details. I told him I had lost a ship. I told him I was decorated. But I didn't – you know why? I don't know if you realize this – when they took us off the ship to a hospital, we were all told that we should never talk about this to anybody. Even the guys in the Army; I met this guy who lives in Forked River – he was on the lead ship, the 515 – and he said that as soon as this thing started popping, they had all the soldiers go down below decks. And the next morning, their commanding officer told them, "Nothing happened last night. Remember. Nothing happened."

Anyhow, I watched the show. And my brother, who lives down in Shipbottom, that particular night my nephew happened to be twisting the TV dial, he came across it and said, "Isn't this what happened to Uncle Angelo?"

My brother is a commercial artist; he works in Manhattan. He commutes 200 miles a day. He's been doing this for 14 years. So the next morning when he goes to Manhattan, he calls the studio and talks to the producer – her name was Nola Safro – and he says, "I watched your show last night on Tiger, and my brother's a survivor of that."

So she flipped. She says, "Where does he live?"

He says, "Right across the river."

She says, "Please, give me his phone number." And the next night, at 5 o'clock, I was eating supper, and the phone rings. It was her. She spoke to me for an hour. She wanted to know everything that happened, the way I'm telling you.

And at the end of the conversation, she said to me, "I have the names and addresses of a lot of your shipmates."

She said, "I have the address of John Doyle," who was the skipper who came back to save us. He lives in Missoula, Montana.

I said, "Please, give it to me." And then she had the name and address of Dr. Ralph Greene. He was one of the doctors. He was a captain in the Army field hospital where we were brought the following morning. I didn't know him then. The next morning, before we got to the field hospital, the head doctor got all the doctors together and said, "You're going to get a load of casualties this morning. Don't take any names. Don't ask any questions. Don't keep any records. Just treat them as they are. Anybody that gets caught talking about this will be court-martialed."

And then we came in, and they treated us, and they wondered, "Where did these casualties come from? What happened?"

After the war, Dr. Greene goes back to his practice in Chicago. He was a pathologist. And every once in a while, he used to think about this.

So in 1974, the government passes the Freedom of Information Act. That was it. He went down to Washington, and went into the archives. He wanted to see the material on Tiger. There still were certain things that were classified, but they gave most of it to him. When he started reading, he couldn't believe it. And he said, "How did they keep this thing so quiet, a disaster like this?"

Guess what I found out at the memorial ceremonies in New Bedford? McGarigal got his hands on some classified material, in England, that proved that there were over a thousand guys killed. They come up with this figure, seven hundred and something, that's bullshit.

Dr. Greene sees all this, and he gets crazy. He decides he's gonna investigate the whole thing. So he spends months traveling all over the country, locating survivors, and when he gets enough good information together, he goes to "20/20." They looked at his material, and they loved it. They interviewed John Doyle, the captain of the 515, and Dr. Greene, and they interviewed Manny Rubin, who stayed in England after the war and married an English girl.

And you know what they did? This is fantastic. I couldn't believe it. They put an ad in a German paper saying, "Would the E-boat captains who remember this attack in 1944 please come forward, because we're going to make a documentary." Three of them came forward, including the skipper who sunk my ship. His name is Gunther Rabe. I saw letters that he wrote to Dr. Eckstam explaining the whole thing, their side of the story.

When she gave me all these names and addresses, I figured the first letter that I want to write is to Dr. Greene. I was so thankful that he went to the trouble to do this. So I write him a letter, and I explain who I was, what ship I was on. And he sends me back a letter a week later. He says, "Please, do me a favor. Put down on paper everything you remember, from the time you left Brixham until you ended up in the hospital. Everything." I put together a six-page letter. He said the reason he wanted to do all this was that he's thinking about writing a book. He was going to call his book "Tiger Burning." Which was an appropriate title, too.

Then I wrote a letter to Captain Doyle and I thanked him, because if he hadn't come back I wouldn't be here today. He saved the lives of 80 to 100 soldiers and sailors that night.

Aaron Elson: Where does McCann come in?

Angelo Crapenzano: Joe McCann was a coxswain on the 515. Doyle was the captain of that ship, and the commander of the group was on it as well.

Some LSTs carried two of these small personnel boats – LCVPs – and McCann was a coxswain of one of them. Now, this guy was an expert seaman. He lived in Washington State. He used to go out on fishing trawlers, and he knew how tohandle the tiller. And here's the thing that's gonna amaze you. He went into the Navy at age 13. He had somebody fake his parents' names. When he pulled us out of the water that day, he was 15 years old.

I wrote to Dr. Greene, to John Doyle, and to my gunnery officer who lived in Texas, Tom Clark.

In the letter to Greene, I explained that I couldn't feel my legs, and I was worried about gangrene, and that they might have to amputate my legs. Now Greene takes this letter, makes copies of it, and sends it out to a few guys. And one of them is Joe McCann.

When I wrote the letter to John Doyle, he wasn't feeling well, and he couldn't answer it. So he called up Floyd Hicks, who lives in California, and who was on his ship. He told Hicks to call me up, and to tell me that Doyle got my letter, that he was glad to hear from me, and that he wasn't feeling well. So one Sunday night I get a phone call from this guy Hicks in California. He said, "I was on the 515 with Doyle," and an engine room guy, too. He said, "I have the address of Joe McCann." He told me McCann was one of the guys who lowered his boat and went around looking for survivors.

I wrote McCann a letter, and I told him about Hicks and Doyle, and I said, "I know that there were two boats lowered that went around looking for survivors, so the odds are fifty-fifty that you are the one who picked me up."

Three or four days later, on a Sunday night again, the phone rings. It's Joe McCann. And I told him, "You know, Joe, I wrote to tell you that being that you were one of the coxswains that picked up bodies, the chances are one in two you picked me up."

He said, "I did pick you up."

I said, "How did you know it was me?"

He said, "The reason I know is because you were unconscious when I pulled you out of the water, and you were mumbling about your legs." He had read the letter that I wrote to Dr. Greene.

Oh, wait till you hear this. I couldn't get over this. I came so close to not making it. He told me that when the captain told him that they were gonna lower the boats and go around looking for bodies, it was still dark. Joe immediately ran to his locker, and he got a Navy lantern. He took the lantern, and he hooked it onto the bow, because he didn't want to go through the water and kill somebody that was alive. So he was just drifting slow, and looking. This is the light I saw. And he said, "On the first run that we made in the area of your raft, we thought you were both dead, and we passed you right by."

Can you imagine? Because I went unconscious, he thought we were dead and they went right past us. Then on the way back they passed us again, and the guy in the boat with him said, "I think I saw one of those guys moving." And sonofabitch – I mean, how close can you come to not making it, after all we went through. I cried. When I hung up the phone, I cried like a baby.

Aaron Elson: Your wife was telling me that the LST that turned around almost didn't come back, that somebody risked a court martial.

Angelo Crapanzano: Oh, God. Here's another thing. We were lined up, eight LSTs, one behind the other, with 500 yards between each one. From the front one to our ship, we were way the hell back. Now the commander of the eight ships knew that these were maneuvers. When we got hit they saw flares, but they thought this was part of the maneuvers. Then when they saw the second one get hit, and the third, that's when the commander said, "This is not maneuvers." So he told all the LSTs to get the hell out of there and go back to England, and the five remaining LSTs took off.

A loaded LST only goes, top speed, five knots. The German E-boats had very powerful twin Mercedes engines that were capable of doing 45 knots.

The five LSTs were under way for quite a while, and the E-boats didn't follow them. In the meantime, Captain Doyle says to the group commander, "I'm turning this ship around, and going back to that area. There's got to be a lot of men alive in that water."

The commander says, "If you turn this ship around, I'll have you court-martialed."

Now, this guy's a commander, and Doyle's a lieutenant JG [junior grade]. Doyle says to the commander, "This is my ship and I'm going back." He wasn't concerned about the Navy crew, but he had all these Army guys. He made an announcement over the PA system. He said, "I'm going back to pick up survivors. Would you rather keep going to England, or go back and fight?"

So they all yelled, "Let's go back and fight!" So now he starts back.

But see, the reason the commander threatened to have Doyle court martialed is normal procedure in the service. You can't jeopardize a ship loaded with guys to go back and pick up survivors. But Doyle knew that when he got back to that area it would be dawn, and once it gets dawn, E-boats don't hang around. They like it at night, sneaky, hit and run. And he was right.

Aaron Elson: What can you remember about the moment you were rescued?

Angelo Crapanzano: Nothing – I was unconscious.

Aaron Elson:. When did you come to?

Angelo Crapanzano: On the 515, in a bunk. And someone was working on me. The first thing I said was, "How are my legs?"

"Oh," he says, "you'll be all right. We're going to take you to an Army field hospital in the morning."

Now this is the comical part of the story. My executive officer, James Murdoch, was one of the few officers who survived. He was a pitcher for one of these Southern teams. Lefthanded. He was really good. He used to walk around the deck a lot of the time with a glove and a ball, bouncing it, and he was a rebel. He was from Virginia. And he smoked cigars. But good cigars. He used to buy them in a box. So I wake up, and I see him standing there in his dry underwear, and you know what he said?

"Sonofabitch," he said. "I had six good boxes of cigars on that ship that went down."

I said, "You sonofabitch! You're worried about your cigars, when all these guys got killed?" I never got over that. I couldn't believe what he said.

Aaron Elson: You've just nearly lost both your legs, you've been in the water for four and a half hours, how did they get you back in shape to send you out on D-Day?

Angelo Crapanzano: Oh, you know about that?

Aaron Elson: It said in the book ("Exercise Tiger," by Nigel Lewis) that you made forty trips on an LST.

Angelo Crapanzano: It says forty? I don't know where they got that. It was in the vicinity of 23 or 24 or 27, I'm not sure.

I'll tell you what happened. I went to the hospital. They checked me out and treated me, and they said, "You'll be all right." They said there was no permanent damage.

They took the survivors, and split them up in small groups. And they put us in what they called rest camps, but I called them isolation camps. Because we weren't allowed passes, or to talk to anybody.

Aaron Elson: The book said that one thing that kept a lot of guys going was the thought of getting 30 days' survivor leave.

Angelo Crapanzano: Oh yeah, I'm coming to this. This is the payoff . We go to this rest camp, and naturally we all know that the rule in the Navy is this: If you lose your ship, you have to go back to the States for 30 days survivor leave because you have to get all your gear back again. We lost everything. When I got there, they gave me Army fatigues, a towel, a toothbrush, and a piece of soap. That's it.

After we're there about three weeks, Murdoch, the executive officer — by the way, my captain was alive when they pulled him out of the water, and when they brought him up to the officers' quarters he had a heart attack and died. He had been on two destroyers in the Pacific, and lost both ships. This guy saw a lot of action. He was a real old salt. When he died, Murdoch took over.

Aaron Elson: How did they break it to you that you were going to be part of D-Day?

Angelo Crapanzano: Murdoch comes out one morning, lines us all up, and he's got papers. I said to the guy next to me, "This is it. We're all going back to the States." So he starts reading them off. He says, "You guys are all petty officers, and all experienced, all went to Navy schools, and you're all going to be reassigned to LSTs to make the invasion of Normandy."

I could feel my blood getting cold. They've got to be kidding. I said, "What the hell are they trying to do, kill us? Chrissakes, it's only three weeks ago we were out there, and now we're gonna go back?" I couldn't believe it.

Aaron Elson: Was it because they were short of crews for the LSTs.

Angelo Crapanzano: Not necessarily, because the LST 294 that I was assigned to had a full complement of men. The problem is this, though. When I went aboard, these guys all knew what happened. I guess word got around, even though nobody was supposed to be talking about it.

I went to the engineering officer, and he was a hell of a nice guy. He said to me right off the bat, "You want to get down in the engine room?"

I said, "All right, let's go." So I went down in the engine room with him. But when I got down there, oh my God, he took one look at me and said, "All right, let's go topside."

You know what I learned at the ceremonies in New Bedford? I was the only guy who got out of the main engine room alive. Not many guys get out of engine rooms. There were five of us down below.

Aaron Elson: What happened to the officer who told you to go up to your bunk when you had the fever?

Angelo Crapanzano: That was my engineering officer, Lieutenant Smith.

Aaron Elson: Was he killed?

Angelo Crapanzano: Yes. And my friend was killed, we were very close. He was a radioman; his name was Joe Grecco and he was from West New York, and he was chronic seasick. I couldn't see why they didn't take him off the ship. He used to stand his radio watch with a bucket next to him. Sick as a dog. He should have never been on that ship.

I'll tell you something else. When we went to Halifax, Nova Scotia, to make up the convoy, there were 40 or 50 ships, and it took us about 11 days to go from Nova Scotia to Ireland. LST's have no keel – they're flat-bottomed – and I'd say that 30 percent of the crew was sick. I mean they got green-looking in the face. And when we got near Ireland, and somebody spotted land, they yelled. All these guys came up, they looked like rats coming out of holes, they were that sick.

A lot of people don't realize this, but when you go below decks, like in the quarters and stuff, the ventilation isn't that good. A lot of guys are throwing up, and with the odor, you get sick even if you're not prone to it.

Aaron Elson: What did it feel like when you went back into the engine room when you were reassigned?

Angelo Crapanzano: It's a funny feeling. I guess it's like claustrophobia. I didn't have it before, though. I used to go down in the engine room and read, and even lay down and take a nap while the engines were running. Nothing bothered me. But now it was different. I went down and it was a terrible feeling. It was like the whole thing's gonna come down on top of me. And I knew that it's a terrible place to be when something like that happens, and that I was very lucky that I got out of there.

Aaron Elson: Did the other sailors press you for details?

Angelo Crapanzano: Yes, but I only told them what I knew. At that time, what did I know? All I know is my ship was sunk, a lot of guys got killed, and I saw the 531 get hit. I saw the 289 get hit. Other than that, I don't know. The Germans didn't even know accurately. The next morning, in the hospital, somebody got hold of an English newspaper, and on the front page it said the Germans reported that they sank a couple of oil tankers. Oil tankers. They'd seen all the flames.

When the E-boats approached us, from quite a distance away, they saw silhouettes, so the E-boat captain who sank my ship fires two torpedoes, and then they watch, and nothing happens. The first two torpedoes went under us. We didn't even know it. One of them scraped the bottom. I never heard it. Some of the Army guys who were on the tank deck thought it sounded like we were making a landing and were hitting a beach. They were depth torpedoes, set for ships with keels. Then the E-boat captain fired two surface torpedoes. One of them hit us and one missed, but that's not the one I saw. That one could have come from a different E-boat.

A lot of the LSTs reported hearing these loud engines, and then complete panic took place. One ship was firing on another ship, and about 25 guys got killed that way.

Angelo Crapanzano: The engineering officer of the 294 said to me, "Wait in my office. I want to speak to the exec." He came back. He said, "Look, don't worry about it." He knew I could type. He said, "You're gonna take care of all the records for the engine room, and work with me in the office, and your general quarters station's gonna be on a gun, topside."

We were among the first LSTs going in to Utah Beach, and we were on the beach when this plane – I think it was an English plane – got hit. I look up, and I see this plane coming down. I said, "Holy Christ! He's gonna come down right on top of us!" He didn't miss us by much. And as soon as he hit the water, the water got all green around it. They had this special dye so when they dunk in the ocean they can spot them to pick them up.

Aaron Elson: What happened to the pilot?

Angelo Crapanzano: I don't even know. There was so much going on. Oh, this is funny: With LSTs, when you go into the beach, especially in France, the tide drops 17 feet. So as you're going in, you drop the rear anchor all the way out, with a long cable, and that lays there. When you go in, you discharge your load. It takes awhile to unload. And by that time the tide starts running out, and then you catch it all the way in to the low tide. You wouldn't believe this – the tide goes so far out, the whole ship is dry. You could walk all around your LST, you could look at the propellers, the screws, everything. Now you have to wait until the tide starts to come back in. So this first day, we got stuck on the beach, then it got dark. All these LSTs are sitting on the beach. And this is D-Day, there's a lot of stuff going on. Everybody's trigger-happy. We're all at general quarters. Every guy's at his gun. So one of the LSTs, way up on the other end, all of a sudden you see all the tracer bullets going up. Then everybody starts firing. All of a sudden, we see this big flash, and a guy says, "We got him! We got a plane!" The captain gets on the PA system. He says, "You guys just shot down your own barrage balloon."

Aaron Elson: What was your impression on D-Day at H-Hour when that artillery barrage came from all the ships?

Angelo Crapanzano: Oh yeah, are you kidding? I always tell this story; we were about a half a mile from the battleship Nevada. So the Nevada is anchored broadside, with the 16-inch guns. And I'm watching it. Everybody was. You'd see the big flame, and then about four seconds later the whole ship would shake from the vibration a half a mile away. They told me they fired a two thousand pound missile eighteen miles. Can you imagine? It's like a Volkswagen or something. Unbelievable. I was so impressed. I said Holy Christ, how about the guys on the battleship? They must have all had earplugs. Look at that disaster that happened on the Iowa. You know, somebody told me – this is true – there's nothing more devastating than Naval power. I'm not talking about aircraft, big, two, three thousand pound bombs. I'm talking about ground stuff. There's nothing more destructive. They were firing at pillboxes, constantly, and the battleships, and still, when they went in on the invasion, them frigging pillboxes were still there.

Aaron Elson: Did you get a Purple Heart?

Angelo Crapanzano: No. I wasn't wounded, physically. I was wounded mentally. They don't give it to you for that.

Aaron Elson: Did you ever talk about it with doctors?

Angelo Crapanzano: The only one I spoke about it with is my psychiatrist.

Aaron Elson: This was before 1984 or after?

Angelo Crapanzano: I had mentioned it to him before, and he didn't seem to think that that was the problem, at that time.

Aaron Elson: When the "20/20" report came out, did you tell the psychiatrist more?

Angelo Crapanzano: Yes. And then a few years after the Vietnam War ended, they came up with post traumatic stress disorder, and found out that this actually happened. It hit me in 1968.

The psychiatrist didn't pump me much. He just said, "What was it all about?" I broke down, and told him what happened, that was it.

You know what I realized, too, Sunday, up in New Bedford? That these "Inside Edition" reporters are all trained – I figured this out myself – they know how to ask you certain questions. They wanted to make me weep on TV. Joe said the same thing. They know exactly the questions to ask you, and make you fill up. And if you don't, they ask you another, and sooner or later they're gonna get you. They want to see this on the camera.

Aaron Elson: Tell me more about your buddy Joe Grecco.

Angelo Crapanzano: I didn't know him till we went into the same crew, and he was from West New York. We hit it off right away, and we always went out together. In December 1943 we went to Chicago – the whole crew went to Chicago to the Great Lakes Naval Training Station for antiaircraft training – and when it was Christmas eve, he and I went walking through Chicago, and we said it looks like New York. And then we went to midnight Mass together.

Aaron Elson: Was he from a big family?

Angelo Crapanzano: He had one brother. Where's that newspaper article I have about him?

Ida Crapanzano [Angelo's wife]: Christmas eves were always sad for Angelo. Even with our kids, we would get their toys together, but it was always very sad for him. I'll tell you, the "20/20" show did a lot for him, because he started to talk about it, and he started to get a lot of correspondence, and he would sit up and write letters.

Angelo Crapanzano: This article about Joe being killed, what's bad about this is that my mother and father knew that we were on the same ship, and this article was put in the local paper, I guess about a week after our ship was sunk. So when they saw that, then they really started to worry.

Aaron Elson: (reading from the article) "Killed in action, Joseph Grecco. Former Dispatch carrier. West New York athlete was radio man…"

Angelo Crapanzano: He was a terrific basketball and baseball player

Aaron Elson: Now it says "Buried Overseas."

Angelo Crapanzano: That was done because they couldn't do anything else with the bodies. It was too near D-Day. But his body came back. I went to see in a funeral parlor over here. He came home about three years after I was married, I guess 1947 or 48. I met his mother and father and brother.

Aaron Elson: (reading) "A telegram from the Navy Department received last Friday by Mr. and Mrs. Frank Grecco, 5400 Madison Street, West New York, notified them that their son, Radioman third class Joseph G. Grecco, was killed in action. The telegram read, 'The Navy Department deeply regrets to inform you that your son, Joseph Gabriel Grecco, radioman third class, USNR, was killed in action in the performance of his duty and the service of his country. The department extends to you its sincerest sympathy in your great loss. His remains were interred in Allied territory outside continental limits of the United States pending cessation of hostilities. If further details are received, you will be informed. To prevent possible aid to our enemies, please do not divulge the name of ship or station.' It was signed by Vice Admiral Randall Jacobs, chief of Naval personnel.

"Grecco, a former Hudson Dispatch carrier , was inducted into the Navy on March 18, 1943, after having graduated from Memorial High School in February. He received boot training at Newport, R.I., and was then sent to Boston, Mass., for training as a radio man. After 22 weeks at school, he was graduated and attained his present rank.

"He was home on leave and upon returning he was assigned as radioman aboard an LST. In March Grecco was sent to England. Born in West New York, he was graduated from School 3, and while in high school played with the Memorial championship basketball team of 1942. He was also on the Build Better Boys team of West New York .

"Besides his parents, he is survived by a brother, Patsy, 14. His father is a veteran of World War I."

Angelo Crapanzano: Joe was a nice-looking boy. He reminded me of John Garfield. He was a cocky type, too. He knew he was good looking.

Aaron Elson: Your wife tells me that Christmas Eve is always a tough time for you.

Angelo Crapanzano: It's sad. It's crazy, I mean, to me it was a sad holiday all the time. It was always like that, from 1944 on.

Ninety percent of the LSTs were built in the middle of the country. We went aboard our ship New Year's Day of '44. Brand new. You could smell the paint. But it wasn't fully equipped. A nucleus crew got on, and they had two pilots that had to take it down the Mississippi. When you get down to New Orleans they put on the guns, the wheelhouse, the mast. They start putting in ammunition, supplies, all that stuff. And then two General Motors engineers came on and we went on a shakedown cruise. Then we made practice landings in Panama City, Florida. And then we went back to New Orleans – that's where McGarigal got on. Then we went back to Florida. This is January. I was standing engine room watch in my swimming trunks, and guys were sitting on the tubs tanning themselves. And as you come up the coast, it's getting colder and colder. The next stop we lay overnight in New York. They camouflaged the ship there. I got home just for the night. Then the Boston fish pier. Then Halifax, Nova Scotia, and that's where the convoys were being formed.

And what happened to us, too – this ship was like ill-fated, because a lot of crazy things happened – when we were in Halifax, we were tied up to a pier that had just the pier and a long metal railing, and when it came time to leave, they never unhooked the ropes, and we pulled the whole fence off the pier.

That was No. 1. No. 2, we were in a convoy of 50 ships, and we had the coffin corner. Of all the ships, this is the last row, and you're over here. That's how they pick off ships, from the back.

After we're under way for a couple days, something breaks on the rudder; they can't steer it now. So we drop out, and we were in the North Atlantic alone. A nice piece of action that is. But we were young, and we didn't worry about things like that.

The favorite expression on my ship was this: We never had to worry about torpedoes because we've got a flat bottom. I don't remember this, but they said it did happen – it could have happened while I was sleeping – they said that something broke on the rudder, and they couldn't steer the ship. So they go down into where the screws are, and they go back where the mechanism is, and you know what they fixed it with? A paper clip.

Aaron Elson: When you finally started to talk about Exercise Tiger, how did that affect your outlook on life?

Angelo Crapanzano: I think it did a lot for me, because the last time I was in the hospital was 1982, and I haven't been in since. So that's 12 years. It made a big difference; I know it did. I've been taking two antidepressants since 1982.

Aaron Elson: Does it make you feel like all of it was not in vain?

Angelo Crapanzano: You mean, like, did I think it was necessary that it happened? See, I sort of have a belief that things happen usually the way they're supposed to happen. You think you have control, but you really don't. Because there's so many things that lead to the fact. Another one of the facts is this: We weren't supposed to be in that convoy. You know what happened? The 508 was supposed to have been in, and two days before she hit something, and we went in her place. We were meant to be there, right?

Aaron Elson: You said you have two daughters. Do they take an interest in this?

Angelo Crapanzano: Not really.

Ida Crapanzano: Now they do. Before they never knew about it. You never spoke to them about it. You never told them stories.

Aaron Elson: How about grandchildren?

Angelo Crapanzano: Well, now the situation with the grandchildren is that, with my oldest daughter, who got married in 1969, I have a grandson who's 22 – he's at St. John's University – and I have a granddaughter who's 19. Now my granddaughter who's 19 seems to be more interested than anybody, although my grandson did bring it up in high school or college. My other daughter, Nancy, got married pretty late, like 34, and her children are too young.

Ida Crapanzano: One is going to be eight, one is five, and one is three.

Angelo Crapanzano: You want to hear something weird again about this thing? In Union City, on the block where I was born, my father had a barbershop. Next door there were people who had a fish store, and then there was a dry goods store, a Jewish couple, Danny Perkel and the girl's name was Romilda Mitrane. And when I went overseas, right around the time that this happened, she dreamt she saw all these Navy uniforms floating in the water, and she went over – she didn't tell my mother, she said to my mother, "Have you heard from Angelo lately?" I guess my mother said no. Romilda didn't tell her about the dream then. She probably told her later.

Aaron Elson: Who was this?

Angelo Crapanzano: A neighbor, a young girl. I played with all these kids, see, when we were small. And the other funny part is – this has nothing to do with the war – when my mother took me to kindergarten, I cried so much and carried on the teacher said, "Take him home. Bring him back next semester." Now I played all the time with Danny Perkel. So the next September, he went to school, and I went with him. The first Jewish holiday he stayed home; I stayed home. I grew up with a couple of Jewish boy friends. Irving Metzger, I grew up with him. He went into the Air Corps. He was a small guy. He was a B-17 pilot. His first mission over Germany his plane gets hit. They were up 40,000 feet. When they get hit, all their equipment flies off, including his gloves. He tells the guys to bail out, and he stays with the plane and brings it down.

When his gloves got blown off, his fingers froze. The German doctors amputated all his fingers. I've often wondered about this, because he was Jewish.

Aaron Elson: It was that cold up there?

Angelo Crapanzano: Forty below. Unbelievable. I went to his wedding, after the war. They lived in Union City for a while, then they moved and I lost track of him.

Angelo Crapanzano: I was what they called a selected volunteer. When I took my physical, the guy said, "You can have whatever you want, Marines, Army or Navy."

My father was in the Navy. He was on a sub tender, and he always said to me, "If you have to go in the service, go in the Navy, because you have a clean place to sleep and good food." But he never told me about the torpedoes.

Aaron Elson: Was he in World War I?

Angelo Crapanzano: Yes. And his brother was in the Army. He was in France in the big battles, and he was gassed.

He was one of the orderlies for Frank Knox, and Knox eventually ran for vice president with Roosevelt, in the Thirties. In fact, one time he was in Journal Square campaigning, and my father and my uncle went up to him, and he remembered my uncle.

Where's that thing I got of his that was made in France? This is a picture of me in New Orleans.

Where were we? In the water or out of the water? My legs are getting cold.

Aaron Elson: What sort of things did you lose when the ship went down?

Ida Crapanzano: He lost my letters.

Angelo Crapanzano: I had about eight dollars in English money, and I had two mandolins. My father gave me one, and I picked up another one. I have two now. Oh no, I sold one. I played by ear, pretty good. In fact, I used to play – see, my uncle played mandolin and my father played guitar, and I used to love to hear that. I used to watch my uncle, and I picked it right up. No lessons or anything. We had a lot of fun on the ship, don't get me wrong. Before this thing happened, it was like one big happy family.

I'll tell you, a lot of horsing around goes on on a ship. Plus there's a lot of card playing, dice playing, guys playing cribbage. All kinds of stuff. And no matter where you go on any ship, you always end up with some rebel who plays the guitar and keeps playing "You Are My Sunshine" over and over, to drive you bananas.

Aaron Elson: What was the food like?

Angelo Crapanzano: Excellent. I mean, I thought it was excellent. I had a very good appetite. Meatloaf. I loved this dish they made, baked salmon, and then they put a crust of dough over it. They give you a lot of fruit salads. But you know the thing that people don't realize is this, too. When you go up in the chow line with your tray, on our ship the chow line was up there and you had to go up a ladder on this side. You'd start here, walk across, go down this ladder, and when it was rough you'd go down the ladder with your tray and hope you didn't kill yourself. I used to sit next to a lot of guys who I knew were seasick and they wouldn't eat, and I'd eat my chow and I'd eat some of theirs. And there were a lot of guys got very squeamish up in their stomach. They'd go in line and then when they sat down, they'd get up and walk away.

"The gal I married, that wasn't her name [tattooed on my arm], and I told her once, 'For a dollar I can get them to ink that over. Do you want me to do it?' She said, 'Give me the dollar. I got what I want.' "

The human aiming stake

John "Bud" Hawk
E Company, 359th Regiment, 90th Infantry Division
Omaha, Nebraska, Sept. 27, 1996

Aaron Elson: Did you grow up in Washington State?

John Hawk: I spent most of my life there. I was born in San Francisco. My dad was a World War I GI student. They had a GI Bill after World War I. He went to engineering school in San Francisco. My mother was going to Mills College. She was from eastern Washington. She was a farmer's daughter up there. I had one sister born in Oakland and one in Sausalito and I was born right in San Francisco.

Aaron Elson: Did your dad ever talk about World War I?

John Hawk: Not very much. He was an artilleryman. And then after the war was over, he was still in the Army and was over on Corregidor and Bataan, in the field artillery. He had pictures of those big disappearing guns, big mortars, that raise up out of the fort and fire and then go back down. He had gotten into photography, too, and he developed a way of taking pictures of their target shooting and calibrating it so that they didn't have to estimate how close they were.

Aaron Elson: How old were you when you went into the service?

John Hawk: Nineteen. My birthday's on the 30th of May. In my senior year of high school, they gave us a 4A classification in the draft. So as soon as we finished school, I think I got my notice two weeks later.

I had just turned 19. So I was just 21 when I got out. When I got home I was 20. Harry put the medal on me on the 20th of June, and I had been 21 on the 30th of May.

Aaron Elson: You went in after Hill 122?

John Hawk: Yes. They were recuperating and regrouping, and I was among the first replacements that they sent over.

We had a nice way to get over there. We were up in South Wales; we'd been over for about a week. We went over on the Wakefield, which was the old liner Manhattan. The Queen [Mary] carried eight thousand, and that thing carried six thousand. Eight days from Boston to Liverpool. I mean, Zoom! We didn't waste any time. We started off out of Boston. It was funny, zigzagging, back and forth and round and round, and pretty soon the scuttlebutt was that they had picked up a submarine behind us. All of a sudden no zig, no zag, no nothing. You could just feel her winding up and going. And they said at the speed we went there wasn't a submarine in the world that could catch us unless we ran over it.

So we made it in eight days, and we spent five or six days in Wales wandering around in the rain. Then they had just finished laying an airstrip down on the beach; they just poured a blacktop strip right on the beach, and they were flying hospital planes over there, old C-47s. Somebody said, "Why are we going to all the trouble to load these guys on a ship and take them across and get them seasick?" So they put seventeen enlisted men and one officer replacement on each plane. And when they landed on the beach, they opened the doors on one side and we got out and on the other side they loaded the wounded in. Never shut off their motors. Turned around and went back. So we flew across the channel and then we just started walking. We walked for about a half a day and we were at the front.

John Hawk: (Showing a picture) This of course is my prize picture.

Aaron Elson: That's Truman pinning the Medal of Honor on you?

John Hawk: Yes.

Aaron Elson: Not pinning. Putting it around your neck.

John Hawk: And I got him to come to me.

Aaron Elson: How did you do that?

John Hawk: Well, I knew a senator, and I said I wouldn't go to Washington. He would have to come to my Washington. So that's on the state capitol steps.

Aaron Elson: Now, those three stripes; you were a sergeant?

John Hawk: I was a buck sergeant. Squad leader. Machine gun section.

Aaron Elson: What happened to the rest of your squad?

John Hawk: Well, this guy here (pointing to a photo), he got hit badly in the shoulder. They were trying to take a pillbox. This little guy's name was McDonald, another sergeant I saw later said he got picked off by a sniper when they got clear up to Czechoslovakia. This guy's name is Frank Lacrosse. He was there when I got there and he was there when I left, and as I understood, he went clear through the whole thing and was never hit once. I had one machine gun section and he had the other. And then whenever we would lose one of the other sergeants, I'd have either both sections or the platoon. Then we'd get replacements. This is a hungry, mean looking bugger, huh?

Aaron Elson: Who's that?

John Hawk: That's me. We were loaded down with so much stuff. As squad leader, I had to carry a pair of wire cutters, a shovel, and I had to carry an M-1 because we needed to be sure somebody had a grenade launcher. I always carried a couple of first aid kits, and enough goddamn ammunition.

Aaron Elson: How many hand grenades?

John Hawk: Usually, depending on what we were doing, I didn't carry any. They were too heavy. When you went into an assault you'd pick up a few from one of the jeeps, but as soon as we got done and had to move out, you got rid of the goddamn things. They were way too heavy.

There's little Mac, I always remember, he was my foxhole buddy, the two of us.

Aaron Elson: What was his name?

John Hawk: His name was McDonald. He was from up in Minnesota or Wisconsin somewhere, and I remember that he had a strikingly beautiful wife and a little boy. He carried their pictures.

Aaron Elson: And what happened to him?

John Hawk: He got picked off by a sniper.

Aaron Elson: Oh, in Czechoslovakia.

John Hawk: Yeah, at the very end. So that's Mac, he got killed later. (Looking at other people in the snapshot) He got badly wounded. And got killed at Dillingen. I know he was badly wounded in the shoulder. But these are our other two sergeants, Getland and Vibey. I know Vibey's dead, I think maybe Getland is. These were taken about the 12th of December. This was before we crossed the Saar River.

Aaron Elson: Were you back with them by then?

John Hawk: Oh yeah. That was just the last time I got knocked out.

Aaron Elson: The 12th of December?

John Hawk: Yeah. A couple of days later, I lost all the dates after that up until I started recovering in the hospital later.

Aaron Elson: How many times were you wounded?

John Hawk: Four times.

Aaron Elson: The first time was in Normandy?

John Hawk: The first time was at the Falaise Gap, where I got the medal. I was shot through the leg, but it didn't stop me. They gave me some rest, and they said I could go to the hospital or stay with the company, so I stayed with the company. That was August 20th. And then in November I got a couple of pieces of shrapnel. Then the record has twice more from that time there and I don't remember the circumstances.

Aaron Elson: Now, did I see a bunch of tattoos on your arms?

John Hawk: Just one.

Aaron Elson: How did you get the tattoo?

John Hawk: Oh, I got that when I was a kid. I wanted to see if it would make my girlfriend mad and it did. Her name's grown over since.

Aaron Elson: Her name was on it?

John Hawk: Her name was right there. The gal I married, that wasn't her name, and I told her once, "For a dollar I can get them to ink that over. Do you want me to do it?"
She said, "Give me the dollar. I got what I want."
She took the dollar and left the name on.

Aaron Elson: What was your wife's name?

John Hawk: My wife's name was Madeline, and that one happened to be Dorothy.

Aaron Elson: Do you have children?

John Hawk: Two. We had three. Our first one was killed by a car when he was six years old. On the way to school. That's a bad scene. Especially if you happen to be a schoolteacher yourself.

Aaron Elson: Was your wife a schoolteacher?

John Hawk: No, I was.

Aaron Elson: I didn't know that.

John Hawk: Yeah. Oh, I got home out of the Army and, boy, you think war is hell? Try going to college when you're beat up mentally and physically, not too smart to start with, and didn't pay much attention in high school. Sweating and worrying about trying to be a romeo and a bread winner and a student all at the same time. I pretty near failed at all three. I wasn't gonna get married because I didn't think I could support the girl. I finally had this one tremendous stroke of intelligence – I don't have many – and married the girl. I held out for three years, but then she finally said, "Go ahead and do it."

Aaron Elson: Tell me about when your child was killed.

John Hawk: I was teaching school at the time, and I would look out at all these kids there. When he was six and a half, he was on his way to kindergarten, he and two other kids. And it looked like the car came on the shoulder, and he didn't get out of the way quick enough. We had the daughter at the time, three and a half. That's a bad, bad, bad thing. A gal that was impaired, shouldn't have been driving a car. She died within a year. It affected her, too.

Aaron Elson: Did she start drinking heavily afterward?

John Hawk: No, she didn't drink. She was partly deaf and had impaired vision. She really shouldn't have been driving a car. She went into shock so bad that she pulled the kid onto the side of the road and got into her car and drove away. Somebody followed her and stopped her within a mile or so. It was about as bad a scene as you can get. I thought I was gonna lose the wife, too. My wife and my dad. I had a tough time with them. My wife was one of those people that was very, very caring, and my dad, he had several grandchildren, but that was his favorite one. They had been very, very close. So that was hard for him. Of all the things that should happen to somebody.

Aaron Elson: Then you had one child after that?

John Hawk: Yes. About three years later I convinced her we shouldn't be raising one. First she said, "Forget it, I've had my boy." And boy, that puts you down. What do you say then? I finally convinced her.

Aaron Elson: How did your wife pass away?

John Hawk: Heart attack. She started to get up one morning and just didn't make it. No warning. No previous history, just a massive coronary. That's the way to go, I guess, but what a shock.

Aaron Elson: That's eleven years ago?

John Hawk: Eleven years ago this November. I'd just been retired two years and was remodeling the house for her, and had it almost finished. Everything but the roof. I'd remodeled the house completely inside.

Aaron Elson: She would have been in her late fifties?

John Hawk: She was 57. Talk about compounding tragedies, our daughter's wedding was two weeks after the funeral.

Aaron Elson: What did you teach?

John Hawk: Elementary school. Fifth and sixth grade. I took a degree in biology. Then I have minors in history and English and geography. I wasn't intending to teach. I was going to teach high school, but there were no openings at the time and I was qualified to teach [elementary school]. I tell you, I did a little ratting around before I figured out how to teach reading. I spent six years just as a classroom teacher, and then for nine years I taught full time and ran the school, too, as a teaching principal. And then the last years I was just a principal.

I struggled, God, it took me over six years to get four full years in. I eventually got in the equivalent of six and a half, seven years. God, that was hard. I could do the daily stuff and everything, but math was hard for me. I couldn't retain the math. But I did real well on the natural science, on the biology. Plants and animals. History and geography I liked, too, so I did that. I had a language deficiency, so instead of taking a foreign language I took so much English I finally ended up with a minor in that.

Aaron Elson: Who were your favorite authors?

John Hawk: I like the kind of the historical novels, even what other people considered horrible ones like "Moby Dick," and those. I like different kinds of writing, and some of them of course that everybody else thought were great I didn't think were worth the trouble, so it was funny that way. I just took that because the only thing they taught when I was in high school were Latin and Spanish and I wasn't interested in either one. I got to college, and of course in those days they said, "If you're going to take a science course you have to have German."

I didn't get along well with the German teacher. And oh, God, was she a German teacher. She was a little spare, kind of spindly gal, always wore a grey knit suit. Her name was Saarlautern. And she's got her hair pulled back and everything.

I had to take some of it. So I was working away at it and I wasn't doing that well. Finally I did some German for her. She says, "You seem to understand it, but you don't speak it or work at it very well."

And I said, "That's probably right."

And she said, "But German is a beautiful language."

And I wasn't feeling that good and I said, "Well, the last time I heard your beautiful language, the people that were speaking it and I were busy killing each other."

She said, "You don't think German is a beautiful language?"

And I said, "No."

And she said, "Then why are you taking it?"

And I said, "Because I'm required to, and that's the only reason." And I could see "D" written in both eyes.

Anyhow, she told me later that one of the people in the class finally came up and told her who I was and about my record. And she said, "I can understand what happened. Maybe he doesn't think that much of the language. It would probably be hard for him to learn."

I told her later, "Well, the last time I got shot I probably forgot all of it." But I struggled and struggled, and finally I married my girlfriend and that took care of breadwinner and romeo. I think the Veterans Administration and the university got together and said if somebody doesn't pass this sucker he's gonna be here the rest of his life. Give him a C, will you?

Aaron Elson: Which university was that?

John Hawk: The University of Washington, Seattle. I made the first year, just barely, and I mean it was tough. I wasn't well enough when I first got home, so they wouldn't let me go to work or anything. I kept saying I have to do something. Well, if you do the wrong thing we'll throw you in the hospital, how's that? That's the ultimate threat.

Aaron Elson: What was the nature of your last set of wounds?

John Hawk: Concussion and combat fatigue. Between the blast that I got and the fatigue, I broke down.

Aaron Elson: How would you describe having broken down?

John Hawk: I was being literally carried out, and I just shut everything down. I didn't communicate. I didn't respond very well. I did what I was told but I wasn't responding.

Aaron Elson: Were you aware that you were not responding?

John Hawk: I just wasn't gonna do it anymore. I said I've had all I can take. Seeing the last couple of guys go, and then ending up like that myself. That was it.

Aaron Elson: And the concussion was from?

John Hawk: One of those big railway guns. Blew up in the bank underneath me. Blew me they said about 90 feet. And no open wounds, just bruised inside. I couldn't drink any water, I couldn't take any food. It all came up. You last a day or two like that and then you fall down. And they were trying to figure out what it was and they couldn't. For a while they couldn't find any open wounds, but then the bruising started to show.

They were feeding me through my veins. Eventually I got to where I could take on some food. And once I got some strength back, I was able to come out of the mental problems. They put me on limited duty, and I went to work for a base post office in Paris.

I'd been there – I don't know, six weeks, two months maybe, I'm very unclear on lot of this – I went from day to day and did everything but it didn't stick, memory-wise. And then they came up with the point system. They finally decided you can't leave men in combat forever; they start breaking down. And here I am with this post office outfit; a lot of those guys had been overseas longer than I'd been in the Army. They'd started off in Africa, and then they transferred them into the Normandy thing and then they finally set up in Paris. It was a big outfit, there were 800 men. But they came up with the points, and you got points for months in combat, and you got points for months overseas and points for being wounded and everything.

So here I had the combat badge and four Purple Hearts and three campaigns and six months up front. When they count up the points I'm the first guy in the post office to get to go home on rest and recuperation. Well, that was fine. They sent us up from Paris up to Le Havre and we waited up there in the ports for a ship to England. While we were there was when President Roosevelt died. And then we got a ship from England over to New York, and they put us on a troop train the next day and headed for the West Coast. We were in Minneapolis-St. Paul when VE Day was declared.

We got through that. We finally managed to get the train on the tracks and get home. I got home on the 10th of May, and my 21st birthday was on the 30th. In the middle of June, I'm about halfway through this furlough, and they finally caught up with me from Fort Lewis and dragged me down to tell me that I'd received the medal. Of course, at first I didn't believe it, I thought somebody was bulling me. And they said, "No, we wouldn't kid about that."

So I said, "Okay, what for?"

And the guy says, "I'm real sorry. I can't tell you what for. All I can tell you is that we have the order that says you got one."

And I said, "Well, thanks a lot. You'd better find out pretty quick."

So they did.

When it came time to make the presentation of the medal, they told me they were going to send me to Washington, D.C., and I could take two people.

I said, "Oh?"

And they said, "On a train."

I said, "What? You mean you can't fly one guy?"

Of course, I was single as hell, and my parents had been divorced during the war. They'd stuck together until my two sisters and I were on our own, and then they went their different directions, which I've always admired them for. They stuck it out, so there was always a family and a home there, and once we were on our own, they went their separate ways.

So I stopped by the state capitol, and I knew Senator Warren Magnuson, who was a ranking senator even at that time. I had grown up with him on Bainbridge Island and he had his home there. I met him while I was in high school. And he called me up and said, "Stop by, I want to say hello to you."

So I visited him and he said, "Where are they going to present the medal?"

And I told him what kind of trouble I was in, that the Army was getting mad at me.

He said, "By golly, I've been looking for some way to get that guy up here." He's talking about Harry Truman. He had served in the Senate with him. Security was fierce. You had to have a reason. So he said, "Now I've got a reason."

Truman was coming to the West Coast for the San Francisco Conference where they decided what to do about Japan. Magnuson got him to come up and he was there for two days and a night, and on one day we had the ceremony. It was great. I had my family in, my father, and my fiancee's mother and sister and all the relatives were there. God, they had a bunch of schoolkids there, and about half of Fort Lewis.

It really meant a lot to me. My dad was a World War I artilleryman from Kansas, as was Harry. So once I got the two of them together talking, I kind of backed off, because I was about ready to break and run. I was really feeling very, very badly about receiving a medal with the serious memories of all the friends I'd lost. In six months you lose so many machine gunners it isn't even funny. So that worked out well. I got that off my back. And then trying to go to school, I wasn't feeling well enough, and they were afraid if I put myself under pressure I'd have a relapse of the fatigue thing. So they said, "You've got to find something to do, but you can't take on anything like going to the university."

So I said, "I'll do it anyhow."

And they said, "You go ahead, we'll throw you in the hospital." So I went back to high school. I had graduated, but I thought, well, knowing my shortcomings I might be able to pick up some of the things that I didn't have, the language and the math.

They were terribly short of teachers at my old high school, and of course kids that had been freshmen when I left were still there. I was gone exactly two years. So I took another year of high school. Actually I ended up most of the time helping the teachers.

Then I tried the university and boy, that first year, oh man, I struggled. Lousy grades.

I took that summer off, went back in the fall and I got sick. I had to drop out. That was the first time. I had to drop out twice before I got done, but I went over to Bremerton and stayed with my dad. They had a junior college there. It was a totally different situation, with twelve, thirteen people in a class. You knew everybody. I had to do something or I was going to lose it altogether. They said, "Well, why don't you try this? Just take a couple of courses." So I did. I took almost two years of credits there and hell, I had a 3.85 grade point average there, compared to my 1.5 at the U of W.

I finally had to go back to the U. The first quarter I went back there I only took two courses and got two D's. So I took some time off again and went back later, and I struggled through. I was trying to take a course that was too hard for me. I was trying to take their fisheries course, which is one of the best in the world, but the competition was just fierce.

The problem that I ran into was that our generous government, after beating up the people in the Pacific, said, "We're gonna help you recover. Send us some of your best students and we'll give them the training." The thing about the fisheries was, they weren't distinguishing the different branches of it. They wanted you to be a chemist and an engineer and a biologist. I couldn't handle the math that was involved in the chemistry and the engineering. The natural science things I did fine on. So finally, I just couldn't make it. I switched over to arts and sciences, and took my degree in biology.

Then, for want of a better thing to do, while I was up at Becket High School they kept saying, "You'd make a good teacher." Teachers were always leaving me with the class. Especially in science, geography and history. They said, "You should really try that." So that was what I did.

In the meantime, I had found a part time job at home. In fact, I worked part time in a Ford garage for almost ten years. The guy said, "That's the longest time anybody's ever worked here." I worked weekends and vacations and stuff like that.

Aaron Elson: Doing what?

John Hawk: I was either a parts chaser, or I ran the wash rack, or I did undersealing. I used to come home from college, go home and change my clothes and go back down to the garage and underseal cars till midnight, and then get up and catch the ferryboat back the next morning.

Aaron Elson: You had to take a ferry?

John Hawk: Yes. From Bremerton to Seattle. It's about an hour ferry ride. Then you take the bus out to the university. You'd catch a ferryboat at 6 o'clock in the morning so you can make an 8 o'clock class. Then you didn't get home until 6 o'clock at night.

I finally managed to survive it and got started teaching. I retired in 1983, after 31 years.

John Hawk: At Chambois, the Germans, they threw everything they had in there, because they were trying to break a hole, and they couldn't get out of the Falaise Gap. That's where I got into it. We had a place there that had a stream and a big ditch, and the German tanks couldn't get across the ditch and our tank destroyers couldn't get across it. And the road ran down like this out in front. The Germans kept breaking across this field, and we were in an orchard. They'd come into the orchard and they blew the hell out of us. And our tank destroyers couldn't see them.

I got chased out of there about three times. They ran over the machine gun [with a tank] once. Hit another one with a shell. I went back and put one machine gun together out of two. Then they came over and chased us out again.

We'd shoot their infantry off the tanks. Then the tanks are blind, so they'd back off.

Aaron Elson: They had tanks?

John Hawk: Yeah. Big Tiger Royals. Where I was, I could see two of them. I could see our tank destroyers and I could see the Tiger Royals, but they couldn't see each other. And we were back screaming at the tank destroyers, "Get those guys off our back!" And they said, "We can't shoot 'em if we can't see 'em."

So I said, since I can see both of them, I'll get out in the middle and line it up. You fire, and I'll give you a correction, maybe we can get them. So we started doing that. And it worked. See, they always parked them in the bushes or behind a building, one of those little old stone buildings. You could put an armor-piercing shell right through it. And hell, there were three tanks there. I know they knocked two of them clear out, and they damaged another one. And the others that were there started backing off. So that worked so good that we started blind-firing into the buildings, and of course that was where they had taken refuge and we started knocking buildings down and boy, the white flags came up. We took probably 500 prisoners there in a couple hours. They just came right across the field. We'd disarm them and send them to the rear.

-169-

Just before the last of that was when I was hiding behind an apple tree, and they machine gunned me through the apple tree.

I was hit once, in the leg. And I think the tank was trying to run over me. The bullet had knocked me down. It was like getting hit with a sledgehammer. I didn't know whether I'd broken a leg or what.

Aaron Elson: There was a tank coming at you?

John Hawk: Yeah. It was as close as right across the room. I thought, "Either I've got a broken leg or I can run like hell," and I tore out of there like you wouldn't believe.

Aaron Elson: With the bullet in your leg?

John Hawk: It had gone through the apple tree and was bent. It went right around the bone. Didn't break any serious nerves or blood vessels. And with my running around to get away from the damn thing, when I finally went back to the medics, he takes a probe and goes in there, "There's no bullet in there." Oh, boy. Hot dog, you know, ye gods. The medic went and looked down in the cuff of my pants where they were stuck in my boots, and there's the bullet. It had worked back out the same way it went in, with all this running around. He puts a big patch on my leg and says, "How come you're still walking?"

And I said, "I've been walking and running."

He says, "Keep on doing it. Do you want to go to the hospital?"

I said, "No." Things had pretty well stopped. They were just rounding up. So we had three or four days rest, and I kept moving. They checked it every day.

Aaron Elson: What kind of a tank was it that was coming at you?

John Hawk: A Tiger Royal.

Aaron Elson: And you were hit by a machine gun bullet from the tank?

John Hawk: Yes. I don't know why they didn't just shoot again. Maybe they were saving ammunition or weren't gonna waste a bullet on one guy. I think they had it figured they were gonna mash me there anyhow. But I tore out of there and went back. I ran around. This is funny but it's not funny: When I took off I went around a building and fell right over the back of another tank. I absolutely ran into that damn thing. Knocked me flatter than a pancake again. I'm rolling around on the ground. I look up and there's a German standing up in the turret. To this day, I would give anything, I almost wished I hadn't killed him so I could find out what he thought, this crazy American attacking his tank with his body. Because I did. I hit that thing, I bet you it made a clang you could hear for a mile. But I was still carrying my rifle. I looked up and shot him and he went plunk, down in the tank. And I took off again. Well, here's this tank and a couple more right behind me. And I'm headed for the tank destroyers, and I mean I'm moving. This tank guy says, "You got about forty feet from this ditch and you just kind of leveled out and went zip." And they started firing. Of course these tanks came around the corner, and I know you can't fire them automatically but they were. And I'm down in the ditch, and every time the damn thing went off, it deafened you. They knocked out two of them and the other one got the hell out of there, and that was the end of it. No more tanks came across. That's when the surrender started.

"I enlisted in '36. And retired in '69. I had 33 years in all. Seven months. And a few days."

The provost marshal

Clifford Merrill
712th Tank Battalion
Bradenton, Fla., Feb. 1, 1992

Aaron Elson: You had told me a story about a prank you pulled in training.

Cliff Merrill: Did it have to do with chiggers?

Aaron Elson: Yes, that's what it was.

Cliff Merrill: We had a guy named Chandler. He was from Maine, and I had come from Maine. There were three of us there from Maine; Chandler, a guy by the name of Webster and myself. What Webster couldn't think up I could. Chandler complained about chiggers around the scrotum. So I said to Web, "I think we ought to get him some iodine." So we got a whole bottle of iodine, and told him that iodine will kill those chiggers. Just pour it on over there. So he did. It killed the chiggers, and it took all the skin off.

Chandler was an individual who always was getting in a little bit of trouble. There was some little thing bugging him and he'd come to us about it. The next incident, he had hemorrhoids, and he wanted to know, "What can I do?"

We told him, "You get a jar of Vicks Vapo-Rub, and just get a lot on your finger and rub it all around." He did. Well, we heard him holler. He said, "It feels like the north wind!"

Aaron Elson: You were from Maine?

Clifford Merrill: Yes. Springfield, just a little town 70 miles northeast from Bangor. It's 24 miles from the Canadian border on the eastern side of Maine. I grew up and went to school there. High school, that's as far as I went. I finished off my schooling in the Army at night – a rough deal.

Aaron Elson: After the war, or before?

Clifford Merrill: Well, it was after World War II.

Aaron Elson: Did you enlist?

Clifford Merrill: I enlisted in '36. And retired in '69. I had 33 years in all. Seven months. And a few days.

Aaron Elson: When were you assigned to the 712th Tank Battalion?

Clifford Merrill: In 1943, in the spring. Prior to that I had been at Fort Knox, instructing. I had a vehicle section there and I was teaching newly arrived trainees how to drive tanks and trucks. It was quite an operation. They rotated companies through, 800 men at a time. I think it was four weeks to get that part of their training.

Then I was assigned to the 10th Armored Division at Fort Benning, and ended up with G Company in the 3rd Battalion. When they reorganized, G Company became A Company of the 712th and I was a platoon leader at that time.

Then we went on the Tennessee maneuvers. While I was there I had an appendicitis attack and had to go to the hospital, and they took my appendix out. When I came back, I was assigned as a company commander. The company commander had transferred out.

Following that, we moved to Camp Gordon and did more training, preparing for combat. Then we moved to Fort Jackson, South Carolina, which was more or less a staging area. That had to be the late part of '43, because in February we moved to Fort Jackson and we did our final firing and what they call Army ground tests. We had moving tank firing and firing with cannons. After that we moved to Camp Myles Standish outside of Boston. That was a final prep prior to getting on board ship. We went across the Atlantic and landed at Gouroch, Scotland. My company was detached from the rest of the battalion. At that time we were at a place called Stow on the Wold. We had other names for it, I forget now. When we were in England, there were all kinds of names like that, like Maughton in the Marsh. That we called Maughton in the Muck. There we had more training firing tank guns. Then we drew our tanks.

Aaron Elson: Were there any casualties in the training?

Clifford Merrill: No, just weeding out. We were over strength. The only casualties were those I didn't want. We weeded them out. For example, at Fort Jackson I had ten officers and I was only authorized four. So I got rid of six of them.

We took our final shooting tests in England. We had moved from Stow on the Wold down to Chiseldon barracks in Swindon and joined the rest of the battalion. Then, all of a sudden, in the middle of the night, they said, "Pack up and go." The Army is noted for that. No advance notice, they didn't want anything leaking out. We were ready anyway. But there was still a lot of confusion.

Aaron Elson: How did you cross the channel?

Clifford Merrill: In an LST, Landing Ship Tank they call it. We went across the channel, as I recall the first tank went off the ramp and just in the water, [only part] of the turret was sticking out.

Aaron Elson: Did it get onto the beach?

Clifford Merrill: We hooked onto it and dragged it on.

Aaron Elson: Was this after D-Day? How many days?

Clifford Merrill: Oh, I don't know.

Aaron Elson: But it was some time after?

Clifford Merrill: Yes, but there was a lot of stuff going on.

Aaron Elson: Was the beach secure, or was it still under fire?

Clifford Merrill: Once in a while you'd get something coming in. Of course, at night everything was blacked out. You couldn't do much at night. My company was assigned to the 82nd Airborne Division, and I advanced through and connected with them. The rest of the battalion went to the 90th Division, and I worked with the 82nd until the 8th of July; this is '44. The 8th of July the 82nd was replaced by the 8th Infantry Division, and boy, we had to break those people in. It was tough. They'd shoot you as quick as they would the Germans. They were scared. I was, too, what the heck. They didn't advance very much. In fact they lost ground. I had one platoon leader that was extremely good, a chap named Ed Forrest. I talked to Ed and the artillery commander of the 8th Division, and we decided we'd stir things up a bit. So I had Ed's platoon advance, but in the meantime we swapped radios, so a spotter plane could speak to Ed in his tank. He had a small receiving set. He made an advance I guess of about two and a half miles. Knocked out a couple tanks. One place they came around – the story was told to me, at that point I wasn't there – they came around this turn in the road with one of their tanks, and here's a bunch of Krauts with a hogshead of cider. They hit the hogshead of cider, and the Krauts.

Aaron Elson: When you say a hogshead, what is that?

Clifford Merrill: That's about 20 barrels of cider in one huge cask. I don't know what else they call it beside hogshead; that's what I learned in Maine. Hundreds of gallons of cider. Too bad to spill all that cider. But Normandy had lots of cider. And Calvados.

Ed made a good advance then. Other places they'd get tied down. Of course I was back and forth across that front all the time. Hell, I never got any sleep. I'd go to sleep standing up.

Aaron Elson: Did you travel in a jeep or in a tank?

Clifford Merrill: A jeep, mostly. I'd have a tank following me, but I wouldn't ride in a tank, because I couldn't see. If I rode in a jeep I could see well enough. And then the final day when I got hit, I went up to one of the leading battalions that was supposed to have been engaged. They'd lost an assistant division commander; he got killed the night before, trying to lead a platoon. Imagine, a brigadier general leading a platoon. He went out where he shouldn't have been. He got hit. Heck, the Germans laid down such fire nobody could bring him out. He bled to death. So the next day I went up in that area, and one of the first people I came across was this battalion commander digging a hole. I said, "What the hell are you doing?" I'm standing up.

He says, "We're being fired on."

I said, "They're not hitting me." You could hear bullets, but that was everywhere you'd hear them. If they hit a tree 30 feet over your head you'd hear the snap. I didn't pay any attention to those. So I said, "I don't see any Krauts around. Let's see what's going on." So I left him and I went along the front line hedgerow, and everybody's hiding down behind the hedgerow and I said, "What goes?"

Well, the Germans are right over there in front of the next hedgerow. There was a captain there, and he said, "There's a machine gun on this side." I asked him, and he explained where the machine gun was. I said, "Well, I'm going to look at it."

I had a tank there that had a 105 gun on it. So I went [on foot] up this little trail. I was armed with a tommy gun; I carried this tommy gun all the time. I had gone up there, and I couldn't see anything. I got down, kind of crawled along, and I looked up, and here this damn Kraut was looking right at me. To this day I don't think he saw me. He had no look of surprise; he didn't do anything. But instinctively I brought that tommy gun up, and I ripped him up.

Then I heard the machine gun, and I could see where the muzzle blast was moving the bushes, and I said, well, I found the machine gun. I guess I'll get the hell out of here. I started back, and they dropped either mortar or grenades, I'm not sure, and the first one caught me right in the back. Knocked me down. As I was laying down another one went off and got my right leg. I had a broken back and two inches knocked out of the small bone in this right leg. And after a while somebody came up and put a patch on me. I made believe I was out. It was a German medic. I lay there, and waited, and they left. My tommy gun was laying in the leaves; they hadn't seen it. I had a pistol inside my shirt in a shoulder holster; they didn't find that. But they put a patch on my back. They figured I wasn't going to go anywhere, and then they jabbered awhile and they left. I picked up my tommy gun. I could walk. I hobbled; I didn't walk very good, but I didn't realize I had a broken leg. And my back didn't hurt, but I knew it was sticky, it felt wet. I walked a couple hundred yards back to the front line, then the medics took over. But I saw the commander of the tank that followed me up there and I told him what to do. I heard him shooting after that, but I don't know what happened. I gave him my tommy gun, too. I said, "Take it into Berlin."

Aaron Elson: That was on what date?

Clifford Merrill: It was the 13th of July. That was all the combat for me. They shipped me back, and I spent a year in the hospital.

Aaron Elson: Was that on Hill 122?

Clifford Merrill: No, we were beyond Hill 122. We had Hill 95, then Hill 122 we kind of circled around it a little bit. But at that point I believe we were beyond; we'd already eliminated Hill 122.

Aaron Elson: How did they designate the numbers?

Clifford Merrill: That's elevation. You figure they weren't very high hills. But in some of those hills they were looking down on you, and some places I think they were throwing the empty shell cases on us. But we'd already gone through La Haye du Puits, we went in there three different times. That's when Hill 122 came into play, the big effect on us anyway, and they drove us out two times. The third time we made it. That's where I liberated some calvados from a liquor store that had been blown up. I had it in the back of the jeep and I thought it would break if somebody hit us, and I'd get glass in me, so the best thing to do is just hide that, so I did. I put it in a hole and covered it up with some brush and dirt and figured I'd go back to it. If I go back to that area I'm going to look for it. Some Frenchman has probably found it.

Aaron Elson: You were in the hospital for a year. Then what did you do?

Clifford Merrill: I went back to Fort Knox. I didn't like Fort Knox. They were supposed to be training people, but they didn't know what they were doing. And I told them so. And the guy who was in personnel was named Heggy; he'd been in OCS with me. And I went in to see him. I said, "Heggy, I want to leave; I want to get somewhere. I want to go to Germany." You'd hear all kinds of rumors about what you could get for a carton of cigarettes in Germany. I said, "I guess I'd better go."

He says, "Okay. I'll put you on orders but I'm gonna put myself on orders, too." He and I both went over, in the same shipment.

Aaron Elson: Then you went to Dachau?

Clifford Merrill: Eventually I ended up in Dachau.

Aaron Elson: What did they do there?

Clifford Merrill: We had war criminals, and we had about 30,000 prisoners of war there. Then we had hard-core war criminals, about 2,000 of those. They were in more or less a big cellblock. It was called a bunker but it was a cellblock. And we had some lesser war criminals; they didn't really pay much attention to them. But the ones we had in the cellblock were really hard-core. They'd been guards at Dachau and other concentration camps, murdered a lot of people. The prisoners of war were not too bad. We had prisoners of war from Russia and the Baltic countries, Ukraine and places like that; they didn't want to go back. Russia wanted them back.

Aaron Elson: They were Russian or they were German?

Clifford Merrill: They were Russian.

Aaron Elson: But they had fought for the Germans?

Clifford Merrill: The only Russians were really those from around the Moscow area, what is the Russia of today. Very few of them were from there, but from Ukraine, and Belorussia, places like that.

Aaron Elson: And they had fought for the Germans?

Clifford Merrill: No, they didn't fight for them but they'd worked for them. Russia wanted them back. We found out they didn't want to go. And when we shipped them out, we had them in railroad cars. Not box cars, regular passenger cars. Boy, they killed themselves, with some of the worst means you ever saw. Break a hole in the window and put their head in and cut their throat. Kill each other, simultaneously, with knives. Bloody Sunday.

Aaron Elson: How many people?

Clifford Merrill: They had a trainload. The first trainload I think we had around eight, nine hundred.

Aaron Elson: That killed themselves?

Clifford Merrill: Yeah. It was a mess.

Aaron Elson: And the ones that went back were sent to Siberia?

Clifford Merrill: They didn't even reach there. Going back, at a certain point, the Russians took over. And even then, they took them off the cars and they stayed in the rain overnight, cold, miserable. You know they're not going to survive like that. They were just as brutal with their people as some of the concentration camp guards were to their prisoners.

Aaron Elson: Bloody Sunday; do you know the date of that?

Clifford Merrill: Pretty close. That should have been, November ... December ... probably the first part of January '46. I may be off on the date.

Aaron Elson: How did the Dachau trials differ from the Nuremburg trials?

Clifford Merrill: Same thing. It was the same idea. We had six members of the court, and they'd have defense counsel, as many as we could get for them. They were well-defended. But they were accused of different crimes. All kinds of witnesses would testify against them for murdering pilots and things like that.

With the concentration camp trials, the Dachau trials, there were guards and those in charge who had killed prisoners. A lot of hanging went on afterwards.

Aaron Elson: What was your position during this?

Clifford Merrill: I was a member of the court.

Aaron Elson: How many other members were there?

Clifford Merrill: I think we had six court members. It varied. Sometimes we had five, sometimes seven.

Aaron Elson: Were there any individuals that stand out in your memory as being especially dramatic? Did any stand out as especially sad, or did it just become repetitious?

Clifford Merrill: Most of it was repetitious, and most of it they'd cry and say they had to do it because they were ordered to do it. In one case we had a young ex-soldier, German soldier. He looked like he was about a halfwit. He had been accused of kicking this pilot. But you got all kinds of things like that. We were skeptical when we'd view these things. In this case I was glad we were. He couldn't kill, he was just showing off. He went along and pushed the guy with his foot. We found other witnesses. He didn't kick him, he had pushed him. So we had a little discussion. We don't want to continue this, let him go. He was grateful. He didn't want his neck stretched. But other cases, it was pitiful in a way – they had kids, their wives would come there, carry on. But Lord, they'd done these things. They'd actually killed people, a lot of them had.

And then we tried this guy Otto Skorzeny. Skorzeny was the German paratrooper, a good soldier, who had planned and carried out the order to rescue Mussolini.

Aaron Elson: How did he do that?

Clifford Merrill: He went in by glider. They snatched old Mussolini out of there. The nationalists had got Mussolini, and he got Mussolini out of there and rescued him. Or he would have had an earlier death than he did.

Then another case was Colonel Peiper, a German officer, and another officer, I forget his name, but the two of them were chief members of the group that executed a bunch of American soldiers, I think they were engineers, at Malmedy, in Belgium. That's near St. Vith. It was termed the Malmedy massacre. Trucks came in; suddenly curtains were pulled back off the rear of the trucks, and here's machine guns and they started shooting at this group of GI prisoners. Some of course feigned death and lay there, and eventually got back to tell the story. The Germans didn't hang around, they figured they'd killed all of them, apparently. So when we had that trial, one of the guys was turned loose and the other was sentenced to hang.

Aaron Elson: There were two people on trial for that?

Clifford Merrill: Two major people. I think there were some lesser people who came in on the trial, too. Hell, the trigger men were not that important; the people that directed it are what we wanted.

Aaron Elson: And what were their ranks?

Clifford Merrill: Of these two? Both were full colonels, I think. I don't think they were generals.

Aaron Elson: What did they say in their defense?

Clifford Merrill: Oh, I don't remember that now. In that case, I really don't because we were so danged, we were tickled to have them and glad we convicted them. Really. Nothing mattered but that we get the rope around their neck, as far as I was concerned.

Aaron Elson: Do you remember the circumstances of the convictions?

Clifford Merrill: I don't remember the circumstances. But I congratulated old Skorzeny myself on getting out of that, because our sympathies were with him. He wasn't in on that stuff. Sure, his troops went in. Some of his troops were trained, English speaking, in the Battle of the Bulge or prior to the Battle of the Bulge, to infiltrate. What the heck is wrong with that? They were fighting just like we were. We were doing the same thing.

Aaron Elson: We were?

Clifford Merrill: Why, sure. All we could. I didn't see anything that would give you a cause to treat him as a war criminal. And as it came out in the trial it was proven; he was nothing but a good soldier.

Aaron Elson: Tell me a little bit about Ed Forrest. You knew him well?

Cliff Merrill: Oh yeah. Ed had worked in a bank, and to look at Ed you'd think, yeah, that's a typical bank teller. He was quiet. Quiet courage. Never raised his voice. Got along remarkably well with his men. [Reuben] Goldstein was one of his men. I thought Ed was the best we had. Of course I didn't tell anybody. I didn't even tell him. But he impressed me as being the best. Always giving, never asking for himself. I think he was hit by one lonesome plane up there, dropped a bomb, and got him. Near the final days. That hurt me more than anything. My first sergeant would write me a lot of letters when I was wounded. I've still got them. He told me all about who was wounded and this and that. The first man in the company to be killed was a lieutenant, George Tarr. He'd say so-and-so joined Tarr's platoon. He couldn't come out and say somebody got killed. The censors would cut that out, or black it out, but they usually cut the letters.

Aaron Elson: How was Lieutenant Tarr killed?

Cliff Merrill: We were just going in, this was our first engagement. I'm not sure of the date. But we were going down this hill. The Krauts had been shelling in this area periodically, interdiction fire I guess you'd call it. And then something happened. George got down off his tank for some reason, I don't know why. I wasn't talking to him then over the radio. He was curious about something I guess. But he didn't get down all the way. A shell hit when he was on the deck and knocked him down, and then another shell went close to him. He just had a brand new baby. Little boy. And I couldn't write that letter. I think I let Ellsworth Howard take care of it, or maybe [Sergeant Charles] Vinson did, because I knew him well. Nice guy. Methodical. Kind of slow. But he'd do anything you told him. Do anything for you. In fact, Ellsworth Howard and I were talking about George the other day. We commented about a train ride from Fort Jackson up to Myles Standish, when we had old George all excited about keeping track of the troops. We said, "George, go count noses." Howard, have you met him? His nickname was the Gremlin. He's a real needler that guy, still is, but he was worse then. And he'd say, "George. Get up there and count noses." And George said, "I did that just about an hour ago."

He said, "Yeah, but you know, we're going to combat. You never know when one of these guys might just take it into his head and jump off this train." We wanted to get him doing something. We didn't want him worrying about his kid, his wife.

"Okay." He'd go out mumbling, and count noses. But he got it organized, he got it down by car, how many in each car. Oh, Lord, I laughed about that. I didn't interfere. Because Ellsworth Howard was the executive officer, let him go ahead, he'd take care of things for me. I can still hear him, "George, go count noses."

This stuff bothers you. And the reaction is later, not then. You don't have time to think about it. But later I had nightmares, I'm telling you. God, I've killed this Kraut a hundred times, for example. Each time he'd come a little closer.

Aaron Elson: Tell me more about the nightmares.

Cliff Merrill: I don't know how they come on really, but all of a sudden, I still get them. It's a good thing we have a queen-size bed and I'm over on one side, way over, and [Jan is] over on the other. And if I start slugging, why, I miss her. I haven't hit her yet.

Jan Merrill: The one in Vietnam is the one that he keeps shooting. I think that's the one he shoots the most.

Cliff Merrill: You do have them, there's no question. I don't know why.

Aaron Elson: I guess it's not unusual.

Cliff Merrill: You sweat. Oh, Lord. You'd be surprised how much they shake you up. Then you don't get any sleep. I don't sleep much. If I go to bed at 10 o'clock, at 1:30 I'm awake. I might get another hour's sleep. Not much more than that.

Aaron Elson: How old are you now?

Cliff Merrill: Seventy-seven. Almost 78.

Aaron Elson: Did you ever counsel younger soldiers, who had gone through the same thing? Did you ever talk to them about it?

Cliff Merrill: I called it guidance. The troops I had under me, those are the ones I'd give guidance to. And I always told them, "Now, I have to give you a little guidance, but don't forget, that guidance takes several forms. Sometimes it's just a tap on the shoulder and sometimes it's a direct kick in the ass." So, that's guidance. I tried to make a joke out of stuff like that. I wasn't dead serious about a lot of things. For example, General Seaman was the commanding general of the 1st Infantry Division. I told him, "I'll get the job done because I'm pretty mean."
He said, "You're not mean. You just look mean."
I said, "Well, I'll get the job done."

Cliff Merrill: I went back to Germany after I'd been to Korea, in '56. Let me get my dates right. We landed in Le Havre, and went on these cars, they called them 40 and 8s. And we figured if they could put eight mules in there they put 40 men in. Boxcars. Cold, miserable. And the trip across, there was a bunch of, oh, humorous as could be things that those GIs did, and I tried to help them along, too. For example, we had no heat in the cars. We stopped where there was a crossing, and the crossing guard had a little shack and a stovepipe. You could see there was a fire; there's smoke coming out of it. Two GIs went out there, and I don't know as they paid for that stove or not. But here they come running, stove and pipe and the works. The fire still in it. Got that up in the boxcar, and got it in operation. And we got coal every time we stopped. We'd stop in every damn railroad yard between there and Germany, and they'd load up with coal. They were warm in that car. But it was cold, God. People were real sick from the cold. That was one humorous incident. Of course there were others. We had extra passengers appear every once in a while. Females. Get a couple of females in a boxcar with forty men, why, it'll get warmer, you know.

Aaron Elson: Tell me once again the story about Omar Bradley's wife.

Cliff Merrill: Well, Mrs. Bradley was rather an eccentric type. When I took the job as the provost marshal in Fort Myers, Virginia, one of the first tidbits of information was that Mrs. Bradley was to be handled with kid gloves. Well, one day she called the office and the provost sergeant answered the phone, and he handed me the phone quick. He said, "It's Mrs. Bradley."

She she said, "Major. There's a great big dog jumping on my little dog."

I thought for a moment. I said, "Is that little dog a female?"

"Yes. But she's been spayed."

And I thought, gee, this is a tough one. I said, "Yes, Mrs. Bradley. No doubt the dog's been spayed, but you know that big dog doesn't know that."

She cackled, and said, "You're pretty smart."

I said, "I'll come right over and handle it personally."

When I went over the dog was gone. But she invited me in to have a Coke. I got along well with her.

Aaron Elson: And then when she was speeding around the…

Cliff Merrill: Oh yeah, she drove pretty fast. She had a kind of a car that looked like an old … what the hell make of a car was that? It wasn't a Reo; it looked like an old Essex. Anyway, she made the turn around the post exchange building and the car leaned over, and went on two wheels. The MPs were behind her. She called me and said the MPs were harassing her.

"No," I said. "They reported it to me and told me about it. They thought there was something wrong with your car, and they didn't know but they might have to render assistance."

"Ohhh." No more said.

We had, even among kids, rank was considered. I caught three of those little kids one day. One was a chaplain's son, another one was General Park's son, and another general's – no, a full colonel's son. They had somebody's hunting bow, and hunting arrows, and they were trying to play William Tell.

The chaplain's son was junior, of course, he had to hold the target. And the others were trying to shoot the bow and arrow.

I put a stop to that. In fact, in the course of doing it, one of those arrows hit them across the ass. That didn't go over good with Mrs. Park.

General Park didn't know about it at the time but Mrs. Park called me. She read me up and down. "This is Mrs. Park."

I said, "How are you today, Ma'am?"

"Don't Ma'am me! That's my son you struck."

"Oh," I said. "That wasn't anything. It was just a reminder to him that he shouldn't be playing with dangerous things like bows and arrows that are steel-tipped." That toned her down a little but not enough to suit me. I didn't say anything further, but she told General Park.

General Park called me. He said, "I understand you had occasion to strike my son with an arrow."

I said, "I certainly did, Sir."

He said, "How did it happen?"

I told him.

He said, "Good. Now I'm gonna whip his ass in good shape."

Aaron Elson: As the provost marshal, what were your duties?

Cliff Merrill: Oh, just the chief of police. Discipline, law and order were the general terms. Anything goes wrong, call the provost marshal. I got calls all the time of the day and night. I'd say, "Call the office. The MPs are well-organized, they know how to handle these things." As long as it wasn't Mrs. Bradley.

But I didn't give a damn then. Understand, at Fort Myers, there were 23 generals. And that meant there were 23 general officers' wives. That was the problem. Keeping everybody happy.

Aaron Elson: And what year was that?

Cliff Merrill: This was in 1950.

Aaron Elson: Was that during the Korean War?

Cliff Merrill: Just the beginning of it. It had started. Because I went to Korea in '52. From Fort Myers I went to officers' career course, and then I went to Korea.

Aaron Elson: About how old were you at that time?

Cliff Merrill: In 1950 I was 36. I was born in '14.

Aaron Elson: What was it like in Korea?

Cliff Merrill: The part I got in on was handling the PWs. In Kojido and then on the mainland, too. On the mainland I had non-communists, anti-communists. They were friendly. But not in Kojido; they were very unfriendly. It was quite obvious in Korea that the prisoners were pretty well-organized. They had an organized resistance, and they had a plan to discredit us because we were our own worst enemy, really. Everybody got shook over what the newspapers were gonna say. Nobody had the guts to kick the damn reporters out of the way. Really. I didn't like them. Same situation in Vietnam. Anyway, to put down a riot, there were no guidelines as to what was a reasonable amount of force. Well, what is a reasonable amount of force when you're faced with ten to twenty thousand screaming meemies trying to crash a fence? What should you do? Let them run over you? If you've got a machine gun you have to use it. What we didn't realize maybe is you could shoot one in the face; that discouraged them. If you shoot them in the torso, it didn't bother them that much. But the disfigurement factor would stop them quicker than anything else. That would change them from looking like a conquering hero, you might say, to a common thug. I think that was part of their philosophy.

There was one battalion commander, a North Korean, Li Hai Ku was his name. And he surrendered. He surrendered his men. But I really believe that was a planned thing to come into the PW camps and there they'd organize riots. They were successful until we finally identified the leaders, Li Hai Ku among them. We isolated them. Put them in solitary, and so forth. Then things quieted down a bit. Their leadership was gone. But on the transfer, what they called the Big Switch operation, we had to watch. They'd try to riot and upset our schedule.

We were moving up trainloads of them and moving back our people who were turned over. We didn't get as many, of course. Theirs went up in the thousands, and the returnees from our side were only in the hundreds, by comparison. I think that was their plan, to disrupt things. They ruined everything they could. They cut up the seats, broke the windows in the railroad cars. We'd transport them from the train station at ... I have to think a minute for the name of that siding where we transferred ... I think they called it

Freedom Station. There we transferred them to trucks. In the meantime, we'd given them new uniforms, new combat boots. Everything brand new. Toilet articles. Really stupid. But you can't criticize your seniors.

Anyway, on the way to near Panmumjon they dismounted from the trucks but prior to getting there, they'd cut all the canvas off the trucks, ruin everything they could. And each time somebody would give us an order to put new canvas on. We had a major general in charge, and I asked him, "What's the sense of putting canvas? These damn idiots don't appreciate it, and they're gonna cut them up."

"That's what we have to do."

So I thought that was rather stupid. After a while they saw it was going to be pretty expensive, and they'd take a whole trainload of people, I forget now how many, but three or four thousand, on trucks. And the way we transported them was, there are seats on the side, two and a half ton trucks with a bench in the middle; they'd straddle that bench. And I forget now, but I think it was forty or more they put on each truck. If they carried GIs it was only 18 to 20 people, but with them we could double it. And the way you'd do that, you'd get all you could get in, the driver would start the truck, and slam the brakes. At that time you could throw in another half-dozen. You learn things.

Aaron Elson: Your position then was what?

Cliff Merrill: I was the operations officer at the Big Switch operation.

Aaron Elson: And what was your rank at the time?

Cliff Merrill: I was still a major. I made lieutenant colonel in '54.

Aaron Elson: And what were you when you retired?

Cliff Merrill: A full colonel.

Aaron Elson: How did you wind up in Vietnam?

Cliff Merrill: I was with the 1st Infantry Division, I was a provost marshal, and we were at Fort Riley, Kansas. Orders came down. Of course we knew where we were going. We went from Fort Riley by bus to Topeka, Kansas, where we boarded planes that flew us to the West Coast. And then on the West Coast we transferred to bigger planes. The plane I was in had most of the division staff, and two jeeps on board the plane. It was a big four-engine plane. And we flew to Guam, Okinawa, and then into Vietnam.

Aaron Elson: Was this toward the beginning or the end of the war?

Cliff Merrill: The beginning. We were the first combat troops of the Army to get in there. I think the Marines had landed up near Hue.

Aaron Elson: So this was what, about 1968?

Cliff Merrill: Oh no, this was '65 I believe. '65 or '66. '65, because I came back in '66. I didn't last too long. Seven or eight months.

Aaron Elson: And your position there was?

Cliff Merrill: I was provost marshal initially for the 1st Infantry Division. Then the commanding general moved to corps and took me with him, and I became the corps provost marshal, which was a bigger job but I actually didn't do as much as I did before.

Aaron Elson: And how did you come into a combat situation?

Cliff Merrill: Combat was everywhere. There were no rigid front lines. You could become a casualty in the middle of any town. I had highway security, amongst other jobs. I had men who were out on the road all the time, subjected to all kinds of things. Land mines were a common occurrence. A daily occurrence really, and we lost troops that way. The way I got hit was, we were in a convoy. I was leading the convoy. I always went out in advance, we had to go over the highway to see what it looked like. And you could sense, you'd go over these highways, dirt roads is all they were, and I was testing to see if I could draw fire. It didn't make any difference, because we were moving right along. We were well-armed. I had machine guns, and a 75-millimeter recoilless rifle; it takes a shell about two feet long. We had an 1,800-head convoy.

Aaron Elson: 1,800 vehicles?

Cliff Merrill: Yeah. We were going up to the Michelin plantation. They had troops going in. We were initial support stuff, supplies; you couldn't fly everything in. They had built an airstrip in the Michelin plantation,but some planes couldn't get in there. Some of the heavy stuff had to be hauled overland, and that's what we were doing. In the convoy was troops, tanker trucks, food, ammunition trucks. And there were three explosions behind my jeep. I thought they were mortar shells. But they weren't. They were land mines.

So I knew the jeep had got hit. I didn't realize I had. See, I didn't wear a vest. I sat on it. To protect the family jewels. We stopped, and I told my driver, "That guy was shooting at us. Those were not mortar shells." So I gave a halt to the convoy, and I was looking around on the hillside. It wasn't steep, it was just rising ground, really. I told the driver to get on the machine gun and I'll go look.

I had hand grenades and a little snubnose .38. That's all the weapons I figured I'd get by with. So I went up this hillside. Through my glasses I could see this change in the contour of the terrain, a little hump. And I went up there, and hell, there was this well-concealed cover for a hole in the ground. I kicked that cover off, and this old guy gave me the Buddhist salute and when he did I shot him through the top of the head. But he had aiming stakes, three sets of them; he'd set off three mines. But he was too old; his reflexes were not too good. That's why he didn't get us. You'd line these stakes up; then, when something comes along, you touch your wires, move over to the next one, touch your wires, and so forth. Simple. Crude. But very effective.

My people were some of the first ones in the division to get killed, so it didn't bother me to kill him. If there had been more of them I'd have been happier to kill them all. I got rid of him.

Aaron Elson: At that time you were hit already?

Cliff Merrill: Yeah, in the upper spine. Little tiny pieces. Nothing showed. Like a faint scratch. I didn't feel anything much. About two or three weeks afterward, my left arm started getting numb. I thought it was a heart attack. I didn't figure I was a candidate for a heart attack; I was always rugged and healthy and all. So I went to the medics and they X-rayed me, and said, "We can't help you here, but get your things together. You're going back tomorrow."

That's how I was evacuated. Back to Walter Reed. And they didn't operate on me either. They said, "Let's wait and see what happens." It got a little better; the numbness was not as pronounced, but I ended up having to be operated on, a very extensive type operation. I lost the use of the arm. It never did come back all the way. And that's how I ended my war career.

Aaron Elson: You were no kid then. You must have been in your forties?

Cliff Merrill: I was 55 when I retired. I retired in '69. But I was batted around. I tried to come back on duty, and went to Fort Dix. I was down there about six, seven months. I couldn't cut it. And they kicked me out. Unfit for service.

Aaron Elson: I know you're very modest about this, but what medals did you get?

Cliff Merrill: Oh, I didn't get many medals. I got the Bronze Star three times I think. Yeah. I didn't worry about medals. One general described it. He said, "You don't toot your horn."

I said, "I figure I don't have to. The results speak for themselves." But a lot of guys tooted their horn. All they were interested in was glory for themselves. I was interested in my men, because I wanted to come back alive, and they were the ones who could see that I would.

There was something ... I thought of it last night ... oh yeah: After I got out of Walter Reed, the First Army commander was General Seaman. He'd gone from the First Division in Korea, field force commander, and went to Fort Mead, Maryland. He called me one day and asked me what I was going to do. I told him I guessed I was going to retire. He said, "I would like you to go down to Fort Dix for me. They've been having problems." The provost marshal there was not successful in keeping prisoners in line. They had a lot of prisoners; I guess over 1,500. The system was, in Europe, all the bad actors, they'd ship them there and hold them awhile pending trial or pending their being put out to places like Leavenworth; long-term, murderers and stuff like that. Real bad actors.

Aaron Elson: Were these American soldiers?

Cliff Merrill: Yeah. And they were kicking up. He didn't know how to handle it. So he asked me if I'd go out and take care of it. I felt pretty good, but I wasn't exactly a hundred percent good. So they tested me, and found I could handle them all right, and they quit. I had an MP battalion there. But I went in with a group of men. I told them how to do it. We didn't use pickaxe handles, we used sledgehammer handles. They're hickory; they don't break. You catch them in the face, it discourages them. What led up to this was the fact that these were old wooden barracks, two-story types, and in each barracks I had unarmed people. To maintain order. If they needed something, they could call, and we'd help them out. They dropped a footlocker on one of my kids. That caused me to take action. We went in. They tried all kinds of things. They tried to set a fire and barricade the doors, but we were determined so we went in and operated on them a little bit. Knocked out some teeth and broke collarbones. A couple of them I guess they busted an arm or so. But we used a reasonable, I termed it a reasonable amount of force. No gunfire or anything like that. We didn't have any guns. We did have those sledgehammer handles. They were very effective, if you know how to use them. But we toned them down. Then this shoulder and arm got pretty bad. I probably did something wrong. I'd already been operated on; this was in '68. So they sent me to the hospital, and I was in the hospital four or five months, taking treatment.

"It was so cold diesel oil froze."

A soldier's life

Wes Boyer
1st Infantry Division
World War II, Korea, Vietnam
Mt. Bethel, Pa., October 1995

Aaron Elson: You know, it amazes me that you were in World War II, Korea and Vietnam. That really puts you in a very small club. There aren't many people who can, from a firsthand point of view, put things in perspective. I've heard stories about how when World War II veterans came home, the reaction they got was tremendous. You hear from Vietnam veterans, how they came home...

Wes Boyer: We didn't get that much. Korea didn't either.

Aaron Elson: What did you think, here you survived World War II and then Korea broke out. Did you expect that there might be anything like that?

Wes Boyer: No, you didn't. No soldier did.

Aaron Elson: Where in Korea were you?

Wes Boyer: In Pusan. That's where our outfit wound up. But they had a lot of people in body bags. Loads of them. Truckloads.

Aaron Elson: So I guess you could say it was worse than...

Wes Boyer: Oh yeah. Because you couldn't see the enemy. It was bad.

Aaron Elson: Did you ever have any close calls yourself?

Wes Boyer: No, I had close calls with the Vietnamese people. We went into a city one time, and there was some sergeant just sitting there. I watched him get shot. I watched the people in the city shoot him. Vietnamese. He was on a bicycle, got off his bicycle and shot him. And then we went after him. And he hid in a village, and we went in all these houses, but those people won't tell you nothing. They'll protect him. We were gonna shoot him up. But we never got him. He got away. If we'd have got him he wouldn't have got away. We'd have shot him.

Aaron Elson: I guess that must have happened more in Vietnam than in World War II.

Wes Boyer: Oh yeah. There was a lot of soldiers got killed in the city, in the towns and villages, for no reason. Because that's where they lived. But you don't know if he was a communist or if he was a good man who lived in the village. You didn't know who it was.

Aaron Elson: In Vietnam, you must have had people who abused drugs.

Wes Boyer: We had a couple in our platoon that had drugs. But they live on it over there. They smoke it over there. That's their life. So it was easy for a soldier to get it. You'd have to look at everybody before you went on patrol, to make sure he wasn't doped up. If he was you'd dismiss him, report him to the c.o. or the colonel, they'd take him to a hospital or something. But that's how they got killed, abusing drugs. They didn't know what they were doing. But we'd dismiss them before we went on, we wouldn't take nobody on patrol that had drugs. We'd get somebody to replace him.

Aaron Elson: Would there be a stigma attached to that, or would you discipline them afterwards?

Wes Boyer: Oh yeah, the commander would. But then if they'd see he couldn't do nothing, they sent him back, send him back of the line, or to a hospital.

Aaron Elson: What can you recall about the first time you saw a buddy, or somebody you were real close to, get killed.

Wes Boyer: Well, you feel bad about it. It hurts. But you've got to keep going. I mean, that's it, he's dead. You've got to go and get somebody else. You can't just stop what you're doing because he died. You just have to put his rifle upside down and put his helmet on there and keep going.

Aaron Elson: You actually did that?

Wes Boyer: Yes. You can't stay there. You've got other men to worry about. We had a couple of them got killed, but out of 15 we might have had 13 come back. The commander would say, "Where's the other ones?" "They're out there in the jungle. They're dead." But you can't take them, you've got to leave them there. Because you've got another 13 men to worry about.

Aaron Elson: What's the morale of the platoon, when you lose a couple of people like that?

Wes Boyer: It's down, a little bit. But then later on it gets all right. They work it off.

Aaron Elson: Did you lose many officers?

Wes Boyer: Yeah. We lost officers. We had a general came, he was giving citations, he was flying in with a helicopter to give citations to the unit, and he was shot when he got out. He was bleeding. But he had his pilot wait right there, and he gave the citations, and he should have been in a hospital.

Aaron Elson: Did he survive?

Wes Boyer: Yeah, he got back in his helicopter and they left. And he was bleeding, because he got shot coming in.

Aaron Elson: Did you ever go into Laos or Cambodia?

Wes Boyer: Laos I did, not Cambodia. Cambodia, we had a lot of trouble there too.

Aaron Elson: But Laos was a secret? Did they make it clear that if anything happened it would be kept quiet?

Wes Boyer: Oh yeah. They wouldn't say nothing. It would be hushed up.

Aaron Elson: Who would explain this to you?

Wes Boyer: Either the captain or the lieutenant. Most of the time it was the captain.

Aaron Elson: And what would you go looking for?

Wes Boyer: Underground installations.

Aaron Elson: Did you find any?

Wes Boyer: Yeah. We found quite a few. But you've got to be very careful in Laos. If you got caught, you had to keep your mouth shut.

Aaron Elson: What would they do if they captured an American?

Wes Boyer: They'd shoot him. Tie his hands behind his back and shoot him. Because they wouldn't take him prisoner. We didn't neither.

Aaron Elson: Did you ever go into any of the tunnels?

Wes Boyer: No, I was too big to go in there. They're small people. They go in them tunnels like nothing. They'd have one in the house where they live, and maybe their wives and children are in there.

Aaron Elson: And they would be Viet Cong?

Wes Boyer: Yeah, they'd go underground. Some of them, you couldn't get in there. Small kids could get in. We didn't bother going in there, we'd just throw a hand grenade in. And I had a firefighter with my platoon.

Aaron Elson: A firefighter like a fireman?

Wes Boyer: No, a flamethrower. We'd open this thing up, and he'd shoot the flamethrower in there. You'd hear 'em scream. Burn 'em up.

Aaron Elson: That must be a haunting experience.

Wes Boyer: But they'd do the same thing to you. They would never take you prisoner. But you could never find their bodies, because they took their dead with them.

Aaron Elson: Of the three wars, which would you say was the most significant for you?

Wes Boyer: Vietnam.

Aaron Elson: Why would you say that?

Wes Boyer: I don't know, it was the country, I think. There was more fighting in Vietnam. There was a lot of fighting in Vietnam. Of course they don't recognize that here. They've still got prisoners in Vietnam. They're not all out. They've got them over there.

Aaron Elson: Why would they do that?

Wes Boyer: They didn't all come home. They're either over there as prisoners or they're over there dead. Somebody's got them. Because they're not all here. There was a lot of soldiers in Vietnam. A lot of units.

Aaron Elson: You were how old when you went to Vietnam?

Wes Boyer: I went to Vietnam when it first started. I was 39 or 40 years old.

Aaron Elson: Were you considered an old man by then?

Wes Boyer: Oh yeah, I was an old trooper.

Aaron Elson: Did they respect you for that?

Wes Boyer: Oh yeah, they listened to me. Even the officers. We had a new lieutenant in one time. Vietnam is very muddy, because they get a lot of rain. And the lieutenant came in, he was gung-ho, shine your shoes, and jungle boots, and all that, and I told him, "You're way off base." I was old enough to be his daddy. And the captain called the lieutenant in. He says, "Let me tell you something. You listen to that sergeant. He knows what's going on. You don't. This is not West Point." I got him clued in. And we took him out one night. He got scared.

Aaron Elson: Like shellshock?

Wes Boyer: Yeah, he got real scared. I told him, I said, "See this, Lieutenant? You don't shine boots here. You'll get shot."

Aaron Elson: But he got scared, and not shot?

Wes Boyer: He got scared to death. He didn't want to go out. And then he never went out again. He wouldn't go on patrol again.

Aaron Elson: What was it that spooked him like that? You must have seen that happen to several people.

Wes Boyer: Yeah, because when we got under fire, he didn't know what to do. They don't teach you that in West Point. In West Point, nobody's shooting at you. But over there, it's the real thing. And I told him, "Lieutenant, we can't do what you want to do. These men have been out on patrol quite a few times. We've been shot at a lot of times. You've never been shot at. Those shiny boots you've got will never give." But he wanted to do like West Point, with everything up to date.

He was gonna come in and be a commander. I said, "We'll never do that."

Because in Vietnam, you know, they trained the bees to know where you are.

Aaron Elson: The bees?

Wes Boyer: Yeah. They knew that American soldiers, when they shave they put certain aftershave, and they trained the bees for that smell. And then sent bees in to kill you.

Aaron Elson: When you were on patrol, you'd be attacked by bees?

Wes Boyer: Yeah, because they'd train them for that lotion that you were wearing.

Aaron Elson: You saw that happen?

Wes Boyer: Oh yeah. I've seen that happen.

Aaron Elson: That must drive somebody crazy.

Wes Boyer: Yeah, because you get bees all over you.

Aaron Elson: What was that like when that happened?

Wes Boyer: Once you get stung, your eyes close up and everything else. You don't know what you're doing.

Aaron Elson: Did that ever happen to you?

Wes Boyer: No. It happened to a couple of people, though.

Aaron Elson: And you saw it?

Wes Boyer: Yeah. You have to douse him down with stuff to kill it. So his eyes don't close up on him.

Aaron Elson: Were you ever in a fire base that was overrun?

Wes Boyer: No. They tried to overrun it, one night. But they didn't get it overrun. Because we had a lot of bunkers, and they didn't know that. A lot of barbed wire all around. We built bunkers ourselves. They tried. But they didn't get in.

Aaron Elson: How close did they come?

Wes Boyer: From here to that house. To the barbed wire. That barbed wire would be right there, where that house is. But then we'd have our bunkers here, and they couldn't get in. We made sure of that.

Aaron Elson: Were you wounded in Vietnam?

Wes Boyer: No.

Aaron Elson: Don't tell me you made it through all three wars without being wounded?

Wes Boyer: Yeah.

Aaron Elson: You either were very lucky or very good.

Wes Boyer: I was lucky. I didn't even get hit when I got the Bronze Star. But I watched everything I did.

Aaron Elson: But a lot of people who watched everything they did, there still was a shell fragment with their name on it.

Wes Boyer: We had someone in Vietnam who had a M-79 shell stuck in him. It didn't go off.

Aaron Elson: Was he killed?

Wes Boyer: Uh-uh. They operated on him and got it out.

Aaron Elson: The doctors should have gotten a medal.

Wes Boyer: They probably did. But they got it out.

Aaron Elson: Did you ever write anybody up for medals?

Wes Boyer: No, I recommended them to General Westmoreland.

Aaron Elson: And what were the circumstances of that?

Wes Boyer: Oh, it was when a guy, he took off to get some people in a village, underground, and he wasn't supposed to go there. But he got sidetracked and went there anyway. We stayed there to protect him, because there was nothing we could do because we were pinned down for a while. And then finally we got up and went over where he was. And he had five or six communists there sitting down with their hands over their head in that one little hut. He routed them out of there all by himself. He's lucky he didn't get killed. Because they had machine guns and all kinds of equipment. But he did it. So we recommended him to General Westmoreland.

Aaron Elson: For what kind of a medal?

Wes Boyer: A Bronze Star. They gave it to him. But there were a lot of people in body bags. They'd load trucks up with twenty, thirty, forty people at a time, take them to the air base. Loads of them.

Aaron Elson: That must be very demoralizing.

Wes Boyer: It is. Especially when they're in body bags. They just unload all the body bags, you'd count 'em, two, three, four hundred at a time.

Aaron Elson: And then when replacements would come in...

Wes Boyer: They'd see the body bags, when they came in, the replacements, at the Air Force base, because that's where the morgue was, where they did identification and all that.

Aaron Elson: Did anybody ever commit suicide?

Wes Boyer: No, I had people shoot themselves in the foot, just to get out of there. Get the Purple Heart.

Aaron Elson: Even if they did that?

Wes Boyer: Yeah, they'd get away with it. They'd do that so they wouldn't have to go out and fight. Shoot themselves in the foot. Stab themselves with a bayonet.

Aaron Elson: Did you yourself have any brush with or indication of combat fatigue?

Wes Boyer: No. It didn't bother me. It didn't bother me at all, what I did. It was a job.

Aaron Elson: What do you think makes that possible for somebody like you, whereas somebody else will go nuts, like that lieutenant, his first day, or the first time he was shot at?

Wes Boyer: It all depends how they can take it, their system and everything. Because later on it was just like a job for me. When I first started it wasn't, but then later on, just like a job. It's just like in the paratroopers. They tell you, when you join the paratroopers, there's a day you join, and don't forget, there's a day you hang your boots up. The day you hang your boots up is when you're up in that airplane and you say it doesn't bother me to jump, because you're gonna make a mistake. When you make that mistake, that chute ain't gonna open, you're gonna hit the ground. They tell you, don't never forget the day you're gonna hang your boots up, because you're gonna make a mistake, you're gonna get careless. When you have to put all those strings together, maybe you'd cross a string that you weren't supposed to. When you pack a chute, you've got to pack it right.

Aaron Elson: Now in all those years, you must have gotten careless once.

Wes Boyer: Oh, I did a couple of times.

Aaron Elson: What happened then?

Wes Boyer: Nothing, really. Just got careless, that's all.

Aaron Elson: But what were the circumstances, one time, when you got careless? Did you say, How could I have done something like that?

Wes Boyer: Yeah. One time. I went out someplace and I didn't have my helmet with me, and everybody else had helmets, and they had their gas masks, and I didn't have any of that with me.

Aaron Elson: This was in World War II?

Wes Boyer: Yeah. I was just by myself. And people started shooting, and I didn't have a helmet. I had my gun, but I forgot the rest of it. I was in a hurry. I shouldn't have been. But I got out of it. But you get careless sometimes. You don't wear this, or you take your boots off. You never take your shoes off. Never. Take your shoes off, maybe you can't get them on.

Aaron Elson: So how long did you keep your shoes on?

Wes Boyer: All the time.

Aaron Elson: For a week at a time, or a month at a time?

Wes Boyer: Oh yeah.

Aaron Elson: I just had somebody tell me he had his shoes on for six weeks without taking them off. Is that possible?

Wes Boyer: Oh yeah.

Aaron Elson: What do your feet feel like? Mush?

Wes Boyer: No, your feet are all right. The boots are uncomfortable, but your feet are all right. Maybe the day when you take them off, that's when you get hit. You've got to be able to move fast, and if you don't have your boots on, you're in trouble, because it's not easy to put them on. Maybe your feet swelled up and you couldn't get your boots on.

Aaron Elson: Was it the same thing with clothes, you wouldn't change your clothes?

Wes Boyer: Yes.

Aaron Elson: What was the longest you'd say you went without changing?

Wes Boyer: Fifteen days. Never shaved or nothing.

Aaron Elson: And slept on the ground?

Wes Boyer: Yep. When you come everybody goes, "Oooh, you stink." And you did.

Aaron Elson: Would you have food with you all that time, or what would you do for food?

Wes Boyer: We had C rations. Little canned stuff.

Aaron Elson: Were they able to keep you supplied?

Wes Boyer: Yeah. C rations. You could take them out of there and carry them anyplace you want to carry them, so they won't be bulky, out of the box. But they were C rations. They taste terrible.

Aaron Elson: What was Pusan like?

Wes Boyer: Pusan was bad. It was a bad town.

Aaron Elson: Did you have to take it or did you have to defend it?

Wes Boyer: We had to take it. We took it. But then we defended it. Because down near the ocean, that's where they set up the camp for R-and-R people, to go back and rest for a while. They could leave you go back for a while and rest. But we didn't do that very often. Our outfit kept moving all the time.

Aaron Elson: Was it cold?

Wes Boyer: In Vietnam?

Aaron Elson: No, in Korea.

Wes Boyer: Oh, yeah, it was cold. It was so cold that diesel oil froze. We had diesel trucks, and you'd go to get a drum of diesel. It was frozen solid. Diesel fuel.

Aaron Elson: How could you melt it?

Wes Boyer: We'd melt it. We even took one truck, and you know what we started it with? Lighter fluid. Poured it in the carburetor. Lighter fluid, that you put in a cigarette lighter. And started the truck.

Aaron Elson: You weren't afraid it would blow up?

Wes Boyer: No, hey, I don't know. It's a chance we take. It worked. It started the truck. We did it to see if it would or not. We had to do something with it. Because the diesel oil froze. That's how cold it gets.

Aaron Elson: Did you have warm clothing?

Wes Boyer: Oh yeah. We had Mickey Mouse boots and all that stuff. We had a lot of warm clothes. Plenty of that. You had to have. Our guards at night, when they walked guard duty, they only could walk so many hours and they'd have to go in and get warm, because they'd freeze to death, even with Mickey Mouse boots. That's how cold it got. Maybe they'd walk four hours, and then go in, and somebody else would come out and walk four hours.

Aaron Elson: Did you do guard duty in Korea?

Wes Boyer: Yeah.

Aaron Elson: That must have been scary.

Wes Boyer: Oh yeah, because you're all fenced in. But you don't know who's on the other side of that fence. They'd try to steal everything you've got.

Aaron Elson: Were these civilians?

Wes Boyer: Oh yeah, anything they could get their hands on.

Aaron Elson: So you would be guarding not only against the enemy but also against civilians?

Wes Boyer: Yeah. Because they'd get in there and steal stuff from you. Anything they could get.

Aaron Elson: Would many guards be killed?

Wes Boyer: No, we didn't have any of them get killed. Got shot at, but they didn't get killed. Because they couldn't get that close to our compound. Then we had the Turkish soldiers there. But that was up in, towards … I forget the name of the town. Anyway, they had a Turkish compound, and they caught a slicky boy, came in stealing their stuff. But they caught him. You know what they did to him? They stuck a rifle rod through this ear and out this ear and hung him up in the front gate. And the commander had to come along and tell them to cut him down. They hung him up there so everybody could see him. Because Turkish soldiers, they're not gonna take you prisoner, they're gonna kill you right away. Because they like blood. They'd kill you right off the bat.

Aaron Elson: Were there ever any conflicts between the Turks and Americans?

Wes Boyer: Oh, no. But they were hard soldiers. The people in Korea were scared to death of them.

Aaron Elson: The civilians, too?

Wes Boyer: Oh yeah, everybody, when they see a Turkish soldier. They're scared to death. The Korean people, it's nothing to see them take a dog and have it hooked up, skinning it. That's their food. If you'd shoot a dog in Korea, they'd get all over you. That was their food. They did it just like a cow. The Turks didn't like that, killing the dogs. If the Turks saw one of them killing a dog, they'd shoot him.

Aaron Elson: Did you ever have any direct contact with the Turks?

Wes Boyer: Yeah, I talked to them. As soldiers, they were all right.

Aaron Elson: Did they speak English?

Wes Boyer: A lot of them did. They didn't bother us. It was their compound, so we didn't bother them either. They had their commanders and stuff. The only time our outfit bothered them is when a general came along with his jeep and told them to cut that Korean down.

Aaron Elson: They took a rifle and they put it in...

Wes Boyer: A rifle rod and stuck it through his ear, in one ear and out the other, and they hung him up. At the front gate, so everybody could see him.

Aaron Elson: When did you two meet?

Wes Boyer: In '75 ... '74.

Aaron Elson: Were you still in the Army then?

Wes Boyer: I'd got out.

Aaron Elson: So you got out right after Vietnam?

Wes Boyer: Yeah. I got out because they wanted to send me back.

Aaron Elson: Really?

Wes Boyer: Yeah. I'd had my years of service already. I told them I wouldn't go back to Vietnam. I didn't want to go back. I said, "Leave it up to the other people to go over there for a while."

Aaron Elson: How did you and Angie meet?

Wes Boyer: We met in Carlstadt.

Angie Boyer: In a bar.

Wes Boyer: At a birthday party.

Aaron Elson: For who?

Wes Boyer: Angie's.

Angie Boyer: That's what I got for my present.

Aaron Elson: Were you a friend of a friend, or you just walked into the bar?

Angie Boyer: No, he was there when we walked in. Me and my girlfriend. And then we went several times, and he was always there. Sometimes we said, we'll go over there and maybe that guy'll send us drinks so we don't have to spend our money. And little by little. …We're married, what, 21 years? It's too bad we don't have any children. I had four already. He had none. I would have had if I were twenty years old but it was a little dangerous, for my age group. You know, menopause. Scary.

Aaron Elson: And what kind of work did you do after you left the Army?

Wes Boyer: I went to work for Tenneco in East Stroudsburg.

Aaron Elson: What did you do for them?

Wes Boyer: I took care of acid tanks. Inside the building.

Angie Boyer: Then he got laid off from that, because he got a rash on his hand.

Wes Boyer: The skin started to come off.

Angie Boyer: And his feet. They said it was from the chemicals.

Aaron Elson: From the Agent Orange?

Wes Boyer: I don't know. They never found out.

Angie Boyer: He never even gave that a thought.

Wes Boyer: Then I started wearing white gloves.

Angie Boyer: And in the meantime, right after he went back to work, Tenneco laid him off. And never called him back. They probably were afraid of getting a lawsuit.

Aaron Elson: Did you have contact with Agent Orange in Vietnam?

Wes Boyer: I don't know if we had contact or not.

Aaron Elson: But did you see it being used?

Wes Boyer: I've seen it used, but I don't think we had contact with it. It's hard to tell if you had contact or not.

Aaron Elson: What sort of after effects would you say you've had? Did you have nightmares, or trouble sleeping?

Wes Boyer: No, I never had nightmares or anything. The reason I never had nightmares is because to me it was a job. And I had to do it, because nobody else would do it. Well, there were other people would do it, but it was my responsibility. It's like me going to work at eight o'clock in the morning. I know what I have to do.

Aaron Elson: Do you ever get reflective, or philosophical, or think about all those years?

Wes Boyer: Sometimes I think about it. I don't get shook up about it much.

Aaron Elson: What do you think about?

Wes Boyer: Well, you think of what you did, it's kind of hard. But if I had to do it all over again I'd do it, if I wasn't too old. I'd go back in the service.

Aaron Elson: What would you say was the absolute worst situation that you were in?

Wes Boyer: The worst? In Vietnam, under fire. That's the worst. Especially when the Air Force was dropping napalm bombs. That was the worst time. That was the closest.

Aaron Elson: Was the napalm coming close to you?

Wes Boyer: Yeah. But they weren't bombing us, they were bombing the Chinks.

Aaron Elson: And about how far away were they?

Wes Boyer: Oh, I don't know, from here maybe across the street. That's how close the napalm landed.

Aaron Elson: They were so accurate that they could do that?

Wes Boyer: Oh, sure. The Air Force?

Aaron Elson: Would they come in at low level?

Wes Boyer: Yeah. You could almost see the pilots.

Aaron Elson: Could you feel the heat from it?

Wes Boyer: Yeah. That's as close as we came to one of them. They dropped five or six bombs. You could hear the people screaming over there. They were hot stuff. Napalm goes right across the ground. It doesn't stop. Those flames just take off.

Aaron Elson: It skids across the ground, giving off flames?

Wes Boyer: Yeah. Burns anything in sight.

Aaron Elson: And is it like a liquid, that if it gets on your skin it keeps burning?

Wes Boyer: It burns everything in sight. Just runs right along. Napalm. I didn't want to get that close to them anymore.

Aaron Elson: Do you have any idea the number of enemy that were involved in that?

Wes Boyer: There were a lot of them. There might have been over fifty. They had to call the Air Force in, because they had heavy equipment. We were only infantry.

Aaron Elson: Did you ever come under any heavy artillery barrages?

Wes Boyer: No, we didn't.

Aaron Elson: Even in World War II?

Wes Boyer: Oh yeah, World War II, but not over there. Mortars or something like that we did, in Vietnam, but not heavy artillery. Just a lot of mortar fire. Of course they were good at that. But their intelligence was good. They knew where the units were all the time. They really did know where our units were at. Not just ours, all the units.

Aaron Elson: That must have been demoralizing.

Wes Boyer: Well, it was, because they could throw mortars into the camp. They did that a couple of times, too, when we were in camp. The whole unit. But their intelligence was good, I'll give them credit for that.

Aaron Elson: Did you ever have any run-ins with officers?

Wes Boyer: I had a run-in with a captain one time. The captain told me to do something. I said, "I ain't doing that, no way. Do it yourself."

"You're disobeying an order."

I said, "Maybe I am. Do it yourself." Because they were under heavy fire. I told the captain, "My squad ain't going out there." You take the squad if you want to get somebody, if you can get a volunteer. Good luck."

"I'm gonna have you put in the stockade."

And I said, "Be my guest." But he didn't do that, because in the meantime we went on another mission. I don't know what he did. He got volunteers to do what he wanted to do, but he didn't come back from his mission. Some of his people did but he didn't.

Aaron Elson: Do you think it's possible he was killed by his own men?

Wes Boyer: He might have got shot with his own people. I knew it was a mission that couldn't be done. Impossible. But I went on a different mission. When I came back, he wasn't there. Some of his men that he took out there were there. I asked them but they didn't say too much about it. I think they shot him. I don't think the enemy shot him.

Aaron Elson: Was there anything humorous you can remember about Vietnam?

Wes Boyer: Humorous? No. Nothing humorous. Not that I know of.

Aaron Elson: Was there ever a time when you felt safe, even?

Wes Boyer: At one time, yeah. But that's when we fell back. Our camp fell back away from the jungle. See, our camp had been right at the edge of the jungle. We used to watch the planes every night, bombing, napalm bombs and all that, all night long. Never stopped. You couldn't sleep. You'd sleep on and off, like naps or something. But as soon as you hear the planes coming in, you knew the enemy's moving someplace, so you'd get up. The commander would get you up and you'd go out in a foxhole. Sometimes we even slept in the foxholes. One guy maybe, two guys in a foxhole. One guy'd sleep, take a nap, wake him up, then the other would take a nap.

Aaron Elson: Was there infiltration into the perimeter?

Wes Boyer: They tried to get in; a lot of times they tried to get in. But they never did. They tried. But we held them back.

Aaron Elson: Were there ever times when you'd find somebody dead in a foxhole in the morning?

Wes Boyer: Oh yeah. But then that might have been his fault. See, we didn't know whose fault it was. Maybe he didn't have his helmet on. It all depends. Or he got careless.

Aaron Elson: Would they try to sneak up on the foxholes?

Wes Boyer: Oh yeah, they'd do that. If they could get past the barbed wire. But usually if you've got barbed wire around, they can't get through there. That barbed wire would tear them up. Yeah, I've seen that. I seen one that lit a cigarette at night. Got blown away.

Aaron Elson: By a mortar?

Wes Boyer: No, by a sniper. You light a cigarette, they know somebody's there. It's at night. That's a good idea for a sniper. Because he didn't have to look, he'd just see the light, and shoot wherever that light is. But that's neglect. They'd tell you you can't do that. We weren't allowed to carry cigarettes with us. We couldn't have cigarettes out there. Because in Vietnam, the Air Force said at 34,000 feet, if you light a cigarette, he can see you, that pilot. He could see that cigarette being lit, at 34,000 feet. And that's the Air Force. So it'd be easy for a sniper to do that.

Aaron Elson: Did you ever have any friendly fire incidents? Or what did people call friendly fire? I don't imagine that term was used.

Wes Boyer: No, not friendly fire. If the enemy's firing at you, it's not friendly. I'll tell you that, boy.

Aaron Elson: But I mean like people who were accidentally killed by American fire?

Wes Boyer: By their own people? Oh yeah, I've heard of that. I think that's how that captain got killed, by his own men, not by the enemy.

Aaron Elson: You can't remember anything at all funny about Vietnam?

There's got to be something humorous that happened.

Wes Boyer: Nothing humorous.

Aaron Elson: Even a good meal?

Wes Boyer: Oh, we had a good turkey dinner.

Aaron Elson: Thanksgiving?

Wes Boyer: Yeah, we went back and had a good turkey meal. Dirty clothes, but we had a turkey meal. Everybody else was dressed up. We weren't. We came in, we were coming in from the jungle.

Aaron Elson: By helicopter?

Wes Boyer: No, we were walking in. Everybody was in this building here, sitting down to eat. Then we walked in. Dirty. Stunk. We'd been gone for ten days. There was a captain over there, "Geez, what are you doing?"

I said, "We're gonna eat."

"Oh, I don't know…"

I said, "Well, we are."

He said, "I don't know if you could eat or not."

I said, "Well, I'll tell you what. These 14 men here say we're gonna eat." I said, "We're gonna eat."

The line was all set up and everything for Thanksgiving. And one of the guys in my squad said, when the captain and a major said, "Well, you'll have to go someplace else," he cocked his machine gun, and he said, "No, we're gonna eat right here." And we did. We went through the line. First ones in the line. We got what we wanted to eat. We sat right down there at the first table, too. Ate what we wanted. And they just kept looking at us – everybody's looking at us. When we finished eating we got up and left. "We'll see you, Major. Thanks."

That wasn't our outfit. It was somebody else.

Aaron Elson: But you were like guests?

Wes Boyer: We made ourselves guests. But they didn't even know us.

Aaron Elson: But you were told to go there, you didn't go there on your own?

Wes Boyer: We went on our own. We saw the building, and we went over there. And they were all sitting down getting ready to eat. We walked in through the kitchen.

Aaron Elson: Do you think they were combat troops or non-combat?

Wes Boyer: Non-combat; they all had clothes on, everything. They looked like they were personnel people; they run the records or something.

Aaron Elson: And they were having a turkey dinner?

Wes Boyer: We had turkey dinner, too. We were the first ones there. Because he cocked that machine gun. He meant it. If they'd have said no, he'd have shot 'em. Because we were tired, ten days out there, laying out there in the jungle. We were trying to get back, because our unit moved someplace and we were trying to get back. Then we left there after we finished eating, and we found the unit. It was back in … what's the name of that town? I don't remember, but we found them.

Aaron Elson: Had they just abandoned you there and moved?

Wes Boyer: No, they had to move.

Aaron Elson: Why was that?

Wes Boyer: They were under fire. They had to move back. That's where we went first but they weren't there. But we got hungry. We ran out of C-rations, and it was something to eat.

Aaron Elson: How many days had you been without anything to eat?

Wes Boyer: Three days.

Aaron Elson: So you had been on the march for ten days?

Wes Boyer: Yeah, we were out ten days, yeah.

Aaron Elson: And when you went back to the base, was it still under fire?

Wes Boyer: No, it was abandoned. But we got it back. The captain said, "Did you have something to eat?"
I said, "Oh yeah. We ate in a mess hall. Personnel department."
He got a letter about that, too. He got a letter down through channels. But that guy would have shot 'em, because we were all on edge. He would've shot 'em if they'd have said no. We'd have been the only ones in there eating. Even the cook got scared. We were hungry. We were hungry, tired and dirty.

Aaron Elson: There was nothing to eat in the bush?

Wes Boyer: Oh yeah, you could pick berries up and stuff like that, and hope that it was any good. Catch a snake, cook it.

Aaron Elson: You would do that?

Wes Boyer: What, snake? Yeah, I'd eat snake.

Aaron Elson: Really? What's it taste like?

Wes Boyer: It tastes good, cooked.

Aaron Elson: Now were these the same snakes that would bite people?

Wes Boyer: Sure. Skin 'em. Cook 'em up. Snake meat.

Aaron Elson: Is there anything I missed, in three wars, that I should have asked you that I didn't know about?

Wes Boyer: I don't think so.

Aaron Elson: Did your division liberate any concentration camps?

Wes Boyer: No, they didn't liberate no camps.

Aaron Elson: But you went in to see them.

Wes Boyer: Oh yeah. I went with some English soldiers. We went down to Dachau, that's where the ovens are. And you see the mounds where the bodies are buried, and the wall where they were shot. Yeah, we went over there. The reason I went over there is, two of the English soldiers that were with me, their brothers were killed there, burned up in the ovens. That's why we went over there.

Aaron Elson: Had they been prisoners of war?

Wes Boyer: Yeah. That's where we saw the steel beds and all that that they push in the oven. We saw the ovens. And the mounds outside. The military took it over, for a museum. So they don't destroy it.

Aaron Elson: How did these British soldiers react, having lost their brothers there?

Wes Boyer: They were sad.

Aaron Elson: I know that the tankers who went into the Flossenburg concentration camp said that even after all they had seen, they couldn't imagine that people could do that to one another.

Wes Boyer: Oh, I know, yeah. But they did. You wouldn't believe that somebody could really do that, kill people like that. That's why they did it. Not just a few people at a time; a whole bunch at a time.

Aaron Elson: Had there been any advance warning or talk about the concentration camps, among the GIs?

Wes Boyer: No, they knew it was there. A lot of people had seen them.

Aaron Elson: Did you have any dealings with displaced persons?

Wes Boyer: Yeah, the only dealing I had with them was selling cognac.

Aaron Elson: Where would you get the cognac?

Wes Boyer: Through the fence. They came up to the fence to sell it. That was the only way you could get a drink. Because it was all fenced in; we couldn't go over there, but they could come up to the fence. We'd be on this side of the fence. Then we had to watch out for the guards, we'd have to do it after the guards passed, then we'd go there. We knew how long it took the guards to go around. So you'd give them a carton of cigarettes and they'd give you a bottle of potato schnapps. Cognac. We called it potato schnapps. We asked them what they make it out of. Potatoes. It did what it's supposed to do. They knew when it was ripe. So we'd give them a carton of cigarettes, they'd give us a bottle. We didn't know if it was any good or not. We'd drink it anyway. Then I went to visit Hitler's nest, Adolf Hitler, where he lived, in Berchtesgaden. We went up there. That's where they searched you. You couldn't go in there with a knife or nothing.

Aaron Elson: How come?

Wes Boyer: Because his fireplace was all diamonds. And a lot of people went up there and chipped diamonds out.

"He told me the name, and I walked over, and I said, 'Right here's his name.' And that really hurt me a lot because that old man fell to his knees and started crying. He said, 'That's my son.' There was a girl there with him. She said, 'That's my brother.'"

The Wall

Cleo Coleman
712th Tank Battalion, World War II
and
Doug Coleman
1st Air Cavalry Division, Vietnam

Pittsburgh, September 1996

Cleo Coleman: My grandfather fought in the Civil War, in Tennessee; that's where he was originally from. He got to Kentucky when he was a small boy, and raised two sets of families. The first time he was married he had a bunch of kids, and then his wife died. The second woman he married had been married before, to a Hatfield, but he died. So they got together and had three more kids – my mother, one sister and a brother.

One morning, when my mother was 13, they were sitting at the breakfast table. It was in the fall, and my grandfather was supposed to pick beans. He was eating breakfast, and my mother asked him, did he ever shoot anybody? He said, "Honey, I don't know. I was shooting at them and they was shooting at me." Then she said, "Did you ever get wounded?"

He said, "No, but I was hit. Through the sleeve, one of my arms, I don't know which one." It went through the sleeve of his coat and missed his arm. But he said that a miss is as good as a mile.

So he went to this field to pick some beans and never did show up and the family was worrying about him, and went to look for him. He'd fell dead from a heart attack. And Mommy was only 13. I don't remember him; this is before she was married.

Aaron Elson: How old are you, Doug?

Doug Coleman: I'll be 48 next month.

Aaron Elson: And you, Cleo?

Cleo Coleman: If I live to see January the 21st, I'll be 75.

Aaron Elson: How old were you when you went into the Army?

Cleo Coleman: Twenty. I was 21 when I was taking my basic training.

Aaron Elson: Did you enlist?

Cleo Coleman: No, I was called.

Aaron Elson: And Doug?

Doug Coleman: I was drafted. At 19.

Aaron Elson: You finished high school?

Doug Coleman: Noooo, I dropped out of school when I was in 10th grade and started doing construction work. And when I turned 18, that's when they drafted me. I got drafted May the 10th, 1968, and stayed in 19 months. But when I came back from Vietnam, I got credit for two years.

Aaron Elson: If you were drafted, how did you get into the Air Cav? I thought that was an all-volunteer outfit.

Doug Coleman: No, I was drafted into that. When I went into the service, I took my training at Fort Jackson, South Carolina, and they made me a field wireman in communications. So when I went to Vietnam they made me a grunt. They used to send me right out into the boonies. I was in a mortar platoon for six or seven months. I never saw a mortar platoon in my life until I got there.

I mean I had no training for it. And I was a medic guard for about three months. If somebody up front of us would get shot I'd go up there with the medic and pull them back to the rear so we could medevac them out.

Cleo Coleman: Didn't you operate a telephone, too?

Doug Coleman: No. Well, I carried a telephone. And when I started having all these problems – I suffer from post traumatic stress – they claimed I wasn't a combat veteran. I had gotten the Air Medal and all of these medals, but they had me listed as a field wireman. And they said, "You were attached to Headquarters Company. You didn't see any combat."

I said, "No, I'm a combat veteran." My mom had kept all my papers over the years. When I went to Vietnam I was a Pfc, and then I made Spec-4. Alpha, Bravo, Charlie and Delta – those are the body companies. It showed in the papers, "Private Douglas Coleman, promoted to Spec-4, Alpha Company." So when I took that to the VA, and he looked at all these medals and he looked at all of my orders that my mother had kept – a lot of Vietnam veterans destroyed everything they had – he said, "Well, you're a combat veteran," and they awarded me a 50 percent disability. That was about four years ago.

Aaron Elson: What was your first Air Cav assault like?

Doug Coleman: I was scared. I didn't know what I was getting into. They'd shown us some films about it before I went to Vietnam. But when I got on the choppers – there'd be anywhere from seven to nine choppers, and they'd each carry five to seven infantrymen, and they might have to make two or three rounds with the choppers to set everybody down in the field – I was real scared. I'd heard of companies being ambushed and wiped out once the choppers left. I know that happened to a couple of companies in my division, like Delta Company, Charlie Company, they almost got wiped out. And you'd hear a lot of talk between the guys, "We hope we ain't in an L-shaped ambush when we get off of that chopper." It happened, like in that book ["We Were Soldiers Once and Young," by Col. Harold Moore and Joe Galloway], when they set down, Joe Galloway and all of them them, that's what was waiting, an L-shaped ambush.

Aaron Elson: Can you describe an L-shaped ambush?

Doug Coleman: It's where you set all the choppers down, and the North Vietnamese army knows that you're coming. When you set down and the choppers leave, you've got fire coming in from two different ways. You've got crossfire and direct fire. In other words, you've been had. So I was always scared. I think I did 25 lifts. That's what you call a hot LZ [landing zone] when you go down. Maybe there might be an LZ that was hit the night before, when they try to overrun the LZ, like a Japanese suicide mission. We'd go in there sometimes the next day, and we didn't know what we would find.

Aaron Elson: What are some of the things that you found?

Doug Coleman: Well, you'd see GIs wounded, or you'd see a bunch of dead gooks laying around. Sometimes they'd already have the Americans in body bags ready to be put in the chopper. I've seen that a few times. But see, I only went through 25 air assaults, but I lived out in the jungle, sometimes it'd be two or three months before we'd come back. I carried my home on my back, and we would walk what you call clicks. In other words, maybe five or ten miles a day, and then at night we'd dig foxholes. We'd set a perimeter up, we'd set our tripwires out, we'd set our claymore mines out and we'd guard all night. And our mission would be search and avoid or search and destroy. If an LZ would get hit, we'd have to clear an opening out in the paddies and all these choppers would come in and pick us back up and take us back into this hot LZ. In other words, we were going where the action was at all times. That's the way the First Cav was.

Aaron Elson: Who would cover you while you were doing the work?

Doug Coleman: Our support was artillery. We had a big base camp. And also air strikes. There'd be napalm and bombs, and then we had the Cobra helicopters. That'd be our support.

Aaron Elson: You must have worked under fire a lot.

Doug Coleman: Yeah, I did. For about ten months. We'd get C rations to last us for five to seven days. We'd carry ten to fifteen canteens of water, all your bedrolls, all your writing material, your smokes. You're carrying that, and every few days you'd get a food drop. I was getting my mail anywhere from three to seven days, when they'd bring our C rations out. Because the choppers weren't coming out to us every day.

Aaron Elson: How high was the casualty rate?

Doug Coleman: Well, I got a list when I was in Washington, D.C. I told them I can't remember names, but maybe I could if I saw somebody's name, I said I'd like to have a list of the First Cav, the casualties, between '68 and '69. I haven't thought about it for a while, but I could go and get a stack of papers, I'd say, up in the thousands got killed, after the First Air Cav was in two years.

There were ten thousand casualties in the First Cav. There were like 58,000 killed in the war.

Aaron Elson: You must have had some close scrapes.

Doug Coleman: Yeah, I have, boy.

Aaron Elson: Can you describe a couple?

Doug Coleman: Well, we got pinned down. We found out we'd run into a North Vietnamese Army hospital base. It was one of the biggest hospital complexes ever found in Vietnam. There were two helicopters shot down and I saw four pilots get killed, and I saw a lot of dead gooks, with their heads blown off.

Aaron Elson: Were you on the ground when you found the hospital?

Doug Coleman: Yeah. See, that's what I was telling you; our mission would be search and avoid or search and destroy. We might walk ten miles every day, and you're walking through the jungle. You didn't know what you were gonna come on. I was down south, around Saigon. I was in Cambodia when we weren't supposed to be in Cambodia.

Aaron Elson: Was the hospital complex heavily guarded?

Doug Coleman: Oh yeah, it definitely was. We had to call another company in to help us take it. I think we called the 11th Armored Cav in, plus all the air strikes. It was all bunkers underground. Above the ground there wasn't very much.

Aaron Elson: What were some other close calls?

Doug Coleman: Well, there'd just be a firefight we'd happen to run up on because it was on the Ho Chi Minh Trail – that's along Cambodia. Then you start shooting at each other, and you call your air support in or artillery. And then, after they put so many rounds in, you go back where you made contact and see if you could find any kills or any wounded.

Aaron Elson: You must have seen some close friends get killed.

Doug Coleman: Yeah. I didn't actually see them get killed, but they got killed at the time all this was going on. There were quite a few guys.

Aaron Elson: How did you react?

Doug Coleman: It got so I didn't care. It seemed like a dead gook, they were like animals. I guess he probably feels the same way; they weren't human. When you saw an American get killed, it bothered you. But you got over it pretty fast.

Aaron Elson: How did you keep your sanity?

Doug Coleman: I used to drink a lot. They sent beer out, like every seven or eight days you'd get beer or Coke. And there were a lot of blacks; they'd go in the rear and they'd come back with a bag of pot and we'd set around at night and pass a joint or two around and take trips home. You smoked a little dope. I didn't smoke a whole lot, really I didn't.

Aaron Elson: Was there racial tension?

Doug Coleman: There was before I came home. That's during all that rioting they had back in what, '69 or '68. And they were starting to come into Vietnam then, before I left. There was a lot of racial tension back in the rear. There wasn't even no war going on back there. There was a lot of crazy stuff. They were pulling grenades out and throwing them in bunkers or in tents.

Aaron Elson: These were blacks throwing them in white tents, or whites throwing them in black tents?

Doug Coleman: I don't know. It happened at night. I know we had a few incidents with some black people. But see, you had a lot going on. Martin Luther King got killed. What else was going on? A lot was going on back in the States, and everybody in Vietnam was replacements. Guys that hadn't got drafted yet were in this rioting going on in the States. Then they were getting drafted, and they were bringing it to Vietnam.

Aaron Elson: How did that affect you? Did you feel abandoned by your own country?

Doug Coleman: No ... I never did think about that. I got drafted in '68, and I wasn't a news person at the time. I didn't really know how much racism and war protesting there was. I found out about it before I came home. They told us to watch ourselves, to hang together, and that there might be a lot of protesters. Then I found this out not too long ago – I never really had thought about it – they started flying the Vietnam vets home late at night so the protesters wouldn't be there.

Aaron Elson: When your nerves started to go, what were you conscious of?

Doug Coleman: I don't know. It's taken me a long time; I'm just nervous about everything, and I have trouble sleeping. I have to take nerve pills to sleep. I'm sort of hyper. I keep busy, or I keep to myself.

Aaron Elson: When you were in Vietnam, how did you get taken off the line?

Doug Coleman: I was getting ready to go on R and R. I took my R and R and went to Australia, and had some dental work done. I had maybe two and a half months left. After I was out of the field for a while, I'd think about having to go back out there, and I started getting all nervous. I started passing out, and I started not eating. I started losing weight. So it had to be the thoughts of going back to my company out in the jungle. I started seeing different doctors. I had something like fifty days left. Then it got down to thirty-some days, and they said, "We're going to send you back home, because we think you have," what did they used to call that? They call it post traumatic stress now. They used to call it shellshock.

When I came home, they told me to take a physical. I went to Cincinnati, and I brought all my medical records. It took all day to take the physical. Then, at the end of the day, they told me they misplaced all my medical records, and I let it go at that. A few years after that I went to reopen my case and they upped my disability from 10 percent to 30 percent. Then I had a nervous breakdown just a few years ago. When I was down in Chillicothe I saw guys that never were in Vietnam just walking around; they were getting 100 percent disability, and I'd been having all these problems, and I was just getting 30 percent. When I went down there – that was about six years ago – I weighed 137 pounds.

Aaron Elson: And how tall are you?

Doug Coleman: 5-10. That's when I reopened my claim again. Then I got 50 percent, because I'd kept all my papers and I proved to them that I was a combat veteran.

Aaron Elson: When you were in Vietnam, what kind of mail did you get? Did you have a girlfriend back home?

Doug Coleman: Yeah, I did. I got a Dear John, which everybody got, I guess.

Cleo Coleman: See, every time I'd get a letter from him, he wanted to know how Linda was. That was before you met your wife.

Doug Coleman: That don't make any difference; that's a long time ago.

Cleo Coleman: I wouldn't say she was out going with another boy, because he was in combat. The way I'd write to him, I'd say, "Take care of yourself, and don't worry about any girls. Go ahead with what you're doing, and don't worry about girls till you get back." Because he was in combat, and I thought he might do something foolish and get killed.

Doug Coleman: Everybody got Dear John letters.

Aaron Elson: What did you do when you got it? Did you get drunk?

Doug Coleman: No … I don't know.

Aaron Elson: How did she say it?

Doug Coleman: I don't even remember.

Aaron Elson: But you and your wife wrote to him, Cleo?

Cleo Coleman: Yeah, we wrote to him a lot.

Aaron Elson: And you wrote home?

Doug Coleman: Yeah, and then I'd write to my sisters, and they'd write me. I got a lot of mail. At night time when I got dug in and all, I'd write people as much as I could.

Aaron Elson: Having been in combat, Cleo, what would you think when you would watch the news, knowing Doug was in Vietnam?

Cleo Coleman: I'd worry about him. It's hard. I know about what he's gone through. It's a lot different from the way I had it. I think maybe he had it rougher than I had it, being out there in the boondocks, living out there three or four months. It had to be worse than what I had. It bothered me quite a bit. I just had to go from day to day, and hope he'd make it. And then worrying about getting a telegram. It's rough. I'd been through war myself.

Aaron Elson: That first day that you were in combat, tell me again what happened with you getting out of the tank?

Cleo Coleman: Well, we landed. We dug in at night. We could hear gunfire. See, I went in about 18 days after D-Day. The front was a little bit in, but you could hear the fighting. They told us all to dig in that night and the next morning, at daybreak, we'd be in combat. They sent out the scouts that night, and they came back with the news that there's no big firearms up there; nothing to fear about, all small arms. My tank was in the lead of the second section of the platoon. At that time I was a loader. I was down in the turret, and all I had was a periscope to look out. I couldn't see much. There was a jeep blew up right beside us, and I didn't know what in all was going on. Then the tank in front of mine got knocked out. The shell went right through the front and cut the driver's head off.

Aaron Elson: Did you see the tank ahead of you get hit?

Cleo Coleman: No. I was down in the turret. The boys told me what happened later. So we moved up, we pushed them back quite a ways, and to our left we spotted a German ammunition dump. [Sergeant Les] Vink, he's the tank commander, told the driver to stop, and he told the gunner to put his sights on it. He gave him the elevation; we could see the Germans running around carrying boxes and things. Vink gave the order to fire, and we opened up on this ammunition dump. That was to our left, but to our right an 88 opened up, and it just missed our tank. So Vink told the driver to back up to a wooded area, and when the driver started backing up, the tank bogged down. The ground was soggy, and he couldn't go any farther. Then Vink gave the order to dismount.

I was the last one to get out the top, and when I was coming out of the hatch, my helmet came off. Louie [Gruntz] was the gunner. He was in front of me, and he forgot his gun. So he's scared, and he sees that I have no helmet on. He says, "You go back and get your helmet, and pick my gun up," and he grabs my gun out of my hand, just like that. And there I was with no gun and no helmet. But there's no way I'm going back.

The tank driver, Freddy Bieber, always told me, "I know where I'm going" – he's the driver; he can see. So I said, "I'll stick with you." And when I got out, Vink and Louie and Bardo [assistant driver Roy Bardo] all took off together. Bieber stayed with me. I was going towards the Germans, because I didn't know where I was. He said, "Follow me." There was a big ditch dug there, and we fell in the ditch and started crawling. A machine gun nest started firing on us, cutting limbs over our back. You had to get low.

The ditch was on a hill, and on the other side of the ditch there were infantry boys digging in. And the Germans were shelling hard. The infantry boys would dig a while, and then they'd have to hit the ground because artillery was coming in. So I walked up – no helmet, no gun – and one of the boys said, "You're in bad shape. One of our boys is laying over there. Go and get his; he doesn't need it anymore."

I said, "No way!" I was scared; it was my first day.

He said, "I'll get it for you." And he went and got that carbine rifle. The boy had a death grip on the carbine. He pulled it out of his hands, and picked up the helmet, which was laying to his side.

There was blood all over the helmet and on the gun. I took some leaves and wiped it off the best I could, put the helmet on my head and got down. And Bieber said, "Let's go this way." I followed him, and there were halftracks and tanks and everything else of the enemy's burning as we went by.

As we were going back, we ran into a new outfit that had just moved in. They wanted to know how it was up there.

"Boy," I said, "it's rough. It is bad."

Aaron Elson: After that first day in combat, how did you adapt?

Cleo Coleman: Well, I thought I was gonna go crazy. I was scared to death.

Aaron Elson: Did you see anybody else go crazy?

Cleo Coleman: I seen one boy. What happened, we got replacements. One boy was called to the Army, and his brother volunteered; at that time they let them do this, to stay together. So they came in as replacements while we were in France. Both of them came to our company. One was in the first platoon, and the other was in the third platoon. So the day that one of them would go out and the other didn't, he stayed behind and worried about his brother. Finally, one day, one of them got it – I think the younger one – and the other one, they sent him back behind the lines. It got to him pretty bad. I never did see him anymore.

Aaron Elson: You've never tried to contact or locate anyone who was in your unit?

Doug Coleman: Yeah, I did. Just before I came here, because this little address book I had, I was gonna tell my dad, I saw a guy in there from Pennsylvania. I gave this old number a call and it was a place of business. I've got a few addresses from guys and I've started to do this a few times, drop them a postcard or something, but I haven't heard back from any of them.

There was one guy that I was with in Vietnam with who got killed; he was from Ohio – I can't remember where in Ohio he was from, and I can't remember his name. I started to get that information before I left Vietnam. I was gonna look his parents up, and I felt guilt. I was afraid his father was gonna jump on me because his son had been killed. If I had been there this wouldn't have happened; I always had it in the back of my mind I would say that.

When I was a volunteer at the Wall, this man came up and said, "I'm looking for a name."

I told him to give me the name, and I went to this book. So he told me the name, and I walked over, and I said, "Right here's his name." And that really hurt me a lot because that old man fell to his knees and started crying. He said, "That's my son." There was a girl there with him. She said, "That's my brother." That's why I wish I would have looked up the father of my friend who was killed. I knew if I had a son I would be wanting to know about how he was killed. I should have done that. I think a lot of us Vietnam vets, we never did do that. That's probably why a lot are getting into it now.

Aaron Elson: Did you marry after the war?

Doug Coleman: Yeah. I got married at 23, and I was really lucky; I've been married for – next July it will be 25 years. I was one of the fortunate ones. A lot of Vietnam vets have been married five or six times.

Aaron Elson: Do you have children?

Doug Coleman: I've got three kids. I've seen my share of bad times; we've separated a couple of times. But the marriage has survived. I got a lot of counseling. I used to drink a lot.

Aaron Elson: Who does the counseling?

Doug Coleman: I've got two; I've got a psychiatrist and a psychologist.

Aaron Elson: Are they veterans?

Doug Coleman: The psychologist is. He was in Vietnam at the same time I was. So it helps a lot – somebody who's been there, he knows. It isn't only about Vietnam, because the focus is the outside world. That's where our problems are.

Aaron Elson: When you were in Vietnam, did you ever think about your dad having been in the war?

Doug Coleman: Yeah. That's what kept a lot of us going. You'd look around, and you'd say, "My dad went through this, and other people went through wars and made it. If they could make it I can make it."

Cleo Coleman: Once you get in, it's like the first day, you're scared to death. That's with you all the time. But you get tempered into it, and you don't fear it as much. You go on. You just hear bullets going over, in the background, maybe you jump a little bit. But you get toughened on it. That's how you survive. It hurt me; I've seen a lot of dead men, I've seen them burned up. But if you get in it long enough, you learn to survive.

Doug Coleman: I saw some things in the war that I don't think you ever tell anybody. There were some things that happened to me. I won't even talk about it.

Aaron Elson: Do you talk about it in therapy?

Doug Coleman: No. You don't have to. They know. Especially the one that's been there. I think a true veteran doesn't tell everything anyway, a combat veteran.

When I was in Vietnam, I sat down in the boonies one night with this old black man. He was a sergeant. I'd been there for maybe two or three months. He said, "Coleman, if you get home one of these days, and you're out in a bar drinking – I know you'll be out in a bar drinking – and some veteran will start telling big old office tales like you never heard in your life." He said, "You just get up and you walk away."

You never will hear the whole truth. I don't care how many books you write, or how long you live, you ain't gonna find out all that went on.

Cleo Coleman: You do things you don't like to do.

Doug Coleman: The things I told you did happen, but there's other things that come along with that stuff, like the looks of people; what they looked like when they were dead. But that's how it is.

Aaron Elson: When you're your father's age, maybe then you'll talk about it.

Doug Coleman: Yeah, you've opened up more; I understand why you said that. Dad, he never did talk about the war.

Cleo Coleman: One time, I know, I did something I didn't like to have to do. There was a small village. My tank commander said, "We seen some people traveling around here. Fire on the village." And I discovered there were some women and children walking around. I told him, "There are civilians in there." He said, "Do this. They're not supposed to be there."
And I had to fire on them.

Aaron Elson: Did you see afterward what happened?

Cleo Coleman: No, I didn't go and see. But I knew there were civilians, women and children. I saw them through the periscope. That's when I told the commander, "I see civilians." He said, "They're not supposed to be there." That's not something to make a big deal out of after all these years.

Aaron Elson: But it had to have affected you.

Cleo Coleman: I didn't mind fighting men.

Aaron Elson: Were you wounded at all?

Cleo Coleman: Small.

Aaron Elson: Where were you wounded?

Cleo Coleman: On the top of the head. We were standing guard under the timberline at the edge of a field, and the Germans threw over a shell. It hit the top of the tree, and shrapnel came down. I was standing guard on top of the turret; I felt something on my face, and one of the boys says, "You're hit."

There was blood running down my face, and about that time they were bringing the payroll out in a jeep, so they took me back over all that open field. There was no protection whatsoever, and I said, "I believe I'd have been safer if I'd have stayed in the tank."

They took me back to the company headquarters, which was on an old farm, and I slept in the barn. I stayed there for about a week. They cut all my hair off, shaved me, and stitched it up. Then here they come with a glass of cognac, and they say, "This'll help you."

There'd been some dead that had been laying out in the field and they couldn't get to them. When they did get them, they brought them back to this farm where the company headquarters was. There was a whole truck full of them – dead bodies, Americans and Germans thrown up there together – and I climbed up and looked at it. It was a terrible sight.

Aaron Elson: What was it that made you want to look?

Cleo Coleman: I'd been in combat for a while, and it was stupid I guess; I wanted to go up there and look and see. I mostly was checking for American boys.

Aaron Elson: What did you see?

Cleo Coleman: Oh, there's arms, feet and legs, thrown all over, bloody, and eyes open, and blood had run out of their mouth and their eyes.

Aaron Elson: And the smell?

Cleo Coleman: The smell was real bad. The Germans had a smell about them; it might have been the clothing they wore, but it's different from ours. Then you'd go out there in the field and see cows with their legs up in the air, and they had a terrible odor.

Aaron Elson: Did it ever make you throw up?

Cleo Coleman: No. Then they'd send us out K rations, and there'd be a bunch of kids, maybe ten or twelve, they'd watch every bite. And I wouldn't have enough to give them all, so I'd throw what I had out on the ground just like a football, and they'd be grabbing at it.

Aaron Elson: Was this when you were recovering from the wound?

Cleo Coleman: No, it was in combat. Going through the little towns. Then sometimes in the wintertime boys would go to one of the farms and kill them a beef, and put the quarters on the back of the tank.

We were guarding a pillbox one time. There was smoke coming out of that pillbox, just a few yards away. We were down in the tank, and we had a Coleman burner. We'd draw straws to see which one would go out there and cut him some steak, and bring it back in the tank so we could cook it.

Then when we did, a lot of times there'd be a German that was kind of a mole. He'd climb up there – you could just see the top of his helmet – and he'd take a shot at us with a bazooka. When we'd start firing, he'd just slide back.

Later on, a night patrol flushed them out with hand grenades. But I thought that was interesting, guarding that pillbox, with them in there under cover, and you in the tank sitting out in the open.

Aaron Elson: Was that on the Siegfried Line?

Cleo Coleman: Yeah. You couldn't knock the pillboxes out. We tried. The walls were so thick, you couldn't get through them.

Aaron Elson: Do you remember where it was that you were wounded?

Cleo Coleman: I don't remember the place. It was in France. Then one time, this piece of shrapnel – I was wearing a helmet; usually a tanker doesn't wear a helmet, but I had my steel helmet on – and this piece of shrapnel big as a quarter went through my metal, into the liner, and stopped.

My helmet saved me that time. And what I was afraid of all the time was mortar fire going down the hatch, and me down in there. I was afraid I'd get wounded, crippled, and I couldn't get out of there, and would sit in the tank on fire and burn.

And another thing I was afraid of was getting captured. I had a German P-38; they were more accurate than our .45s were, and I carried one all the time. I said if they get me, it's death. They'd kill you right there. Especially the SS.

They don't take many prisoners.

Aaron Elson: Now, that happened on both sides.

Cleo Coleman: Uh-huh. We had a tank commander in our platoon who was killed, Stanley Muhich. I was right beside him, the next tank over. I don't remember the town now – it was a small village – but anyhow, a shell got jammed in the chamber. So you've got a big rod; you have to get out there, stand at the end of the barrel and push the shell out. That's what he was doing when a sniper got him. They loaded him up and we moved back to this little town. That evening a sniper was brought in – he was bound to have been a sniper; he had a camouflage uniform on – and one of our boys – Muhich was one of his best friends – I saw this boy march the prisoner out behind a stone wall and close the gate. I didn't pay much attention, but I heard a gun fire. And he came back through the gate and his face was white.

One boy says, "He shot that prisoner." And we went to look. He had a hole between his eyes. Nice looking man. But I never did say nothing about it.

Aaron Elson: Do you think this was the sniper who had shot Muhich?

Cleo Coleman: He took it that it might have been. Later on – after I came home – I got a letter from Muhich's sister. She wanted to know how well I knew her brother, and did I know how he got killed. I wrote her back and told her just exactly how he got killed.

She wrote me another letter; she said, "Did you ever hear of Stan ever saying if anything happened to him, he wanted to be buried over there?" I wrote her back and told her I never heard him say anything; I said we didn't talk about things like that.

So I don't know what happened. He was a cavalry man. I think he cleaned out the stables, Stanley did, in the horse cavalry, in California. That was his job.

Aaron Elson: His buddy was white as a sheet when he killed the prisoner?

Cleo Coleman: Yeah. It did something to him when he shot that man in cold blood. I wouldn't have done that. The last day of action, we were going across this field, and they started firing on us when we got about halfway. Then the Americans started throwing artillery in, and we blasted it, too, with our tanks. We had the doughboys beside us, and they hit the ground.

There was a wounded German. He was down on his knees, and two doughboys walked up with a rifle. I hollered, "Don't do that, boys!" They just shot him anyhow. Killed him. The last day of action.

After a man's captured, I wouldn't have done that. They'd have probably done me that way, the Germans, if they captured me, but I couldn't do it. I wouldn't want to do it. After a man's captured he should be treated like he was captured, not killed. Unless he did something real, real, real bad. But he was fighting just like me; that's the way I see it.

Aaron Elson: Now, when Doug came home, he suffered from post traumatic stress. How about yourself?

Cleo Coleman: I was all right. My problem was it was so many months, maybe a year, I'd dream about being in combat. Every night. If anything moved or fell beside me, I'd jump.

Doug Coleman: I've heard my dad; he's told me a pretty lot about the war, but I never have really told you anything, did I?

Cleo Coleman: No. I know you had it rough. You didn't have to. I know.

Aaron Elson: The things that you won't talk about, have you seen anything similar in movies?

Doug Coleman: I've seen things in movies that I relate to. The movie "Platoon," that's the way I lived. The guy that made it, he was there.

Dale Albee: May I say something? [Lieutenant Dale Albee, of the 712ᵗʰ Tank Battalion, was sitting in on the interview] I was going to say the same of "Platoon." Do you remember when that Vietnamese ran, and the guy shot him; did you see that puff of dirt come out of his back?

Doug Coleman: Yeah.

Dale Albee: That's exactly what you get when you hit a guy. When you see a guy running and you shoot him, that's exactly what you get is that little puff. That was one of the things that I remember about "Platoon." Because that's actually the way it happened.

Doug Coleman: And I'll tell you, the life I live right now, believe it or not – and he can tell you that, I mean I laugh and joke about it, and my wife laughs and jokes about it, my kids even laugh and joke about it – I live like Forrest Gump. I mow grass for I don't know how many hours. I live out in the country. I hardly ever see anybody. That's the way I live.

Cleo Coleman: Just like me; I want to be by myself a lot of times. I just don't know, if the war did anything to me or what.

Aaron Elson: When did the dreams about being in combat stop?

Cleo Coleman: They probably went on for six months or a year. They slacked off gradually. But I was always fighting. If something moved behind me or would make a noise, I was aware.

Aaron Elson: Did you marry after the war or before?

Cleo Coleman: After. I raised six kids – three boys and three girls. One of them's dead.

Aaron Elson: The one who died, how did…

Cleo Coleman: She was very young; just a little girl, about 18 days old.

Doug Coleman: And I have a sister who got killed when she was 19.

Cleo Coleman: In a freak accident.

Doug Coleman: Drunk driving. Her husband killed both of them.

Aaron Elson: She was 19 and married already?

Doug Coleman: Yes. She had a little girl, which we don't know where she's at. His family took off with her, and we haven't seen her in 16 or 17 years. See, my sister's husband got drinking one night; they hadn't been married long, but she had a little girl – she was three weeks old – and my sister got mad and went out looking for him. She found him in a bar; that's what they told us. It was 2 o'clock in the morning, they were on their way back home, and he was driving at a high rate of speed. It was raining that night, and evidently they must have been arguing. They said he hit his brakes, and he crossed four lanes and hit a curve and went airborne into a gas pump and burned the car.

Aaron Elson: Did that accident bring back any flashbacks of the war?

Doug Coleman: For me it did, oh yeah.

"I said, 'General, do you remember when you raised the missions from 25 to 30?'"

Jimmy Doolittle and me

Dr. Gerald Levine
VA Medical Center, East Orange, N.J.
and
Jerry Rutigliano
8ᵗʰ Air Force

East Orange, N.J., May 1994

Aaron Elson: I'm looking for information on post traumatic stress as it manifests itself in World War II veterans.

Gerald Levine: PTSD became part of the diagnostic nomenclature around 1980. A lot of the World War II vets did experience symptoms. They tried to normalize their symptoms, they thought that everyone had those symptoms, and they didn't really know that there was help to be had or how to go about getting it. So I think the label PTSD legitimized it as an impairment.

Many of them, early on, report a lot of anxiety related problems. Problems falling asleep, problems staying asleep, intrusive memories of their war experiences, nightmares, these are all reexperiencing phenomena. They would have intrusive thoughts, nightmares. To a lesser degree I hear about flashbacks; not real sustained flashbacks, but with a flashback what happens is that something can trigger it, a smell, a word, a sight, even something symbolic like an anniversary, and for the moment the person is transported back to the scene of the traumatic event, and they forget where they are. These flashbacks can last for a second, or they can go on for hours. But we see that a lot more in Vietnam vets than we do in World War II vets.

Aaron Elson: Why do you think that is?

Gerald Levine: I'm not sure. It may be that they're closer to the event even though this is 20 years later, but it may be something that recedes over time. That's one possibility, that some of the reexperiencing phenomena, they just somewhat decrease over time. That's probably the more likely thing.

With Vietnam vets we've seen a greater degree of anger and mistrust than World War II vets. I think part of that is due to the fact that with World War II there was a clear moral right and wrong, and with Vietnam the country was very divided about our presence in Vietnam. And many of the people in the country didn't separate out the war from the warrior, and so treated the homecoming Vietnam vet in a rejecting way. So a lot of Vietnam vets came back feeling like they were betrayed after serving their country, and that sense of betrayal led to mistrust of authority, and a feeling of real hurt and rage and bitterness. We don't see that in the World War II vets, and it may be that they won a war, and they were received as heroes.

Aaron Elson: One thing I've noticed in the interviews I've done is that these men cut off their feelings, and they almost were aware of it. You couldn't feel anything after a certain point. And yet they did have feelings; if a friend was killed, they would still be overwhelmed, but in order to go on, they would see things, and it would almost be like looking at a photograph. It's hard for me to conceptualize because I never was in a situation like that. How does that affect someone?

Gerald Levine: It's called emotional numbing, and it's a very common feature of PTSD. What happens often is that a person feels alienated. They have great problems with intimacy, great problems feeling softer, more tender emotions. Often the only feelings they can feel are more intense feelings of rage, and when they're very stimulated. Like a lot of vets who are numb are drawn to more daredevil activities as a way of feeling something. And now actually there's some important research going on. We don't know whether that numbing is due to a natural occurring opiate which is released in the body, and some of the drugs that are being explored are opiate antagonists. One of our psychiatrists is involved in that research. It's being used in an experimental stage. It's just preliminary data, but the fact is that this is a very common complaint, and it's a common complaint of the families, that these men are cut off from their feelings. They say that they just can't feel closeness for anyone; they can't really be touched, although when they talk about World War II vets and losses there, they get very flooded emotionally. Somehow that overwhelms them.

War is one of those experiences that most people, unless you've been in war, you don't have a parallel experience to relate to, and a lot of combat vets, whether it's World War II or Korea or Vietnam, they feel that either there's not going to be an interest in what they have to say, or they'll be judged by their activities, or they're just simply not going to be understood. So there is a lot of withholding. I think as the World War II vets are aging and they're becoming more aware of their mortality as they see their numbers decrease, I see them reaching out more and feeling a need to talk more about their experiences with family.

I at one point was co-leader of an ex-POW group here. We thought, we didn't get it off the ground, of doing oral histories, videotaping some of that. But I think it's very important that that generation bear witness to their experiences and pass it along to the next generation.

Often the stories are very painful. There's a lot of avoidance in recounting painful material. At least that's what we find here.

Aaron Elson: I know that when they have told the stories they seem relieved.

Gerald Levine: Sometimes they've never really told it. Part of the therapeutic task, the kind of therapy you do with people who have been through these kind of traumas is, you're not a removed kind of therapist, you have to be active and engaged and very real. And you simply follow their lead. Some people would call it a kind of dosing model, or they gradually tell more and more as they're comfortable. You certainly don't push it with someone in over his head, but the aim is that the emotion that surrounds the event gradually gets neutralized as it is retold. That seems to happen. It doesn't always happen, but some of the charge is taken out. And especially when there are some feelings of guilt associated with the event.

We see two types of guilt. We see survivor guilt, which is usually associated with the loss of a buddy. During war people develop close attachments and then when someone close to you dies, it's more than a feeling of sadness over the loss; it's a feeling that perhaps you could have done something to prevent it.

There's an almost mystical sense that if someone had to die, why was it that person and not me; if that person had lived they would have done something more worthwhile with their life than I'm doing with my life. So it just shifts their sense of the world, so there's that kind of guilt. With survivor guilt you get a depression and a sadness, and part of the task is to help the person separate that you can be sad for someone else and at the same time be happy for yourself. You don't have to hold yourself hostage from experiencing joy in order to keep the memory of that person alive. So there are those issues. And then there's the kind of guilt that you might call moral guilt, that people violate values that they've grown up with, and they're involved in killing. So that's very different from hurting someone's feelings, or the kind of neurotic guilt that therapists usually see. So that's always a struggle.

Aaron Elson: Some of the World War II veterans seem to compartmentalize their life. There was the period before the war, there was the war, and there was after the war. Many have had marriages that lasted 50 years and been exemplary family men, whereas the next generation has been full of divorce. Does this tie in to their experience during the war? Did that make them value family more than the next generation?

Gerald Levine: I don't know that the war relates to that. I will tell you that a lot of them came back feeling that now they were back home and they had to get on with life, and they really did throw themselves into work and raising a family, and that distraction really, in many ways, made them not address the kinds of symptoms they were experiencing. Now we're finding that as men retire and they don't have the same activity level, some of them are having a recurrence of the PTSD symptoms. And we think that some of it is that their daily structure is not competing with those thoughts. They have more unstructured time, and so there's more reverie about the past. As far as the divorce rate and all that, I think it's probably more a comment on shifts in cultural values. I mean, certainly people who served in the war, many of them take fewer things for granted. That is one of the lessons or gifts they take from the suffering that they went through, so there often is a greater appreciation.

Aaron Elson: Can you give me a couple of examples of people you've treated who have developed symptoms after retirement?

Gerald Levine: Last week I saw a World War II veteran who was a pilot whose brother died. His kid brother died in World War II, and he still carries that grief with him, and it's very raw. With the approach of D-day and the approach of the anniversary of a lot of events, it's triggering much more intensely a lot of memories. I think last year the guys who served in the Pacific theater were experiencing some symptoms with the anniversary of Pearl Harbor. So some of it is an anniversary reaction. Some of it is that the whole issue of mortality stirs up a lot of feelings. Wanting some sense of closure, everyone has that, it may be, I have found with some World War II vets, they are sharing experiences that they have never shared before, because I think that they are aware that their time is more limited now, and there is a greater need to share.

Aaron Elson: What makes someone in that position seek treatment?

Gerald Levine: First of all they're informed that treatment is available. I think we need to get the word out, especially to the Persian Gulf vets, but usually it's an exacerbation of symptoms. Usually with World War II vets it's anxiety related symptoms or depression. It's often depression. Medication is really an important component of our treatment.

Aaron Elson: When you say anxiety related symptoms, here you have a guy who was in World War II, basically went his whole life without recognizing symptoms...

Gerald Levine: They often recognized them.

Aaron Elson: Or concealing them, because they didn't feel it was manly, or right.

Gerald Levine: That's a good point, that while they were proud of their record in the service, they didn't feel that it was manly to seek treatment. I mean, there is a whole thing about self-reliance and dealing with things on your own, and I think that some of them, as we've begun to understand more about PTSD, the people providing treatment are more responsive. Some of them felt unresponded to when they did seek treatment in the past. So there's a greater awareness of people providing treatment as well. At this point, many of them are having a great degree of anxiety and pressure, sometimes nightmares.

Aaron Elson: Sometimes during an interview the person will say, "I had a nightmare once, but only once," or once or twice. I get the feeling that they had them more, but they were minimizing it.

Gerald Levine: Well, it's on a continuum. We get people with nightmares several times a week, we get people with nightmares once or twice a year, there's a difference between nightmares and night terror. Some people have night terrors which occur at different stage of sleep, and the person might not have a recollection, but often it's their spouse or their bed partner who will say that the person was shouting or flailing around and was very agitated. And the individual himself, striking out, defending himself. So it's often at another stage of sleep.

Aaron Elson: What are some of the nightmares like? Are they related to specific incidents?

Gerald Levine: Some of them are actual replays, reliving of events. Sometimes they're not. They're often about vulnerability, being under attack, either feeling helpless to defend oneself or trying very hard to defend oneself. The man who's here today, I think he's had some interesting dreams which he could tell you. He was a pilot, and he had recurring dreams about one more mission, being called for one more mission, so I would suggest that you speak to him.

I also wanted to say something about some of the issues with the Gulf War. We're finding that there's a great concern about health. There are a number of differences with the Persian Gulf War vets. It was the largest call-up of reservists, I think 18 percent of the people called up were reservists, 50 percent were reservists and National Guard. And often these people had civilian lives, and their lives were disrupted, so we're finding greater family problems with that disruption. There was a concern that Iraq would use biological or chemical warfare, so a lot of the vets were inoculated, and also took pills. Now it turns out that some of those inoculations had not been FDA approved yet, they were still in an experimental stage, and they produced their own effects. So the veterans are concerned about the effects of the medications. There is some question about whether in fact biological warfare was used and whether they were exposed. They certainly were exposed to, you know the oil refineries were burning so they were exposed to burning fuel. So there's an uncertainty about their health, and they also have the usual PTSD symptoms of some nightmares and vulnerability and anxiety, and vigilance. We're first beginning to see this emerge, although certainly apparently something like 34 percent of Persian Gulf veterans have some distressing symptoms, and 9 percent are diagnosed with PTSD.

Aaron Elson: One other thing, have you seen people who cracked under pressure, like combat fatigue, and later lived normal lives?

Gerald Levine: I think you can make a distinction between acute trauma and post traumatic stress. Many of the vets who had what they called shellshock, which really was acute trauma, did not go on to develop PTSD.

(Jerry Rutigliano enters)

Aaron Elson: You were a pilot?

Jerry Rutigliano: I was an aerial gunner, on a B-17.

Aaron Elson: Is that your unit, the 381st?

Jerry Rutigliano: Right. This was written by the chaplain, Dr. Brown. Actually it's a diary of every mission they went on, shot down, captured, killed, POWs like I was. I've got a page, where was the invasion...

Aaron Elson: You were in the invasion of Normandy?

Jerry Rutigliano: No. This is a listing of every mission that the group went on, and the dates, and the city. The yellow is the missions I went on. And these two are D-Day. I missed D-Day. I was on my 27th mission when we got shot down. See, what happened, when I first got there you had to do 25 missions, and Jimmy Doolittle took over in January or February of '44, and my first mission was in February of '44. We got halfway through, and he raised it to 30 missions, and we got shot down on our 27th. I was a POW for eleven and a half months.

Aaron Elson: Twenty-seven missions was a lot more than the average, wasn't it?

Jerry Rutigliano: The life expectancy was less than half of that. But the odds against making 25 missions are right in the front of the book, about five to one.

Aaron Elson: You were a tail gunner?

Jerry Rutigliano: I was a waist gunner. We were in the middle of the aircraft. We used to have 10-man crews, two waist gunners, then they cut it down to one waist gunner, when the fighters weren't as thick as they used to be. On our 27th mission we were leading the squadron over Berlin.

Aaron Elson: Over Berlin?

Jerry Rutigliano: Yeah, I had six trips over Berlin. The first Berlin raid was March 6, 1944, we lost 68 bombers. That's 680 men. We made it through that mission. We stayed down on the 7th, and went again on the 8th of March. We lost 37 more bombers. And then on the 9th of March...

Aaron Elson: This is like history. I've seen this on documentaries.

Jerry Rutigliano: I had six trips over Berlin. The sixth trip was May 19, which was a couple of days ago, 50 years ago a couple of days ago. May 19, 1944, we were leading the squadron. We turned on our IP, our initial point. When you turn on the IP, you have to stay straight. The bombardier takes over, and there's no way you can go but straight ahead. No evading flak or anything. You had the bomb bay doors open. We got two direct hits in the bomb bay. And I was in the waist. The plane caught fire.

Aaron Elson: Where is the waist in relation to the bomb bay?

Jerry Rutigliano: Midship, not far from the bomb bay. The bomb bay was between the pilot and the radio room, and we were behind the radio room.

We peeled out of formation, but we couldn't get out, we were on fire. Our intercom was shorted out. And our alarm bell was out. Later on I found out that everybody went out the front, the pilot, co-pilot, navigator, bombardier, and engineer. And the radio operator turned to me and said, "Help!" I could see the blaze from the bomb bay. So just before I went out, I couldn't get the tail gunner, so I kicked the door off, and it went flying back, he saw the door, and he started crawling into the waist. The ball gunner, the guy in the lower ball, he came up, he was in a bit of a panic seeing the plane's on fire, and through lack of oxygen he collapsed.

I had my chute on ready to go out, and I saw him laying there. So I went back, and me and the tail gunner revived him, and put oxygen on him. We smacked him, revived him, and we went out, one-two-three. The plane exploded. And a fellow who used to be in my crew was flying in another plane, he told me many years later that he told the tail gunner to keep an eye on our plane, and the tail gunner told him that it exploded and nobody got out. That's the way it appeared to him.

So the pilot – I didn't see him until 35 years later – told me the navigator's parachute didn't open, and he was killed.

I was captured by civilians. They beat me up.

Aaron Elson: Really?

Jerry Rutigliano: Well, some other fellows were shot, by civilians, and hung.

Aaron Elson: By civilians?

Jerry Rutigliano: They didn't like us. And when they got us, they said, "You're bombing the women and children." That's what they said we were doing. Then I went to a local prison, the soldiers took me down there. It's a long story, I don't want to go too long.

Aaron Elson: Where did you land?

Jerry Rutigliano: Right in a farm. The civilians beat the hell out of me. First of all, I was running. I hit the ground hard and I had hurt my ankle. I was running away. It was a bright day like today, it was May 19th. I hit this plowed-up field, and I started running away from the farmers who were chasing me with a dog, when up out of the wheatfield pops this German with a big rifle, and a big mustache, he was gonna shoot. I had my hands up. And he told me to walk towards him. So I walked towards him. He searched me. He asked if I had a pistol. I said no. We weren't allowed to carry pistols anymore because the civilians were shooting the guys with their own pistols. We used to carry .45s. So by the time I'm talking to him, the civilians catch up and they start beating me. Then the soldiers came, and they took me to a prison.

Aaron Elson: When they started beating you, where did they hit you, in the face?

Jerry Rutigliano: In the face, the hands, they were swearing at me. I was a rough kid from New York, in fact I was just 20 years old the week before, I went on my 25th mission on my 20th birthday. It would have been a big surprise for me to go home.

So I got down in this prison, and they came to take us out, and we saw a couple of other crew members. My co-pilot had a hole in his leg. He was bleeding. So they told me to pick him up, and I picked him up and carried him up this narrow stairway, one time I hit the wall with his leg and he started screaming, so they put him in the back of a truck and I told them to get him to a hospital. That's the last I saw of him. I went to Tempelhof Airfield, on the ground, there were about 50 other GIs there who were shot down. To make a long story short they took us by train to Frankfurt, interrogation, solitary, threatening, we got on a train and went to Grosteitschau, which is near Danzig, up in Poland. On the way up there we stopped, the air raid alarm sounded, we were locked in the train, the air raid alarm sounded, and we were out there. The guards took off and went to the air raid shelter, and we were in a marshaling yard in broad daylight, and they started bombing. Our own planes. Fortunately we were not hit.

Aaron Elson: What went through your mind, being on the receiving end of a bombing like that?

Jerry Rutigliano: There's nothing you can do. You can't scream or holler,

"Let me out of here!" You just have to sit there, and you hear the flak going, bouncing off the roof of the train. So that was one crisis. Then after the all-clear sounded we went up to Poland, to Grosteitschau, Stalag Luft 4. They must have had over 50,000 Air Force POWs. They shot down like 4,000 airplanes.

We stayed there for nine months. And the Russians were coming from the East. So they told us they were going to evacuate the camp, and we were going to march for four days, to another camp. It was Feb. 5, 1945. So we took everything we owned, which wasn't much. We took what food we had, and started marching. We marched 86 days. Five hundred miles, in the snow, rain, sleet. Crap. We lived in barns. We slept on the ground. We lived like animals. Eighty-six days we never had our clothes off. We wore the same clothes, were lousy from head to foot, full of lice. We went through bombings, strafings. Part of that time we went on a train, there were 57 of us in this train, freight trains, we all had dysentery or diarrhea. There were no toilet facilities, of course. Half of us had to stand up and half of us had to lay down, we couldn't all lay down. And we did what we had to do to relieve ourselves. As I said, we had dysentery and diarrhea. They wouldn't let us out.

We got out of that, and we marched, from February 5th to April 25. They never marched us at night, for obvious reasons, because there were about 4,000 of us in this march, all Americans. We marched to this roadblock, with SS troops, we marched through the roadblock. They put us in this field. We saw German soldiers on patrol. They had switched guards on us. They gave us the old Wehrmacht guards, old men, home guards, in their sixties. They told us, you're gonna sleep here tonight on the ground, you're gonna get up tomorrow, you're gonna march eight kilometers, that's around five miles, to the American lines. They didn't want to have anything to do with the Russians. We thought they were full of baloney because we couldn't believe anything they said, we didn't believe anything by this time. You can imagine what we looked like, all of us 20, 21 years old. I lost 80 pounds. We ate out of the ground, raw potatoes, raw kohlrabes. Turnips. It got us sick but it kept us alive. Dehydrated sugar beets, anything we could get our hands on.

When I was 15 years old, I joined the 27th Tank Corps, at the Kingsbridge Armory in the Bronx. Two months later I turned 16. We lied. You had to be 17. We got a dollar a drill; we went after that buck a drill. And we went to Canton, New York, on maneuvers, in 1940, this is before World War II. So in October, the draft took effect, and Roosevelt federalized the National Guard for one year. I was still in high school. So I wanted to go. I was gung-ho. My father said, "If you go, I'll tell them you're underage." He didn't want me to go because he was sick. So I got out. And I enlisted in '42. In the Air Force. But I was driving a tank in the city dumps at 15. I didn't have a driver's license, I'd never driven a car. …Where was I?

Aaron Elson: You were being marched back toward the American lines.

Jerry Rutigliano: We were bedded down, and they said you're gonna march to the American lines tomorrow morning. To make a long story short we got up, we started marching, and sure enough, we saw an American jeep, a GI, and a rifle, First Army, 104th Infantry, the Timberwolves. We naturally went nuts. There was a major there who shook hands with everybody. So we marched across the Elbe River, and we were liberated. We had K rations. Which to us was like a steak dinner. We went back for seconds on K rations. The rest was all history, we finally got a shower, a bath, clothes.

Aaron Elson: What happened to your guards?

Jerry Rutigliano: They became POWs. They weren't the bad ones, the old men, like I am now, 70 years old. We had some bastards in there, but that's something else.

Aaron Elson: Dr. Levine said I should ask you about the dreams you've had. He said you described one nightmare in particular about going back, being assigned one more mission.

Jerry Rutigliano: Oh yes, for a long time I was in a barrack and they awaken us, at one or two o'clock in the morning. They say you're going on another mission, last mission, and we get in the plane, and we always crash. We never make that mission. But I used to dream about this all the time. In the beginning, I dreamt of it constantly. In fact I used to wake up screaming sometimes. My wife says last night I kicked her, screaming.

Here's a crucifix my mother gave me. I carried it on every mission. I never left the ground without it. And this part that's holding it together is from an old Klim can, that's milk backwards. When the Germans caught me, they examined this, they thought it was something to do with spying.

Aaron Elson: You were a sergeant?

Jerry Rutigliano: A staff sergeant. Here's a picture of the first day we were liberated, in Bittesfeld, Germany. I weight about 115 pounds, from 185. Here's a couple of days later, after we got a change of clothes. That's at Hermann Goering's airfield. And there's Jimmy Doolittle. That's me and General Doolittle in Washington, D.C.

Aaron Elson: Did you ever forgive him for increasing the number of missions?

Jerry Rutigliano: That's exactly why he sat me down. This was in 1976 at an 8th Air Force reunion in Washington, D.C., and I went to see him, there were a whole bunch of people to see him. I said, "General, do you remember when you raised the missions from 25 to 30?"

He said, "Yes." He was a little bit of a man.

I said, "Well, I got shot down on my 27th. And I was a POW because of you." I was joking, really.

So he said, "Sit down." And he put his hand on my shoulder. He sat me down, there's hundreds of people waiting to see him, and he's explaining to me why he had to raise the missions. He's a general. I became a little bit embarrassed. Here I am asking him, here's a guy that took off from an aircraft carrier with no hopes of getting back for that Tokyo mission, he was a great, great, great general, a great soldier, I admired him, and I told him that. I didn't want him to have a guilty conscience.

He said we needed experienced crews. He was apologizing. And he wouldn't let me go. I wanted to leave because it was getting embarrassing, people wanted to see him, and he kept talking to me. He just died recently.

Acknowledgments

One day in 1994, I was riding in the elevator of the high-rise in which I live, along with two other passengers. One of them knew I was looking for D-Day veterans to interview. He pointed to the other and said, "He was at D-Day." "Wow!" I said. "Which outfit were you in?"

The veteran said nothing, and glanced toward his crotch.

I hesitantly looked down, and saw a large belt buckle with an eagle.

"Oh!" I exclaimed. "You were in the 82nd Airborne?"

"The 101st," he said.

That veteran, Maurice Tydor, invited me to a meeting of the General Anthony C. McAuliffe chapter of the 101st Airborne Division Association. There, he assured me, I would meet plenty of D-Day veterans. I did, and I also met plenty of veterans of the Korean and Vietnam wars.

The chapter has an annual "Nuts" dinner at West Point in honor of McAuliffe, who was immortalized by his response to the German demand for the surrender of his division at Bastogne.

It was at that dinner in 1994 that I conducted a somewhat impromptu interview with Len Goodgal, Mickey Cohen, Frank Miller, John Miller, and Bill Druback. John Miller passed away in 1997. His estate paid for an open house dinner at the Bayonne chapter of the VFW.

The Eisenhower Center in New Orleans sent me the names of some D-Day veterans it had interviewed. One was Ed Boccafogli. Another was Dr. Vincent Del Guidice, who had been a pharmacist's mate aboard the USS Bayfield. When I met Dr. Del Guidice, he had just been speaking with a former shipmate, and suggested I look him up as well. That shipmate was Lou Putnoky.

Putnoky wasn't home when I called, and I spoke briefly with his wife. She said that when I interviewed Lou, I should make sure he told me the story about meeting the father of the boy who drowned. She said Lou gets very emotional when he talks about it, and might not bring it up.

When I last saw Lou, he had just returned from a reunion of the Bayfield. He said he got up and for the first time in public related the incident in which he told Scotty about the fate of his son.

I discovered the 712th Tank Battalion at a low point in my life, following the breakup of a relationship, when I moved temporarily into my parents' old apartment. One day a newsletter from the 712th arrived. It was addressed to my father, who had passed away six years before. As I read it, I remembered the great stories he used to tell. I wrote to the newsletter's editor, Ray Griffin of Aurora, Neb., and asked him to put a notice in the next newsletter asking anybody who remembered my dad to contact me.

Ray forwarded my letter to Sam MacFarland of Pittsburgh, who had been in my father's company. Sam wrote and suggested that I attend the battalion's next reunion. Which I did, in 1987. I found three people who remembered my dad. And simply because he had been with them for the handful of days it took for him to get a pair of what he called million dollar wounds, the battalion's veterans have embraced me as if I were a member of their family. It is a welcome for which I have always been grateful.

If Chi Chi Press were a book, it would be "The Little Engine That Could." You could fit its entire staff in the cockpit of a P-47 and have enough room left over for a wedding. Its editor, Susan English, transformed a collection of often rambling interviews into compelling conversations, without interfering with the individual voices of the veterans.

The Bergen Record has provided me with the photography of Carmine Galasso, Beth Balbierz and Don Smith. Thanks also to photo editor Rich Gigli and Terri Auchard.

Everybody's a critic. I'm glad I can say that about Bill Newton, who pooh-poohed my penultimate cover design and suggested the arrangement of photos that I finally used; and also Paul Lapidus, who insisted I come up with a better title than the original, which was "Conversations With Veterans."

Thanks also to Al "Smitty" Smith for confirming my belief that this was indeed a book, and not just a bunch of interesting transcripts. And from cyberspace, thanks to Mario Paesani's web site for the Mae West tank graphic; to Pat Lowe of the Will Rogers Memorial Library; Wesley Johnston of the "Dad's War" web site; and Calvin C. Boykin Jr., the author of "Gare la Bete: A History of the 814th Tank Destroyer Battalion." I had to make a judgment call – Will Rogers' account places the date of the incident with the two German tanks as Dec. 23rd. Pete De Vries' Silver Star citation says it occurred on Dec. 19th. I have seen enough inaccurate records to feel comfortable in believing they describe the same event.

When Ted Weiss said he could print my first book, "Tanks for the

Memories," but that he wouldn't have time to read it, I suggested that he keep a copy in the bathroom and read it there. Sorry, Ted said. That's the only time he gets to read the newspapers. Nevertheless, I appreciate his guidance and the printing skills he brings to his work.

The stories in "A Mile in Their Shoes" didn't take shape in a vacuum. They were told to me, and I related them to others – most notably the regulars in the Bookaccino and the members of Hilda Bary's writing workshop – before I knew that they belonged in a book.

Above all, this book would not have been possible without the sacrifices and the cooperation of the veterans who allowed me to record their contributions to history.

Appendix A

A Churchgoing Man

I never got to interview the late Sergeant Max "Lucky" Lutcavish. This account of his light tank's encounter with a German Mark V tank – which is referred to in the interview with George Bussell – is taken from the 712th Tank Battalion's D Company log.

While moving in the lead vehicle of a platoon of light tanks up a road northeast from Alencon, France, the following action took place on the 12th of August, 1944:

Upon rounding a curve we suddenly came upon an enemy truck loaded with Germans. Before my gunner, Cpl. [Fergus] O'Farrell, could fire, the truck stopped and backed around the curve. We pursued it and directed fire with the 37-millimeter and coaxial guns at a group of dismounted Germans by their truck.

About that time I heard a terrific explosion. I looked to the rear and the tank directly behind me was in flames. I caught a glimpse of a whirl of dust caused by a muzzle blast to my right. Immediately I spotted the position under an apple tree at about 125 yards away. I didn't know for sure what it was or whether it could be knocked out with my 37-millimeter, but knew I had to do something quick because it was already traversing its gun on to me.

There was no cover or no way to go back because of the burning tank behind me. Again I heard an explosion and felt my tank lunge forward. A bazooka had hit me in the rear and set the rear end of the tank on fire. What a position for a churchgoing man to be in! There was nothing else to do but to dish it out, so I directed fire on the gun position that looked like that of a tank.

That gunner of mine was plenty fast. In less time than it takes to tell he threw eight well-placed rounds of armor-piercing into that position and had it on fire.

Now we could definitely tell it was a tank, a huge one with a gun that made our 37 look like a pea-shooter.

While we were wiping the cold sweat from our brow another enemy tank crossed the road about 400 yards ahead of us. We swung the turret in that direction hoping that we could chalk up another one, but the tank disappeared in the brush before the gunner could fire on it.

By this time my tank was burning badly, so I ordered the crew to abandon it – disregarding the numbers system – and we made our way back to the rest of the platoon, toot-sweet, on foot.

Appendix B

The following is an excerpt from a letter from Gunther Rabe to Dr. Eugene Eckstam. Eckstam is a survivor of Exercise Tiger. Rabe was the captain of the E-boat that sank LST 507.

Dr. Eckstam,

Thank you for your letter dated 27th August, 1984. I am just coming back from a short trip to Normandy, where I visited the Utah and Omaha Beach memorials, our old chateau, and other sites from the last war. Please accept that this will only be a very short reply to your letter, because I am leaving Germany for a three-week tour to Portugal early next week.

You certainly will understand that the copy of the quotes you sent to Dr. Greene have struck me deeply. When in action at war and feeling you had success with a mission – this feeling is very very different from that being confronted with the scene, which you illustrated in your letter, showing the event from the "opposite side." You will believe, that for a man who went through the longer part of his life in the meantime – today these events look very much different. I think we in our generation have to do everything possible to prevent that governments repeat the same mistakes again.

Sincerely yours,

Gunther Rabe
Kapitan zur See